C000140933

The Secret Life of
Joan Denise Moriarty

The Secret Life of Joan Denise Moriarty

A biography

by

Sandra MacLiammoir

BLACKWATER PRESS

Editor
Deirdre Bowden

Design & Layout
Paula Byrne

ISBN
0 86121 728 4

© 1995 The right of Sandra MacLiammoir to be identified as the Author of this work has been asserted by her in accordance with the *Copyright, Designs and Patents Act 1988.*
The Author hereby asserts to the Publishers her moral right of paternity in the work.

Produced in Ireland by
Blackwater Press,
c/o Folens Publishers,
8 Broomhill Business Park,
Tallaght, Dublin 24.

All rights reserved. No part of this publication may be reproduced, stored in a retrieval system, or transmitted in any form or by any means, electronic, mechanical, photocopying, recording, or otherwise, without the prior written permission of the publisher.

This book is sold subject to the conditions that it shall not, by way of trade or otherwise, be lent, re-sold, hired out or otherwise circulated without the Publishers' prior consent in any form of binding or cover other than that in which it is published and without a similar condition including this condition being imposed on the subsequent purchaser.

While considerable effort has been made to locate all holders of copyright material used in this text, we have been unable to contact some of these. Should they wish to contact Blackwater Press, we will be glad to come to some arrangement.

For

Fon, Tara, Conn and Sarah

Acknowledgements

Joan Moriarty and Aloys Fleischmann, who placed their papers at my disposal, gave interviews, and offered other help, facilities and materials. Aloys Fleischmann opened his entire archive to me, and was generously hospitable at all times. Many others co-operated. My thanks goes to all those who kindly consented to be interviewed on tape for this biography. Amongst these are Peter Mackay, Lord Inchcape, who, with his wife, Georgina, Lady Inchcape, was most helpful, particularly regarding details of Glenapp Castle in Scotland. Others include ex-Taoiseach, Jack Lynch, and ex-Arts Council officers, Mairtin McCullough, Colm O'Briain and Arthur Lappin. My thanks to Martin Drury, also of the Arts Council. I am grateful to Dame Ninette de Valois, and to her secretary, Helen Quinnell, for their help and co-operation. Ethel Beare also kindly contributed on tape, as did Brenda Sexton, Beatrice 'Billie' Hunt, Pat Murray, Tom Donnelly, Pat Leonard, Pat Fleming, Sean Cunningham, Roz Crowley, Frank Sanquest, Katherine Lewis, Alan Foley, and Eileen Flynn. My thanks also to interviewees Madeline O'Connor, Sheila Rafter, Kieron Bolster, Myra and Catherine Greany, David Willis and Dr Derek McCoy. My thanks to Ita Power in Mallow for her help and hospitality. A number of off-the-record interviews are also deeply appreciated. I am also grateful to Canon O'Callaghan, of Mallow, for opening the parish records, and to Martina in the records office for her help. My thanks to Tim O'Mahoney, of Cork City library, to Tim Cadogan, of Cork County Library, and to Noel O'Mahoney, of Bantry Library for their help and co-operation. Appreciation is due to Debbie Sparshott, Examinations Manager of the Royal Academy of Dancing, to Jane Pritchard, of the Rambert School, and to Catherine Browne, Head of UK Exams and Membership, Imperial Society of Teachers of Dance. Thanks also to Conn Woolridge, to Tara Woolridge, and to Joan O'Donovan for their advice, and to driver Mick Leary for organising my UK itinerary. Thanks to those at Leeds Register of Births, for allowing me personal access to the birth records, to other agencies in the UK who afforded personal access, to all those who patiently answered my many other questions and finally to my editor at Blackwater Press, Deirdre Bowden.

Contents

Preface xi

Introduction xv

  1. Origins 1

  2. Orphan 6

  3. Early Life Reinvented 20

  4. Glenapp Castle 24

  5. Back in Ireland 31

  6. Friends 38

  7. Soulmate 45

  8. The Bad Years 53

  9. Aloys' Life with Ann Madden 64

10. Collaboration 71

11. Showdowns 81

12. Poetry 91

13. Irish Theatre Ballet 100

14. Dijon 112

15. Schools 116

16. Legend 125

17. Swan Lake 136

Contents

18. Irish Ballet Company 145
19. 76&77 155
20. The Playboy 164
21. Cresting the Myth 173
22. Crisis 182
23. The Firkin Crane 196
24. The Brinson Report 207
25. Aftermath 219
26. Honeymoon 228
Epilogue 238
Appendix 241
Bibliography 247
Index 249

Preface

I first met Joan Moriarty in 1988 when I interviewed her for a newspaper profile. Piano music had been floating down from her studio as I went up the stairs, as though she herself was playing. I found her standing alone near a record player, leaning on one arm, a faraway look in her eyes. The mirrored walls in the big bare room glittered, the wood floor shone. The music evoked sadness, isolation and loss. It was as though she was using the empty room as a prop; an image. She had created a mood and, as she had intended, I was immediately drawn into it. On that first day, as she wistfully sketched for me the story of her life, volunteering what seemed like much personal detail, I addressed her as 'Joan'. It's alright between ourselves, she smiled softly, but for the newspaper, she'd prefer 'Miss Moriarty'. It was a slapping-down.

She was anxious to know how I'd obtained her private number, but it had just been a matter of asking at the office of the Irish National Ballet in Cork. There seemed to be a gap between her obsessive sense of privacy, and the casual way someone else had passed over her number.

Some of my questions were blunt. She was appealingly vague, but there was something unconvincing about the too-pat answers; something steely in the gauziness. I felt sorry for her, and left with a feeling that she didn't add up. It was obvious to me that she was in the business of concealment, but it was none of my business.

Like every other journalist who had interviewed her, I wrote up the story of how she had nearly died twice in the early days, exactly as she gave it to me. It was the 'starved-for-her-art' story of how the struggling dance-teacher was rushed to hospital with malnutrition and given the last sacrament. 'That was it,' she lied to me in her seductive voice, as she had lied to others. 'That was how dance came to Ireland.'

My approach to her years later, requesting co-operation on an intended biography of her, was made after I had secured agreement for his co-operation from Aloys Fleischmann, the person whom I by then understood to be the key figure in her life. I made no promise, no commitment, or made any of the right noises. I did not refer to her 'contribution' in any terms, and made no reference to her status in the dance world. I made it clear from the start that the project was mine, and that the story was to be real. It was their relationship, I indicated, which I intended to focus on.

I have since asked myself, as the real story began to fully emerge, why she co-operated, and instructed her friends to do the same. In the light of the deeply secret nature of her life, why should she place revealing personal papers and correspondence at my disposal? Why should this woman who had resisted a previous attempt at a biography which promised to reflect all her sacrifice and hard work, suddenly say yes to this newspaper journalist who was a comparative stranger, and who promised nothing, but who was obviously on to something?

Joan's intuition was legendary; she was famous for rejecting people who might not subscribe to her myth, but she handed everything over to this outsider without asking one anxious question, or making any demand whatsoever. So why?

There is more than one answer: The first and most simple, but very important reason, is that Joan did not want to die. On a personal level, she dreaded death. As this work shows, she had been led to believe that by some means she could aspire to immortality. Bricks and mortar were part of her plan for this in the shape of the Firkin Crane building, which she planned as a home for the National Ballet Company. Another obvious legacy for posterity would be a book about herself. For this, anyone could simply have listed her achievements and left it at that.

But there were other, less conscious reasons why she agreed to co-operate on this particular project and with this particular person. Joan Moriarty did not know who she was. She did not know what her own value was in a very literal sense, and she also did not know the value of her work. Throughout her adult life in Cork, decades of sycophancy and adoration had not answered any fundamental questions for her; the right noises had never yielded the kind of answers she was looking for.

Neither did she know, to the end of her life, whether she had failed or not, and in that first interview, she had looked to this complete stranger for an answer. 'I don't know; have I failed or haven't I failed?,' she had faltered, in a bid for sympathy, but her confusion was genuine. Two professional companies which she had started, had been closed. There were all sorts of reasons for this, but deep down Joan did not understand why, and neither did anybody else. She did not know why she had been deposed from her position at the pinnacle of Irish dance, and she did not know whether, ultimately, there was any significance in what she had done for dance in Ireland. She needed to know.

So, at the end of her life, Joan instinctively did what she had done once before when a likely stranger appeared, who had the vision, the energy and the power to create her—she submitted. She parcelled herself up, papers, videotapes, photographs and all, and she handed herself over to be created.

The first time she had done this was with Aloys Fleischmann. Created in his terms, Joan the person became lost, and 'Miss Moriarty' the superhuman 'goddess' took over. This time there is to be a reversal: 'Miss Moriarty' the icon will be dismantled, and Joan Moriarty the person will be recovered.

Joan believed that she was having one of the great love affairs. She logged dates and other details on undated personal correspondence. It was Joan's intention to leave her hoard of intimate letters behind when she died. Against her will, the main bulk of these were destroyed by her protector, but a certain amount of personal correspondence remained available to me. These form an integral part of her real story.

Aloys did not understand why Joan preserved evidence of her real life story any more than he understood the significance of the love letters she could not bear to destroy. I came to believe that one of his secret and unspoken reasons for co-operating so fully, was that he hoped to manage the project, to turn it into his own hymn of praise, and to present it as his last gift to Joan.

In a sense, Joan was also entering the confessional for the first time in her life, as well as the last; she was putting her internal affairs in order. She had a deep need to allow herself to be truthfully evaluated and therefore validated, and for that she had to step outside the charmed circle she had so painstakingly built up. She did not have the courage to do it in life, so, by allowing access to her papers, she did it in death.

Her hope was, as false and baffling as her existence had become, that someone else would be able to make sense of her; that someone else would somehow legitimise what she had actually experienced and done, rather than what the public thought she had done. But her hope above all, was that someone else would discover in her as a person, an authenticity that she herself had never been able to find.

Introduction

Joan Denise Moriarty, elegant and beautiful, with a high-profile, glamorous career as Ireland's First Lady of Dance, seemed hugely successful. Understood to be a solicitor's daughter from Mallow in the country, it was said that she almost singlehandedly managed to establish the first national ballet company in the country. That she did so, not in Dublin, the Irish capital, but in Cork, the second city, was, champions argued proudly, against all the odds. The influential army of patrons and supporters that was assembled included Jack Lynch, head of the Irish government, and Dame Ninette de Valois, founder of the Royal Ballet in England.

Appearing frequently in public, surrounded by people in thrall to her magnetic aura, Joan's aloof and enigmatic presence gave an impression of ease and confidence. She managed eventually to become a sort of icon of dance, an emblem of chaste and hard-working Irish self-sacrifice in the cause of her art, and she lived out her career celebrated as an ascetic legend.

She was treated to a marvellous, even rave, press. Her achievements were heralded routinely, unquestioningly and extensively, and were eventually rewarded with many honours, including an honorary doctorate from the National University of Ireland. Her work appeared on Broadway, at Sadler's Wells, and in Europe. The hard times establishing herself in Cork, her abstemiousness, her punishing daily regime, her dedication to work, and her scanty appetite were widely regarded by admirers, as tokens of her near-sainthood. That she was a woman of few words added to her allure.

After nearly forty years in the business, and more than a decade of huge state subsidies, the Arts Council suddenly and inexplicably demanded her resignation, and then completely withdrew the grant from the prestigious National Ballet Company. How this could have happened to the admired ballet figurehead has remained a mystery.

Who she was, how she had achieved such celebrity, and how she could have been deposed have never been discussed. Of the little that is known about Joan Moriarty, most of it is fictional. She was a woman with many secrets.

Born secretly in England to a daughter of a Lord Justice of Appeal for Ireland, Joan also believed herself to be the illegitimate child of a British Lord, the second Earl of Inchcape, in Scotland. Unwanted and unacknowledged, she was put into an orphanage in the North of England, where she was raised in unhappiness and poverty. She was later fostered out to a series of people in Liverpool and the south of England. Her ballet training was scant, she received no education at all, and she had no dancing qualifications.

When, as a sick, depressed, and difficult child she was sent to Ireland to live with a distant cousin, she was treated like a kitchen maid. In the city of Cork, she struggled unhappily, but could not cope alone, and had a series of nervous breakdowns. The turnaround came when she managed to find an influential protector, the composer and university music professor, Aloys Fleischmann.

Together, under assumed private names, they created the legend known as 'Miss Moriarty'. Her public career was in reality an elaborate private game of mythical 'battles' played over decades with her lover. The 'battles' were performances, and the ballet companies they formed, were symbolic 'children' born out of the battles. The greater the struggle, the better they liked the rewards. Their game was fuelled by his imagination and skill, together with the talents of many artists. It was also fuelled by money—the generous charity of Cork people and businesses, and the big government subsidy dispensed initially by friend and ballet fan Jack Lynch.

For Aloys Fleischmann personally, Joan was a 'goddess', and he was in love with her. It was Aloys who was by far the most influential figure in Joan's personal and professional life. Her love relationship was an essential component of her work, and without it, there would have been no Irish National Ballet.

'Miss Moriarty' the icon did not exist. She was a work of the collective imagination, initiated by Joan Moriarty, taken up ruthlessly, with her willing complicity, by the creative force of her lover, and perpetuated by acolytes. One factor which kept everything validated, was that, as was to be expected through the ballet artform, audiences were provided with a vehicle for their own dreams.

The glittering and expensive product had little to do with Joan's abilities, but was unquestioningly hyped by the media, led by *The Irish Times* columnist, Seamus Kelly. Queenly, statuesque, and mysterious, Joan came to embody for the Irish public, figures of myth and folk-memory. Queen Maeve, the beautiful, red-haired, battling goddess of legend, was the image her creative lover fashioned, and this duly percolated over decades into romantic Irish minds. Her asceticism, aloofness and spinsterhood led also to associations within the Irish consciousness, of the archetypal chaste virgin female of Irish morality. It was partly for this also, that she was revered. She became a model of femaleness.

But behind the evening dresses and bow-ties, the gaiety and the success, it all became too big for her to handle. Joan's professional life was a constant torment of debilitating doubts and fears, and she could not sleep at night. Her own real battles were with depressions, and many physical illnesses. Her silent presence at gatherings and her distaste for small talk were due to fear. Having little education, she was afraid to speak and afraid to write. She dreaded being found out.

Behind it all, for his own personal reasons, her whispering paramour secretly reassured her of her greatness, showering her with overblown praise, and seducing her with mythical imagery, into a false professional heaven in which she reigned as a wonderful queen.

Her life as 'Miss Moriarty', ascetic ballet teacher and choreographer, entailed the strain of wearing an elaborate mask, not just in public, but in private, too. There was much she dared not tell even her closest confidante. Throughout her life, the wearing of this mask meant unremitting vigilance. She fought hard to keep her position, but the strain of being the Artistic Director of the national company made her physically ill and psychologically shattered, and eventually became the albatross which she allowed to fell her.

Established in her false roles, and unable to let go of the power, prestige, and money that they brought, she trusted the man who had formed her, and subscribed to her own myth. She allowed the many days, years and moments at which she might have considered retirement to pass. When she eventually panicked, and offered to abdicate, it was too late. She had to remain and be publicly, and ignominiously toppled.

When 'Miss Moriarty' overreached, Joan Moriarty the person, was the victim. The one she trusted was looking the other way when it happened. She played the victim, but the irony of this was, that all her life she had been not a victim, but a survivor. Disgrace came, and disabled by her unacceptable secrets, she faced her public humiliation bravely and mutely. She never knew that it was her own trust in her most cherished supporter which had really destroyed her, and it need never have happened.

When at the end of her life the honeymoon finally came, promising fulfilment and peace, that too, turned to ashes in their mouths—Joan had another accident, and embarked on her tragic, terminal decline.

Ashamed to live, she spent her existence living out lies; afraid to die, she never wanted to wake up from her dreams. She died as she had lived—alone, in pain, and desperately afraid.

1
Origins

From time to time throughout her career in ballet, Joan Denise Moriarty gave the press a potted version of her life story. It was almost entirely false.

She was believed to have been born in Mallow, County Cork, on 22nd July 1920. This is the date of birth in her driving licence, and the day on which she celebrated her birthday, but there is no record of her having been born in Mallow on that date. Neither is there any record of her having been born in Mallow on any other date.

The founder of the Irish National Ballet was not Irish. She was, as many suspected, older than she claimed to be, but just how much older, even she herself did not know. Though she lived in Ireland most of her life, she never became an Irish citizen. She was British, and travelled all her life on a British passport. The date of birth in this is 22nd July 1916, exactly four years prior to the date she always claimed. Her passport states that she was born in Leeds, in the UK. But there is no record of her having been born in any Leeds parish, either on that date, or on any other date. She never had a birth certificate, and though she tried, she was never able to obtain one. She told her closest confidante that she never knew exactly how old she was.

Neither did she know exactly who she was. Her first memory was of being in an orphanage, and of being deeply unhappy. She was a scrawny, deprived, cross little infant, and she was known as Mollie. Though she didn't know it for years, she came to believe that she was the unacknowledged, illegitimate product of a secret love affair between a female relative of her adopted Mallow family, and a wealthy British Lord called Kenneth Mackay, the Second Earl of Inchcape, who owned the vast estate at Glenapp, in Strathnavar in the West of Scotland.

Sometime before the heather came into bloom in the summer of 1915, Kenneth Mackay, Viscount Glenapp of Scotland, strode into his father's study, and expressed his intention to marry Caroline

Frances Joan Moriarty from Dublin, the beautiful younger daughter of the Rt Hon. John Francis Moriarty, Lord Justice of Appeal in Ireland. The Irishwoman was known simply as Joan, and her intended husband was an upper-class barrister who had met her father on the legal circuit. Her father had been HM's First Serjeant-at-Law in Ireland from 1908–1913, and was Attorney-General for Ireland from 1913–1914. The couple would have had an opportunity to meet first at the fashionable Irish home of a brother of the Earl.

Within two years of her marriage to Kenneth Mackay, Joan Moriarty was to go and live in the splendid castle on the Glenapp Estate, owned by his father. The Irishwoman knew that with this young aristocrat she was to become titled and rich, and believed that she would eventually become mistress of the thousands of golden acres of moorland and the purple hills comprising the estate. But her privileged life with the Earl was to be deeply unhappy, and her marriage was to be under strain from the start.

The Second Earl had a roving eye and Joan had an elder sister—Marguerite, also beautiful, and also moving within his circle of friends. Marguerite, who had been born in France, was nearly thirty years old, and was faced with the embarrassing social pressure of her younger sister showing signs of getting married first.

The father of the Moriarty sisters, the Rt Hon. John Francis Moriarty, had been born in Mallow, and was one of the colourful, admired figures of Irish legal life on the Munster Circuit. He was a talented opportunist with a good brain, and he got by on nerve. He had a reputation for being clever and hardworking, but he was what is known in Ireland as a chancer. He liked to amuse himself at work, going in for risky maneouvres in court, for his own enjoyment, and wittily entertaining his colleagues. He lived a high life, running up plenty of debts, with little regard for the circumstances of his unpaid creditors. When one of his creditors came to court looking for payment of money, complaining that he was bankrupt and ruined, the judge was asked by a colleague what he was going to do about paying the man this debt. Justice Moriarty flippantly said that he could offer the man a cigar. Moriarty had married a wealthy widow, and the couple had run through her fortune, mainly on the racetrack.

If the first Earl of Inchcape knew anything of the lifestyle of the Irish Justice of Appeal, which he probably did, he would have been disapproving of the Moriartys, for he himself was an abstemious, hardworking Scottish businessman who rose from nothing at all, to very high government advisory positions, as a prestigious adjunct to his considerable skills in the world of shipping. He was extremely influential in Anglo-Indian affairs, and had amassed a considerable personal fortune in business. Everything Lord Inchcape did in life was touched with a high morality and a sense of correctness.

Whether or not he disapproved of Joan's father, it is certain that the self-made millionaire was disappointed in his heir's choice of wife, on the grounds that Joan Moriarty was a Catholic, and he did not want any Catholic inheriting his swelling Protestant wealth. But the sport-loving Kenneth was determined to go his own way and marry the lovely Joan. His father then explicitly stipulated that if he went ahead, any sons of this marriage were not to be brought up Catholics. The threat was that he would disinherit his heir if this was not agreed. He meant it.

The ageing Irish judge had imposed another shaming domestic pressure on his family a few years before this, particularly on Marguerite. In 1909, when he was 57 years old, widower John Francis Moriarty had married Mabel Agnes Dolphin, a 28-year-old Galway woman, whom he installed in his townhouse on fashionable St Stephen's Green, in Dublin, to preside over the household in which Marguerite still lived. He provided his new wife with three servants, allowed her to bring her friend, Constance, over from Galway to keep her company, and went back to his legal work, which involved much travel. Mabel was just three years older than her stepdaughter Marguerite.

Not long after this, the displaced Marguerite had a love affair with Kenneth Mackay. Their passionate liaison may have taken place in Ireland, in Scotland, or both, when the old Lord was safely away in his office in London. Whilst Marguerite was making secret love to Kenneth at country house parties, she may have been expecting him to marry her. He may not at the time have been her younger sister's beau. It is possible that she was genuine, that she was making a foolish mistake, and that he may have jilted her. But this is unlikely, since it would have been the behaviour of a cad, and her family would have got to know and been scandalised. Perhaps he had intended to marry Marguerite at first, and that he had later fallen for her sister. It could even be, that the lovers' passion cooled, and they ended their affair mutually and amicably, before either knew that Marguerite was pregnant. On the other hand, he may

3

have been engaged to Joan at the time of this affair, and both himself and Marguerite may have been caught up in the senseless urgency of an illicit passion. Both may have gone into the affair knowingly for the sake of the immediate thrills, experiencing indecent delight, in the knowledge that they were cheating on the innocent Joan, and under her nose.

Whatever the reasons of the lovers for behaving as they did, by the time the charming Kenneth married his Joan, he may already have impregnated her sister. If his affair with Marguerite was not already over before Kenneth's marriage to Joan in 1915, then it took place either at the same time as his marriage, or very soon after it. Whether Marguerite had a love affair with him beforehand, or whilst he belonged to Joan, either by betrothal, or by marriage, their affair became an issue when, at some point, Marguerite discovered that she was pregnant.

However much time she had spent in Scotland, in the company of the young heir to the Barony at Strathnavar, the increasingly pregnant Marguerite now could no longer be seen there, or remain in Dublin high society. The wedding of Joan and Kenneth went ahead, and by the time her younger sister had become legitimately pregnant by her new husband, Marguerite had already undergone a withdrawal in disgrace from the scene, to the refuge and protection of some faraway mother-and-baby home.

There was the usual dreadful stigma attached to being an unmarried mother, and Marguerite went to great lengths to avoid discovery. She decided to stay in Britain and travel down to England to have her baby. The usual place of refuge for an Irish Catholic girl in this predicament, was behind a convent wall, with the nuns.

Whether Kenneth Mackay himself cared about the welfare of his child isn't known, but it is likely he would have known that Marguerite had gone off to have his baby. The young people may or may not at first have concealed the truth from Kenneth's father, the Earl of Inchcape, who was becoming increasingly intolerant with age. What is certain, is that it was Joan herself who later took a compassionate interest in her sister's little daughter, to whom she was related both by blood, and by marriage.

So around 1915–1916, the middle-class Marguerite Moriarty, single unmarried woman aged around thirty or so, checked into a Catholic nursing home in the UK, and gave furtive, shameful birth to a dark-haired, pretty little daughter. As if in apology, she gave her new baby the first name of her little sister, whose position as wife to a man who was soon to be a Peer of the British Realm, she may herself have wished to occupy. Then she paid the price, and abandoned her child forever.

Her baby was to be transferred to an orphanage to be adopted if possible or at least fostered. Marguerite supplied a name and address which the nuns might contact in the case of an emergency.

Then she turned and walked toward the convent gates, left the Catholic nuns behind in England, and went back to her fashionable townhouse on St Stephen's Green in Dublin. With the help of a cook, a housemaid and a parlourmaid, she got on with the rest of her life.

On 18th August 1916, less than a year after her marriage, Joan Mackay, soon to be Lady Inchcape, gave birth to the first child of her marriage, a little girl who would grow up rich and privileged. She named her baby daughter Patricia. Joan was never to become mistress of splendid Glenapp Castle in the West of Scotland, but Patricia was later to meet and befriend a poor-relation 'cousin' who came on holiday from Ireland to stay at the castle, a dark-haired little girl called Joan Moriarty.

2
Orphan

J oan Denise Moriarty spent her earliest years in an orphanage in or around Liverpool, where she was very unhappy. She could remember being sent from the orphanage to be fostered at the age of about two, and of feeling that her life was even more miserable. She ran away from her foster parents. She was sent back, but they couldn't cope with her, and returned her to the orphanage. She would have been very young at the time. She remembered being fostered out again, and becoming dreadfully upset by the move. She eventually managed to run away again, and was sent to another orphanage.

Around 1916, there was no love in orphanages. There were no hugs or comforts for abandoned children; no understanding of the basic human needs of eye-contact, and physical contact. The basic care sustaining their young lives, consisted of inadequate food, clothes that were not warm enough, and shelter that tended to be cold and cheerless.

Children who have survived this situation, and who later describe orphanage experiences, say that the isolated feeling they are left with is indescribable. They talk about an anguished existence of deep loneliness, and of disabling feelings of rejection. Joan's memories of this time were very painful, and she was unable to talk about it. From other records of conditions at that time, however, it is possible to guess with accuracy at the circumstances of Joan's earliest years.

Joan Moriarty would have been washed and dressed in a brisk, businesslike fashion, and told to keep tidy. There would have been no kisses on her cherub's face. Breakfast every grey morning would have been warm gruel. She would have been commanded to eat it all up, and firmly told that she was lucky to be getting a hot breakfast. She might have been given some toast and an egg once a week, but she probably was not. Then she would have been ordered outside in cold weather, to take the chill, smog-laden air, the wind on her bare,

6

thin legs, along with a group of similarly unwanted and unhappy orphans. Every six weeks, she would have stood in line in a corridor, with a row of other little ones, outside a heavy door, waiting for her turn to go in, and have her thick, dark hair chopped off again. Before she was allowed to leave the room, her hair would have been routinely covered in some medicine with a horrible smell. Then it was back along the dark corridor, the cold air harsh against the back of her neck, towards the smell of potatoes and gravy, where she would queue again, her spoon in her hand. From the moment she was born, there would be no fond tucking-in at night. No nun or staff member would have been allowed to become attached to a child, or show favour, even if she had wanted to. The message Joan would have received from the adults around her, was that she was not wanted in this world, that she herself was to blame for this, and that whatever she got was purely on sufferance, for which she would have to be grateful. She would also have been disciplined fairly rigorously. Other abuses, cruelties and deprivations for little ones in these prisons were commonplace.

Though most orphans tend to adjust to whatever treatment they find, it sometimes happens that young children do run away from foster homes. Some children, after having known only institutional care, become frightened and deeply overwhelmed by life in a normal family. Having no experience of what is 'normal' in a family, they are unable to adjust. This is what happened to Joan when she was sent to her first foster home. She was one of these highly-strung infants, with a deeply entrenched sense of insecurity, which came out in enraged behaviour. She instinctively fought to go back to the impersonal privations of the orphanage.

Since adjustment to new situations is most difficult for infants at the age of two years, she may have been around that age when the orphanage first found a foster parent for her. Her life situation gave plenty of reason to be angry. She could have knuckled under, and become passive and acquiescent, as many do, but she didn't. She cried a lot, and was difficult to manage. Spirited and independent, she was in the fighting phase of her life, and she didn't stand a chance.

When she was a little older, she was fostered out more successfully with another family, and spent some time in Worcester, where she was known as, 'Mollie', and where she made her first communion at the age of eight. She had by this time matured enough to call her foster parent 'mother'. The whole of the first ten years of her life were spent in this way, but she was never reconciled to it. Unwanted and unloved, she remained unhappy throughout her childhood.

The earliest photograph of Joan Denise Moriarty shows a thin, worried-looking infant in a crumpled smock, standing in front of a high brick wall, between two bigger boys who look equally unhappy, and who are dressed identically in crumpled cotton sailor uniforms. The children all look tired, and do not appear either clean or well-nourished. The boys look bewildered, mistrustful, and eager-to-please. The infant Joan Denise has swollen eyes and an angry scowl.

As well as showing her unhappiness, her early pictures reveal her changing fortunes. At the age of about three, she looks fatter, but solemn, in a cotton gingham dress, crumpled and worn. Yet another photograph shows her with a too-short, plain hairstyle, a downturned mouth and another plain dress. By the time she is photographed at the age of around four, she looks much better-nourished and cared for. Her face is fat and pretty, her swept-up hair is longer and glossy, and her dress is edged with lace. She holds a large racquet in her hands, and a soft ball sits to her right. But the eyes are downcast, the mouth is turned resolutely down, and the facial expression is sulky.

It is certain that before she came to Ireland, Joan Denise spent some time in Worcester. In the missal that as an adult she kept precious personal clippings in, is a faded fragment of a mass card, on the back of which is written in a cursive hand, recognisable as her own: 'Joan Denise Moriarty took her first communion at Worcester'. The card is torn in such a way as to suggest that the date, and possibly an address, may have been removed from it.

This must have been written retrospectively, for there is another card in the missal, in a child's early script. It says, 'To Mother From Mollie on my First Communion Day 11th April 1924'. It is likely then, that she had been known as 'Mollie', since she first started to talk. When asked her name, a very young child trying to pronounce the name, 'Moriarty', might well pronounce it 'Mo-ollie'. For a child who could not yet say 'J', or finish words, the name 'Joan', would be lost in the pronunciation, and reproduced simply as a long vowel sound of 'oh'. Thus 'Joan Moriarty', said by an infant just starting to talk, would be 'Oh Mo-ollie', and in this way her name would become 'Mollie'.

She remained known by someone as Mollie, well into her teens, and possibly beyond, for on the back of a picture of herself as an adult walking a dog, she signed it with love from 'Molly'. Added to this is the question 'Liverpool?' She had hardly known where she was.

Later in life, when she was giving interviews about her career, she tended to begin the story of her early years by saying that she'd gone on holiday from Mallow to London at the age of about six or seven, and on seeing a ballet at the theatre, had fallen in love with the idea of becoming a dancer. In reality, she did not see Ireland until she was ten years old, when, after a serious illness, she was sent from England on the brink of death, and as a last resort, to stay with Marion Moriarty, the woman whom for the rest of her life she was to call mother.

She'd become an embarrassment to everyone around her by getting scarlet fever. In the days before antibiotics, this contagious illness was dreaded, and regarded as a sort of plague. It started with nausea, vomiting and headache, and then fever, with hot, dry skin. After a day or so, a bright rash appeared and became widespread. The tongue became bright red, and after a week or so, the skin began to peel. Scarlet fever can last weeks, and leave the sufferer with ear or kidney infections. Not every child actually got it. The weakest and most puny member of a family would be most likely to get this prolonged illness with such troublesome symptoms, and if Joan was with a foster family at the time, they would have guarded against the other children getting it by having her hospitalised and, subsequently, when she was no longer contagious, they would have had the option of either taking her back, or trying to return her to the orphanage.

Since the illness could last for weeks and was very troublesome, as well as contagious, they would have kept her in the isolation hospital whilst she had fever and vomiting, and whilst she had the bright red rash all over her. Once she was no longer contagious, she could have been returned to her foster home, or to the orphanage. But long after her skin started to peel, and she was no longer contagious, it turned out for this child that after her serious illness, she was returned neither to a foster home, nor to an orphanage.

It became clear that the puny Joan Denise Moriarty, who didn't get enough milk as a baby, who was always cold, and who never had enough to eat, was taking too long to recover. The illness had knocked the remaining fight out of her and, alone in her sickbed, she had finally faced the truth of her situation. With a spirit that had ebbed to a dangerous low, and nobody to hold her hand, the ten-year-old had faced her lot, and decided that it was not worth the fight. When the time came for her to start eating again, she turned her face to the wall.

It was one thing to see a child that was fading to skin and bone. It was quite another to see her hollow-eyed apathy. With a frisson of horror they realised that the troublesome child seemed to have lost the will to live. As the days went by, her once-reddened face became like parchment, and she grew thinner. The foster parents and the nuns became alarmed. When it was feared that she might die, they no longer wanted to be responsible for her. It was time to look up the emergency address, and to discreetly inform her nearest relative that they could do no more with her.

As an illegitimate child who was known by her family only dispassionately and from a great distance, little Joan's existence was an embarrassment which was a secret. If she was in fact dying, they needed to let it be done decently, but still from a distance. So when nobody in charge of her could do anything with her, her mother was contacted, and informed of her near-critical condition. A way had to be found, and the obvious solution was to send the child to disappear into the country, as far away as possible.

Perhaps before her illness, she had been disciplined as a method of breaking her spirit. It was felt at the time, that strong and consistent discipline based on a punishment regime, was a cure-all for behavioural problems. The action of trying to trace relatives, may or may not suggest some degree of guilt on the part of someone.

It went completely undiagnosed, but what Joan was really suffering from at the tender age of ten, was her first bout of serious reactive depression, triggered by her physical illness, on top of an already deprived life. Nobody around her realised it. Her apathy and loss of appetite alarmed people mainly because she had lost so much weight, and showed no signs of recovering. Children can experience serious depression, but it was not usual at the time for those in authority to be much concerned with psychological well-being.

The Moriarty family would have taken care to avoid the shame of publicly acknowledging the child, and the father of the child was probably not consulted. Marguerite had an uncle Michael Moriarty, her father's brother, whose immediate family had remained in the extreme south of Ireland. Michael may have by this time been dead. If not, he would have understood how difficult these things can be, since he himself had sired an illegitimate child. The authority in charge of Joan Moriarty in the filthy air of the industrial North of England, had sent out an appeal, saying that the child had better somehow be sent away to get some cure-all fresh air somewhere else. She needed either to convalesce, or else die.

It was somehow decided from a distance that the ailing girl was to be sent to Ireland, deep into the country, to the wife or widow of this most raffish and least respectable of the Moriarty clan, in the quiet, small town of Mallow, down in the County of Cork. It was hoped that, one way or the other, the family would bury the child quietly down there.

Michael Augustus Moriarty was born at Sandfield House, one of the big old Protestant houses on the edge of town, into a fairly wealthy legal family. A solicitor, he practised at Bank Place in Mallow, and would have been thought of as belonging to the local gentry. He was an overshadowed younger brother of the successful John Francis, Lord Justice of Appeal, who left Mallow for Dublin, and became His Majesty's first Serjeant-at-Law for Ireland in 1908, and also Solicitor-General for Ireland in 1913. Another brother, James, was a barrister.

Michael Augustus Moriarty was one of life's losers. He was a high-stake gambler; an indiscreet womaniser; a depriver, and possibly a deserter of his wife. It was said that in a shooting accident, he'd knocked out the eye of his old neighbour, John Bolster. It was also said that everyone knew he had an illegitimate son by a woman who lived down Berry's Lane. He was a foolish gambler: a man who tended to stake—and lose—not only his money, but also his property, including his own dwelling houses and farms. He is known to have lost one of his houses by staking the lease at a game of poker. By the time Joan Denise arrived, Marion Moriarty and her sons were far from Sandfield House, and were temporarily renting a smaller home. When she first arrived in Mallow, he would have been nearly seventy years old, if still alive, and for some reason had spent a lot of his time in the North of England, away from his family. It was this man whom Joan referred to as her 'father'. She was later to say that her father had died when she was eighteen months old, and that she had never known him.

In the absence of her husband, Marion, wife of Michael Augustus, agreed to the request of the family she had married into, and allowed the girl to come to her home in the small, quiet town of Mallow, in Cork, to live with herself and her three grown-up sons, Sid, Jack and Gus.

Marion belonged to a family of small business working people, the McCarthys, who owned two public houses in the town, the Clockhouse Bar and the Horseshoe Bar, as well as several small terraced houses on Bridgeview, in Broom Lane, Ballydaheen, which overlooked the river Blackwater on the edge of town. Marion inherited the houses, and collected rents from them.

When Joan arrived to the fresh country air of rural Ireland, she was worn out and frail. The first house Marion took her into, to be introduced, was that of Mrs Greaney, her closest friend, who rented one of the McCarthy houses at Bridgeview. Marion did not even try to hide the fact that the sickly Joan was not her own. It was believed by some locals that Joan had been born in Scotland, but Marion Moriarty did not talk about it. She told her friend that she thought the child wouldn't survive, and Mrs Greaney was touched by the frailness, and the beautiful hair.

It was not unusual in Ireland, for illegitimate children to be hidden in the country with near or distant relatives in this way. It would also be possible to conceal a birth, both in Ireland and in England. Formal adoption acts in both countries came later. In England, informal adoptions took place until 1927, and in Ireland an adoption act was not passed until the 1950s. Even now in Ireland, retarded, or otherwise unwanted children are sometimes informally given over into the care of another, usually single female member of the family, who may still be living in the rural homeplace. Communities as well as authorities usually accept this without fuss. It would often have been expected that a child might have been unwanted because of some physical or mental defect, and since such cases went untreated anyway, nobody would have spent any time trying to decipher the state of Joan's mental health. People with disabilities were often left to rot indoors, or to do menial work around farms, and denied contact with the outside world.

Neither would it have been considered in any way remarkable, given Joan's dreadful start in life, that she was so unhappy. There were plenty of others like her. She would have been considered quite lucky to have moved from the raw, smog-laden air of the industrial

North of England, to the fresh air of Ireland to convalesce, and it is likely that this had a good effect on her spirits.

It was hoped that Ireland might save Joan from wasting away. But as she perked up, it didn't escape her notice along the way, that her apathy and her refusal to eat after the illness, had resulted in people taking quite a lot of notice of her. Somewhere in her young, uncherished mind, a pathetic victory was taking place, with an expedient logic. Her behaviour had thrown a scare into those around her, and they'd been forced to act in an entirely new way. She had won by getting anxious attention, and it had been an easy triumph in which they'd felt helpless. Previously, she'd always been the powerless one; shifted around like a neglected pawn by nuns and a succession of foster parents. Suddenly, nobody punished her when she lay silent and still—people became tender, and this was the only power she'd ever had over people. It was a lesson that seriously ill children quite often learn: sickness and refusal to eat leads to considerable power over parents. For Joan, it was a lesson that she could not possibly ignore; a weapon that she was to employ again and again.

The moment she stepped onto Irish soil to meet the new stranger that was to be her mother, she was schooled in the art of deception. Marion did not know Joan's exact age, but if anyone asked, Marion instructed Joan to say that she was six years old. This must have been difficult for the convalescent girl, for, as thin as she must have been, she was tall for her age, and would already have begun to assume the introspective thoughfulness of the pre-pubescent girl, rather than the headlong innocence of the six-year-old child. Even at ten, she would have felt keenly that it was impossible for her to be presumed to be a six-year-old. Weak after illness, in a new country, and insecure with a large stranger, she did as she was told.

Marion Moriarty must have had her reasons for pretending that Joan was six years old, rather than roughly ten. Mixing up ages is a good way of concealing origins, and covering tracks, but it would have been enough simply to have altered Joan's birthday.

In later years, Joan herself said privately, that her educational level was always well below what would normally have been expected. If she was unable to read at this stage, it could have been shame which motivated Marion to pretend that Joan was younger, and there would also thus be no danger of Joan having to go to secondary school and of disgracing herself. She had been institutionalised during and after the First World War, when her chances of education must have been remote. She had also been unsettled by going in and out of foster homes, and had been ill for a lengthy period. On the other hand, she was able to write by the time she made her first communion at the age of eight. Joan always claimed to have taught herself to write.

In public, her new mother bravely passed the child off as her own. But Marion, who was born in 1876, was aged around fifty when she took Joan in, and had finished having babies about twenty years previously. When Marion suddenly appeared with half-grown Joan, the neighbours knew at once that the girl could not possibly be her own, because not only had the girl suddenly appeared from nowhere, but they felt that Marion was too old to have been her mother. They also realised immediately that Joan was far too big to be six.

So little time did she spend in the smaller country house which Marion had taken just outside the town, that Joan was hardly sure of the name of it. In one of her photograph albums is a picture she entitled 'glengarrett house'. This is crossed out, and corrected to 'Ballygarrett House'. They rented it for a very short time when Joan first came. The house no longer exists. The only buildings left are the stables, now used by a stud farmer.

Joan was not there long. The suffering and shame of her early upbringing were only the beginning. The secrets and intrigue gathered momentum. From such a turbulent start in life, Joan came to Ireland, expecting a rural haven, to find that there was to be no stability or security, and she had more to tell lies about than how old she was, and who her mother was.

Her 'father's' whereabouts were a mystery. He had gone to the UK for some unspecified reason, and may have been dead. He may simply have deserted, but whatever Marion's secrets were, she didn't confide in Joan. Her new guardian's life was in a state of upheaval, and Joan was to lead a nomadic life with her new mother.

Her new brothers were much older than Joan; nearly old enough to be her father. In days of prosperity they had been sent to public school in England, and with their legal background, they were still thought of by local people, as being gentleman types. Local people thought they were her uncles, but she saw little of them.

The men she referred to as her brothers, benefited little from their educational experiences abroad. Firstborn Jack Moriarty, 'a bit of a toff', was at least twenty years older than Joan. Jack at first worked in a car factory in London, and later, together with his brother Gus, worked as a mechanic in the riverside garage the brothers owned at Ballydaheen, just outside the town. Jack Moriarty was not much of a businessman, though, and he took little real notice of it.

A thin, glamorous man with gold-rimmed glasses, who wore good tweed and a velvet cap, Jack was a dissipator and a loser, like his father. He spent his time amusing himself rather than working, and was fairly simple-minded. One of the few people with a car, he enjoyed the company of Kieron Bolster, a young neighbour, with whom he often went shooting in the mountains. He amused himself by spinning far-fetched stories from the wider world, deliberately baffling the country lad. He could while away hours throwing stones into the river for his labrador, Sam, to fetch. He was naïve in business, and thought everyone honest. Jack Moriarty lost money on his business, mainly, it has been said, because he was an easy touch for giving credit to horsey pals, but he was never without a cigar. He drank, and was fond of women, but he never married. A spender, money meant nothing to him, and when he died, all he left was a couple of old guns. Jack saw Kieron Bolster every day, but during the years that Kieron knew him as a close friend, Jack never once mentioned his younger 'sister' Joan.

Heavy-set Gus was a well-known handballer, who was also famous for his bowling and hurling. Gus was keenly interested in amateur sport, and did not marry until 1950, well after his mother died in 1940.

Denis, the youngest, was known as Sid. Sid had the bright cheeks and terrible cough of tuberculosis, and he died young, in 1947. He was a solicitor who did not do well. He worked amongst the poor people, for low fees but had few clients, and did little business.

A new sense of insecurity would have been dawning on Joan as she made her way through those first few months in Mallow—the shameful insecurity of being in a family that was on the slide, and going from bad to worse. There was to be no trace in Joan's photograph album, for example, of the modest little terraced house she later spent ten years in. Marion's personal anxiety—more potent for its unspecified nature—would also have communicated itself to her.

No sooner had Joan fattened up a little, playing amongst the buttercups near the wide Blackwater river, than Marion started packing her bags. She was on her way back to England, and would take Joan with her. As part of the disintegration of this family, Joan herself had no option but to leave the newfound grasslands and river behind her, and to accompany Marion back to built-up city life in the North of England. To enter her teens leading an insecure, nomadic life, completely at the mercy of Marion Moriarty, and baffled by this world full of secrets, must have been a bitter disappointment to Joan.

Marion moved back to England with Joan, and went first to Liverpool, where it is possible that she may have been searching for her husband, who had spent time at the nearby seaside resort of New Brighton. Joan had no recollection of her 'mother' being with her 'father', but she did recall moving constantly from place to place, she did not know why. They also went to Manchester. Marion was alone with her adopted daughter, and travelling. She must have been looking for something. She would have needed some good reason to comb the North of England with a young girl in tow.

Joan later told a close friend that she was never treated like a daughter by Marion Moriarty. She was dragged around, she confided, from place to place, and was treated merely as a sort of lady's servant for the stern and forbidding Marion. During this period in England she went from school to school, where the girl was usually academically so far behind that she had the humiliation of sitting in classes with children much younger and smaller. She was tall, and felt her inappropriateness keenly. Bewildered by the changing syllabus in the different schools, and unable to keep up, or even relate to the work, she applied herself to the business of finding out merely how to read and write, and she did that, shaky and unsure, for herself.

What her adopted mother was doing in the North of England, Joan never found out, but later confided bitterly that no priority whatsoever had been given to her education. Joan had strong traces of Manchester and Liverpool in her mixed accent.

It is likely that Marion, who had the child foisted on her when she herself was well past childbearing age, when her own family was grown, and when she had no male supporter, had a very high level of resentment against the job of looking after this unhappy child, who was neither well-adjusted nor easy to manage. If she thought Joan was dying when she agreed to take her, perhaps she believed that the duty would be a temporary one, and that she would eventually bury the child. Maybe the arrangement at first was that she would simply nurse the child back to health and then send her back. Whatever the dynamics of their relationship, Joan later reported that she felt neglected by Marion, and that she did not like her.

When she became famous, Joan talked publicly of having won a scholarship to the Sheila Elliot Clarke School in London during childhood. She later told the press that she'd also attended the Espinoza School, but her private claim that she taught herself to read and write, shows some neglect of her education on the part of those responsible. She may well have attended these dancing schools, but there is no proof of any sort. It seems unlikely, in view of the lack of priority given to her general education, that she had seen much in the way of expensive dancing classes during early childhood. In the same way, if Marion later completely neglected to have Joan educated during the time she was in England, as Joan said she did, and treated her as a servant, it is difficult to see how she would have prioritised dancing lessons.

But nobody could prevent Joan from dreaming. In her own, mostly made-up version of her life story, which in later years she used to recite to the press, she had a few little anecdotes about childhood, in which she used to quote things her mother was supposed to have said to her as a child. Significantly, not one of these little quotations is positive or supportive. She used them only to illustrate her own stories, but all are negative.

'We'll see, dear. Hush, now,' her mother is supposed to have said when as a six-year-old, Joan informed her, during a performance of *Swan Lake* or *Giselle*, that she wanted to be a ballet dancer.

As a child, she used to sit staring into the fire for hours, she related. She could see all sorts of things in there. 'Your imagination will be the death of you', was the pretended quote from her mother, which Joan used to tell, to illustrate the fact that she had a developed imagination.

In another anecdote, she said she used to practise dance steps under the table, in the house of people she was staying with in London, where she'd been sent at the age of six, because there were no ballet schools in Ireland. 'Can't you keep your feet still?' was what they'd said. She intended these to be gentle memories of childhood days, but clearly, the young Joan Denise didn't know what support, love and encouragement was.

If Marion had gone to England in an effort to return the now comparatively healthy Joan to those who were more closely related to her than Marion was then, she may have been looking for those who had put the girl into the orphanage in Liverpool. If Marion treated the girl as a servant, she would have made it clear to Joan that the young girl was not particularly wanted or appreciated as family. A woman in this position would justify such behaviour by feeling, like most of her society of the time, that the stigma of illegitimacy carries blame for the child.

There is evidence to suggest that Joan's personal recollection of the nature of her relationship with Marion was rather different from the perceptions of onlookers. This in itself isn't neccessarily significant, but it may be.

Accounts from Mallow neighbours would indicate that Marion was far from stern; that she loved her adopted daughter very much indeed, and that Joan herself adored her adopted mother. There is also similar evidence that some of her own recollections of the nature of her relationship with her brothers, differs dramatically from the observations of others.

Under the circumstances, it was to be reasonably expected that Joan would work at concealing the truth of her origins from the public and press. But she made a lifetime habit of presenting her realities, even to her closest friends, in ways that didn't add up. She would never forget her bad start. Increasingly as she grew older, she contrived to present information about herself in a manipulative way, a way that was designed to get sympathy. She also had a deep need to be noticed, to be admired. She knew she needed help, and using every tool at her disposal, she worked out her own ways of getting it. By the time Joan was a young woman, she had developed a remote, secretive, and manipulative personality.

These early years formed the basis on which Joan Denise Moriarty made her life choices. She was to remain frail for the rest of her life, and had frequent bouts of illness, both physical and mental. She was subject to severe depressions, and for the rest of her life, was aware that her mental state was fragile. Her command of spoken language was shaky forever afterwards, and she was afraid of saying anything in company. She had no aptitude for spelling, and had no confidence in her ability to write. She needed help to formulate sentences. She could read, and was willing to learn, but she felt ill-equipped and poorly-educated. For these reasons, as well as her feelings of inferiority, she was deeply afraid of meeting people. Socially, she always secretly felt out of her depth, and kept quiet. For the rest of her life, her personal attachments were cool and distant, and she continually sought out conditions of privation.

Illegitimate, rootless, and rejected, Joan Denise Moriarty was damaged. The sense of desolation, first known as an infant, would remain with her, as would her lack of trust, and her sense of being unloved. But there would be no overt rage. Buried deep inside, anger is an emotion that abandoned, wounded, neglected people are unable to express. It usually comes out in other ways. She was hurt and shamed by her secrets, yet her trials were far from over. Not only were there to be more secrets, there were plenty more lies to be lived out.

3

Early Life Reinvented

The story that Joan Denise Moriarty related so many times to the press contained enough invented little snippets to cover roughly half a page. Sometimes the facts differed a little bit, but basically it was the same story.

She always presented herself as extremely hardworking; someone who worked until she dropped. But the rigors of her early life, which she related as an adult, her impossible work schedule and cheerful dedication to it, is pathetically far-fetched, even by Irish work-ethic standards.

When she was six years old, the story ran, she went on a holiday to London, where she was taken to see the ballet, either *Giselle* or *Swan Lake*. By the time Act II came around, she was sure of what she wanted to do with her life. Tugging at her mother's sleeve to the point of maternal embarrassment, and to the annoyance of those around her, she insisted that she wanted to be a dancer. 'Yes, dear, sshh. We'll see. Keep quiet now,' her mother replied.

Back in Ireland, the story continued, she kept nagging until her mother made enquiries about dancing schools. There was no school of any reputation or standard in Ireland, and so at the age of six and a half, Joan Denise went to live with relatives in England who had three young children, and became part of their family. Assessments for talent and physique were followed by a year at the Sheila Elliot Clarke School of Dancing, and she then took up study of dance at the Espinoza School of Dance in London. Even at six and a half years old, she said, she loved the thousands of exercises and limbering routines, and all the sweat and tears, and was always very enthusiastic.

A dancer, she said, in describing the routines of her early life, must be well-educated. To this end she had to be up by 6.15 in Winter and Summer, to catch an early bus into the centre of London. At the terminus another bus took her out to her educational school, where she had to be in class by 8.45. After the whole day at school, she took a bus back into town and to her dance school, where she then remained for three hours of classes. It meant getting home very late, and after her evening meal, there was homework, and it was as late as 11.30 or 12.00 every night before she was in her bed. The day she had loved most, the adult Joan related, was Sunday. Every Sunday after church she put on her practice clothes and all day long, practised everything that she had learned the previous week. So active was the young dancer that at meals, the family she was staying with always used to ask her to keep, for heaven's sake, her feet still under the table. A late addition to the story was the Goddess of Dance, an image which she said she had looked up to thoughout her career. But this Goddess of Dance was not mentioned throughout the whole of her career, and came up only towards the end of her life.

So that was her own story of her early life. The family she stayed with in England, must in reality have been a foster family. They may have sent her, along with their own children, to ballet lessons, but this is unlikely.

Above all Joan's story shows her out-of-touch with normal childhood routines, inventing one she considered admirable and worthy. She was unaware that it would be very unusual for a child to be sent from Ireland to the centre of London at such a tender age to study dance, even with relatives. It also shows that the child-identity she later chose to re-invent, was superhuman; a six-year-old, single-minded ascetic who pushed herself and punished herself beyond reasonable bounds, in the cause of her art. Her own early life was so awful, that she retrospectively invented a super-childhood that pleased her, which contained an ambitious little budding ballerina.

Her own story of early days continued with a brief reference to the summer holidays with her cousin Patricia, at 'Glenacht' Castle in Inverness, Scotland. This is the part of her own story which had some basis in fact. In the mornings the girls would hear ex-pipe major Daly of the Gordon Highlanders playing the pipes for Lord and Lady Inchcape. And in the evenings, when they were supposed to be in bed, the girls would creep down and listen to his piping just before dinner. Joan Denise wanted to play the pipes, but wasn't allowed. Eventually, after much pestering, her aunt allowed her to take lessons from this pipe major, in Scottish dancing as well as in piping. A keen student at the pipes, she related that she became the first girl to enter the Highland Games, where she came third in her class. At fifteen, she said, she won an Irish stepdancing championship. In 1936, or 1938, she entered the All-Ireland Piping Championships in Killarney and won. She said she was sixteen when she beat the men at this instrument, and got her name into the newspaper. This section of the story—upper-class, grand and acceptable—had no need of re-invention, and is authentic. But the 'highland games' she referred to were a tiny little event in the vilage of Coull, and she was more like twenty years old when she entered the competition at Killarney.

In those days, people went to work at the age of thirteen and fourteen, particularly those who were not being educated. She said she'd worked as a waitress in London at some time, and in later years, when people wondered why she never married, she told them that at this time she had been betrothed to a violinist who'd died of consumption before she could marry him. Even a close and loyal friend of later years, was sceptical about the truth of this romantic story.

Whether or not she nagged anyone to bring her to dancing classes, and whether she had to pester her aunt to allow her to learn piping, which she did learn, it is clear that she was a loner and a dreamer. But she was aware that her own account of her life was thin.

'This seems very rushed and glossed over,' she apologised on tape, 'but it is a long time ago and it is hard to remember'.

She said that she won a scholarship to the Rambert School, paying no fees, and that she cleaned and tidied the office for a small sum. She did not say when, and there is no evidence available to support her assertion that she trained with Rambert. There is no record of her attendance at the Rambert School, although indexing, which goes back to the twenties, is incomplete. Neither is there any record of her performing with Rambert, and it is likely that she did not.

She also said that she had been to a newly-opened Rambert school in Paris for three years, to study staging, lighting, choreography and management, but there was never a Rambert school in Paris as such. Marie Rambert used to recommend pupils to individual Parisian teachers for short courses. In any case, Joan was in Ireland at the time she was supposed to be in Paris.

However, a lot of dancers did tasks at the school, as she said she had. She also appears to have had some perspective on Marie Rambert's approach, and must have had some opportunity to familiarise herself with the older woman's ways. She related that she considered Marie Rambert 'marvellous', with whom, like everybody else, she'd had a love/hate relationship. One possible later source through which she may have picked up some Rambert anecdotes, was Charles Lynch, a storytelling Corkman who had been a pianist for Rambert, and who later was employed as pianist for the Irish National Ballet. If Joan herself ever did come into contact with Rambert, it would have been briefly, and possibly not even as a dancer. Whatever the facts, she was capable of inserting herself into Rambert stories, and used the idea of the strict Frenchwoman as a role model.

The formidable Rambert, she related, told her that she'd never make a dancer. One reason was that, at five foot six, she was too tall. In such circumstances, other disciplines peripheral to dancing tend to be tactfully suggested, which would be more suitable to the student's aptitudes. She'd be better off going home, she was told, and doing something like starting a school in her own country.

In reality, she had almost no general education, and Joan Denise Moriarty does not appear to have obtained any dancing or teaching qualifications at all. In terms of her eventual exalted position in Ireland, this lack of training seems odd, but in terms of running little schools in provincial neighbourhoods for small children, it was not unusual for dance teachers in the thirties to be scarcely trained. Standards were not uniform, and when it became the fashion for teachers to put young pupils in for exams, the teachers themselves were not neccessarily required to hold qualifications. By the sixties, a more stringent system was in operation. From that time, teachers entering pupils for exams needed to be of a certain standard themselves. Joan started teaching dance in the very early thirties, when she was still almost a child herself.

In August 1963, at the age of about forty-seven, she applied to take an elementary executant examination with the Royal Academy of Dance, but she became ill and did not keep the appointment. She never made another.

4
Glenapp Castle

A brief life of wonderful privilege and opportunity, in a setting of unbelievable romance and splendour, suddenly opened out to the young Joan Moriarty, in magnificent contrast to the heavily-populated, impoverished, industrial North of England. Whatever threats or blandishments Marion used to secure this, she managed to send Joan during the holidays to Glenapp Castle, in Ayrshire, Scotland, to stay with her Aunt Joan and her cousin Patricia.

Glenapp provided an avenue towards a kind of healing for Joan, and gave her a deep and almost mystical love of nature. Surrounded by majestic purple hills, fifteen thousand acres of land rose up in a great sweep of sensational open landscape from sea level, to a height of nearly two thousand feet. The castle nestled in thirty-six acres of gardens. The view from young Joan's bedroom window looked out over the treetops across the lonely island of Ailsa Craig, and extended to the Mull of Kintyre. The turreted castle overlooked deep glens and dense woods full of bluebells and squirrels, birch, pine, cedar and ferns. There were extensive moorlands thick with the smell of heather and the call of game birds. Twelve miles out to sea lurked the treacherous Inchcape Rock, which was submerged at high tide. Secretive loner Joan, at her most impressionable age, adored the wild spaces and drank in the fairytale.

Little Joan knew Patricia's father, Kenneth as 'Uncle'. She did not suspect at first that the Earl was her father, and she had no notion that Patricia could be her half-sister. Neither did anyone else discuss it. The family welcomed her, but there was no acknowledgement of her, other than as a cousin from Ireland, a poor relation.

James Lyle Mackay, the first Earl of Inchcape, Patricia's indulgent grandfather, bought the castle and estate in 1917 as a family seat, and kept his large yacht moored in nearby Loch Ryan, which opened out onto the sea. Decisive and brilliant in business, he was variously described as a 'hard man' and a 'ruthless man', but he was 'never cruel to little people'. He was from the little east coast herring town of Arbroath, and had started his working life at 15, as a scrivener in a lawyer's office.

When he first travelled to India as an assistant to a Scottish business firm, he found that Scotsmen were well established in Anglo-Indian trade. He joined them, seething constantly with new ideas, all of them new ways of making money. One of his first ideas was to establish a bank, the P and O Bank, which had branches in India. He rose fast, and was eventually made President of the Indian Currency Association, arguing for the gold standard. He became big in shipping, and ended up with the whole of the combined fleet of the P and O Company, and the British India Company under his control.

After the First World War, he argued for the fleet to be released for trade, and oversaw the sale of the ships himself, as well as hundreds of enemy ships. He would guard pennies eccentrically, but was personally generous. He was a man who liked to work a sixty hour week, and could never understand why workers were fighting for a forty hour week. In old age, he went to the office every day when he was in London, and at the time of his death at the age of seventy-five, he had four secretaries.

James Lyle Mackay ran Glenapp almost feudally, with himself as king. Eighty-eight men and women were employed in his forests, gardens and castle. He entered his servants' lives to the extent that they became devoted to him. His gun-loader considered him a mystery, with a fearful, piercing eye. His butler said it was 'exciting to be near him, for there was something terribly beautiful behind all he did'. He left legacies to his servants. Even at Glenapp he was extremely busy, opening the day's telegrams whilst his servant struggled to remove his shooting boots. His employees had to be as perfectionist as he was. Everything around him had to be immaculate, every rug lined up, and picture frame straight. No speck of dust was allowed in house or yacht. Thirty crew looked after his yacht, *Rover*, yet he always kept a wet mop handy to personally remove any little blemish that may appear. He caught mackerel by the hundreds, and it was his pleasure to stop at every house on the way home to distribute his catch.

There were eight hundred brace of grouse to be bagged in a season over the expanse of his moorlands. In the shooting season, privileged friends and business contacts came up from London to enjoy his hospitable house parties. Servants stood by after a day's stalking, to take off guests' boots. Log fires blazed in their bedrooms as they changed for extravagant dinners of salmon, trout, venison and game. Friends that came to join the big shooting parties at Glenapp, included cabinet ministers, and all sorts of influential people like Lord Kilbracken, Lord Churchill and Lord Rawlinson.

His son and heir Kenneth, who became the second Earl, had a great love of sport and the sea, and became an active businessman, working in the P and O Company. In 1916, within a year of his marriage to the beautiful Irishwoman, Joan Moriarty, he spontaneously joined up, and went off to war in France leaving behind a wife pregnant with his first child.

Kenneth's three legitimate children were christened Catholics for his wife's sake, but the boys were later converted back to Protestantism. Joan was allowed to bring up Patricia, their eldest child, as a Catholic, and Patricia remained a devout Catholic all her life.

In the twenties, Aunt Joan was perceived as having a sad life. This may have been because of the roving eye and habits of her husband, or she may have had an undiagnosed depressive illness. At the time, there were no drugs for depression, and the condition usually went untreated. In any case, the rearing of her young family may have given Aunt Joan a reasonably optimistic outlook at this time and she seemed to welcome little Joan into this more upmarket branch of the family. She may have felt that a Catholic girl of the same age as her own little daughter, would be a fit companion for her, and she may also have felt some responsibility for young Joan, the product of her own flesh and blood.

On the other hand, perhaps it was her husband who gave permission for his illegitimate daughter to stay. Aunt Joan may have felt that the girl was foisted on her, and she may have been upset but weak and powerless to resist whoever was exerting pressure for little Joan to come and spend some time at Glenapp.

There are signs, from the way Joan thrived, that the people she found there were to some extent able to open their hearts, as well as their home, to their young relative. The Glenapp climate and attitudes towards young people were such that, for the first time in her life, Joan Denise Moriarty began to experience happy times. For the few years that she went for brief summer visits, she flourished in this fairyland of opulence, and in her new found freedom, she learned very quickly.

It was here at Glenapp Castle, which all her life, Joan Denise called 'Glenack' that she first bloomed. Cousin Patricia was keen on ballet. This affluent family with an interest in their children's accomplishments were in a position to offer Joan also, the opportunity to learn ballet. It is certain that Joan developed an interest in Scottish/Irish dancing at Glenapp. It was here that she learned to play the bagpipes, known in Ireland as the war pipes, and it was here that she began entering piping competitions.

It was also during holidays at Glenapp Castle, where she spent days and nights with this aristocratic family, that she saw her first justification to put on real-life airs and graces. She had a ready-made real-life family of cousins to fuel her imagination—the grand castle full of grand people.

She and Patricia giggled on the stairs at night, listening to the adults thronged over cocktails after the day's shooting; watching as they made their way in evening dress towards the dining room with its heavy carved oak table, to the echoing formal accompaniment in the Great Hall of a Scottish piper. Little Joan was transfixed by the loud majestic wail of the bagpipes that nobody could ignore, and entranced by the dignified stage presence of the piper. The piper captured the splendour and tradition of Scottish-baronial Glenapp life. She wanted to play like this piper, and be majestic like him.

A ballet teacher would have come to the castle to teach Patricia dance and so it is likely that the girls did class together, and that they practised together, with Patricia teaching Joan some steps she didn't already know. Joan would have made a welcome addition to the dancing class, partnering Patricia, who was the only little girl in the family.

James Mackay had built a large and beautiful room onto the castle, with two great windows. One faced the sea, and the other looked out on extensive lawns, massed rhododendrons and a forest of firs. Curios from all over the world were assembled neatly in here, amongst the tapestries and silver models of sailing ships. He was indulgent with the children, and later the grandchildren, and welcomed them into this room. Patricia, though getting a bit too big, would have brought Joan to visit this dear grandfather when he was home from the office in London, or from his yacht. He would have opened the gold and turqoise musical box in the loving little ritual that Patricia had known throughout her childhood. For fun, he would have studied their adolescent eyes in the magic moment as they watched the intricate little bird with real feathers rise in the box, and sing sweetly. He had a special talent for enchanting young people, and his own children called him 'father-man'. They were not allowed to touch things he kept in his room, but he organised a 'touching drawer' especially for the young ones, that they could rummage happily in during their daily visits. There was no bullying with him, but plenty of praise. When anyone was naughty, they were sent to his study for a stiff lecture. If they cried, he told them always to remember that he was their friend.

His favourite child was not one of his sons, but Elsie, a remarkable and wild girl who had inherited some of his force and personality. He adored her spirit. He encouraged her to be brave, and to do everything a man could do, and more. The headstrong Elsie's marriage to Dennis Wyndham, of the Wiltshire Regiment, lasted five years. After that, she resumed her maiden name and took a lover. It was Elsie who assumed control of the decoration of the ships in her father's fleet.

When young Joan Moriarty showed an inclination to learn the bagpipes—a pastime not altogether usual for a girl, the old Lord would have let her be encouraged in this. In later life, she said that she had been the first girl to enter the Highland Games at Coull. It is true that the Highland Games was a man's world, and also true that the grandfather would have seen to it with relish, that any ambition on the part of a young girl to invade male arenas, was facilitated. He admired spirit and backbone, particularly in a girl, and it was his habit to give people the benefit of the doubt first. This little cousin from Ireland was like his daring Elsie and the rootless cousin herself rejoiced inside at the possibility of being a little like the already legendary Elsie.

Braemar is the main venue for the true Highland Games, but apart from this event lots of minor ones take place all over Scotland. Coull is a tiny place on a minor road, a long way away from Glenapp, across the Grampians, near the east coast and Aberdeen. The only logical justification for being on this side of Scotland could possibly have been a visit to Abroath south of Aberdeen, the first Earl's birthplace. Perhaps a touring party which included Joan, was in the area when they happened upon the little Highland Games going on in some field, and they indulged her when she wanted to join in.

In the early Spring of 1928, during one of her adventures, Elsie met a tragic death. One of the first female pilots in the world, her ambition was to fly the Atlantic. Accompanied by her lover, she set off West to East from America, in a two-seater. The plane went down, and she was never heard of again. Her father was devastated. Those close to him said that he never got over her death. It was but the first tragedy to darken the family at this time, and overshadow young Joan Moriarty's brief times of uneasy bliss.

Soon an even greater tragedy unfolded. The wonderful Glenapp world of summers that they knew was to fall apart totally, and for all of them. The happy summer of sharing that Patricia and Joan had known together as they grew up was to be destroyed by a dreadful series of events. After about fifteen years of marriage, during which time he gained a reputation for his affairs with other women, the Second Earl finally fell completely in love with Leonora Brooke, known as 'Nonie', the daughter of the last white Rajah of Sarawak. Nonie inhabited the same ruling-class level of society as his own family, and the India connection was very strong in both the Brooke and the Mackay clans. Kenneth decided eventually that he wanted to marry her.

In 1931, he divorced his beautiful, sad Joan, and his link with the Moriarty family was severed. The death aboard his yacht in 1932, of the old grandfather in Monaco, and the final upheavals of separation and divorce, meant that everything was changed, and that there would be no more Glenapp for the teenaged Joan, ever. Her brief Summer visits to this idyllic place were over, and by 1931, she was permanently back in Ireland with Marion. Her times with her relations in Scotland had been her important times, but they had been overshadowed by the secret sadness of Aunt Joan, and heavy with the silent and unacknowledged adults' secret of her own illegitimacy. A dark and uneasy atmosphere was what Joan knew as reality.

Aunt Joan slid into a deep despondency, and subsequently became depressed to the point of feeling that she had nothing left to live for. Less than two years after her divorce, at the end of February 1933, the year in which her ex-husband was to remarry, she committed suicide. Still lovely, she was in her thirties. Aunt Joan's sons were in their early teens when she died, and Patricia was seventeen. Three months later, Kenneth, the new Lord Inchcape, married his Nonie.

Though she was far away when her kind Aunt Joan died, young Joan had intuitively experienced at puberty some of the internal family tensions as they became terminal. The pall of tragedy darkened the memory of the only happy times she had known. Everything in the jigsaw of memory was changed forever—the leaf-dappled river gardens; the forests of rhododendrons; the heady scent of moorland heather; the morning mists; the solid, dark oak of the beautiful furniture with the beeswax smell—all were suddenly starkly laden with a vivid sense of annihilation. Though she came to realise that in a sense she belonged there, she also knew that she could never have Glenapp. Deep within herself was the knowledge that she could never go back. Joan's anguish contained a new sense of preciousness. The acres of ordered splendour, and the fine things she had briefly enjoyed, had imprinted in her needy heart and mind, a first deep love; the loner's passionate love of nature. In future, the beauty of nature, and of fine things, would powerfully attract her, imbued with the sense of poignant loss that she already knew so well. This almost morbid, internal passion would become a focus. It would almost comfort her in its familiarity. There were no cold, dark corridors with antiseptic smells in nature; there were no starched humans that never embraced her. Nature she could allow to reach her, deep inside. She would cherish it forever.

The suicide of Aunt Joan showed Joan Moriarty a distorted truth, that this life contains much bleakness. The lesson for her young mind was that these happy and contented times she had discovered, were to be deeply mistrusted. Now her privileged cousins too were without a mother. Her sense of personal loss deepened. There was no security to be found anywhere.

The kind Lord was an enormous unconscious influence on Joan. She now had a clear sense of what a good 'father-man' was. He was someone who was aristocratic, with morality, fine manners, gentleness, and in his own autocratic world, a benign ruler. He was loving and indulgent to females, showing them fairytale, foreign worlds, and putting on enchanting little displays especially for them. For the first time, Joan had experienced male loving care. It was good. She had never met anyone like the eccentric and famous first Earl before. Amazingly, she would again.

5
Back in Ireland

I t was mostly said by Joan Moriarty herself, that she came back to Ireland in 1945, and immediately began laying plans to form a ballet company. She also said she was in Mallow forming a school in 1944, or even earlier. At other times, she acknowledged coming back to Ireland in 1938, claiming much intensive studying in the UK and Paris. The facts are that she came back in 1931, and that before moving permanently to Cork, she remained in Mallow for a decade, never returning to the UK or anywhere else during that period, or subsequently.

She probably celebrated her sixteenth birthday in Mallow. Packed amongst her luggage when, at around the age of fifteen, Joan Moriarty accompanied Marion on the boat back to Ireland, were souvenirs from forays to Glenapp Castle. Amongst her things there was a set of bagpipes, a kilt, and a pair of ballet shoes with hard toes. A testimony to the only education she'd ever had, these were to become the tools of her trade. At first she lived with Marion in a flat in Fair Street, Mallow, over the office of Marion's solicitor son, Sid. At night, the noisy wail of the pipes could be heard on the street below, as she practised in the flat, the sound rising and falling jerkily. As she marched up and down in the confined space, passers-by had no alternative but to notice her.

The bagpipes, or war pipes, as they are known in Ireland, are not the easiest instrument for a young girl, but Joan took the encouragement that she had been given extremely seriously, believing that at last she had some aptitude and flair of her own. She also wanted to be different, and the pipes gave her a legitimate focus. She had glimpsed Elsie's against-the-tide talent through the admiring eyes of the old Earl, the man who had also seen something in herself. Her feeling that she had inherited something of that talent, gave her courage to do it.

Marion had by now inherited five terraced houses in the town, and after a short time, instead of just collecting the low rents, they managed to get a vacancy in one of these and move into it. Along with Denis, Jack and Gus, Marion and Joan took up residence in Bridgeview, Broom Lane, amongst Marion's tenants in the adjoining houses. Though the houses would have been an acceptable source of income for Marion, actually moving into one of them was something different. Socially, it was a very big step down as a dwelling, since Marion came from the propertied small-business class. Worse, for a family with a big-house history on the male side, their presence amongst their mother's tenants highlighted the inadequacy of the three brothers.

Sid was ill, and worked only some of the time, giving very favourable rates to his poor clients, and Jack was a too-generous spender, indifferent to work. Big brother Gus, the sportsman, was very involved with the GAA, and it was part of his brief to put on the St Patrick's Day concert every March. Joan wanted to be part of it, and asked Gus to allow her to be on the bill. He indulged her. Out of her suitcase came the ballet shoes. She would, she told Gus, perform *en pointe* before the audience. He gave her an early spot in the show.

When the big moment came Joan she did something that was to become rather a hallmark of her early performances—she fell. But she didn't just stumble momentarily and then get up and carry on; she fell heavily and irretrievably, wrenching her ankle severely. Whilst the audience waited in distress for her to get up and continue, she lay for awful moments, stretched full-length across the stage, unable move. It was a serious accident, and the end of her solo performance. Eventually she was carried off and the curtain brought down. At the end of the show, when the cast lined up to take their bows, Joan was revealed sitting on a chair in the middle of the stage, unable to walk. She got plenty of attention.

It was usual for whole communities to go to these events whenever they got the chance, because without even radio at the time, it was the only sort of entertainment on offer. Joan was a novelty to watch, whether she was doing Irish dancing, this new-fangled ballet, or playing the equally strange instrument they hadn't seen before. The traditional Irish pipes, known as the uillean pipes, have a softer, quieter note, with less wail. Air is put into the bag, not by blowing with the mouth through a heavy reed, but by a bellows operated by the left arm. The bag of the Scottish war pipes is inflated by lung-power. Joan's ability to play the foreign ones gave her credibility.

Many of the neighbours had never before seen this girl who played the noisy, unusual pipes, and with her budding beauty and her dancer's ideas, she was enough of an exotic curiosity to be stared at. She demonstrated ways of walking, of moving, and of holding herself, that won her an audience of locals on the street. It is likely that they admired her cheek. Young Irish girls were never like this. Ballet was foreign, and foreign dances had for centuries been culturally and morally extremely suspect. The art and pastime of dancing had long been a matter for guidance from the pulpit. The clergy of the previous century had fought very hard to keep a strict yoke on their flocks, and had developed the habit of suddenly appearing brandishing sticks wherever people were dancing, and then chasing them all home. Revellers fled when they heard that the priest was coming. The population had grown accustomed to these clerical interruptions, and even in 1930, Ireland expected much guidance from the church on how to behave.

Young girls in the early thirties would never have been encouraged in body disciplines which showed off their curves. The well-clad performance art of Irish dancing was regimented, predictable, and safe. The nation was still more-or-less in the grip of the clergy. Girls were required to demonstrate modesty and obedience. Signs of vanity were stamped out; looking in the mirror was frowned on, and mirrors were literally removed from the gaze of young girls. Joan's half-schooled style, peculiar to herself, came from across the water, and she knew nothing about Irish customs, or how it was that she was a curious attraction in the locality.

Joan's approach to dancing and performing was based partly on her own deep need for love. She also didn't know what else she could do, so she gave dancing her whole commitment. When she performed, she had found that she got some attention. Misfortune was also still getting her attention and approval. She was suddenly getting noticed, not as an unwanted kid who had to be fed somehow and billeted somewhere, but as a particular young woman, Joan, who was dancing and charming people, and getting their sympathy. When she danced she became someone. It gave her individuality.

Since she had never before been personally valued, this gave her some sense of worth, but like all rejected and unloved people who become performers, she equated people's approval of her performance, with their approval of herself. So she put everything she had into it. It was her very life. When children are in difficult life situations which hurt them, they devise some strategy that enables them to cope with the chaos around them. Joan Moriarty, in the midst of a flux that was unstable and very insecure, picked dancing. That was to be the constant factor in her life which gave her some control.

Audiences didn't know this. All they saw was a young struggling girl. She was rather desperate. Her actressy ways didn't just proclaim, 'look at me'. They also said, 'this is all I've got'. People know a survivor when they see one. They liked her. She was an innocent abroad, and her naïvety was her safeguard. That, and the big heart they sensed, initially saved her from being cast out.

Joan was different, and little girls in audiences were mesmerised by it all. By the time she started looking for young pupils for her dance classes, the community knew what she was all about. It was 1932, and she was about sixteen. The venue for her first class was to be the Shorecastle Hall, but few girls came.

Brenda Sexton was one of the first Mallow children to attend the new dancing class, and she was nine when she started. She had watched Joan dancing on stage and had been mesmerised. She had also seen her fall, and knew it was possible to come back from a drama so awful as a bad onstage fall. Brenda's father was dead. Her mother loved dancing, and Brenda was thrilled to be going to dancing lessons. So were Bobbie and Lana O'Connor, daughters of the County Engineer, who lived at Clydaville, one of the remaining big Protestant houses outside the town. These two girls were from a well-off family, whose parents could afford to pay. There was to be no hit-and-miss approach; Joan had things all worked out. The first thing the little girls were told by the now beautiful and athletic amazon standing before them, was that their teacher was to be addressed as 'Miss Moriarty'. Then, they were told, they were immediately to get dresses made to her design, or bring the money. The short tunic was to be in dark green cotton cloth with short sleeves, and they were to wear white ankle socks. It was almost like dressing-up and childhood backyard theatricals.

Brenda's feelings towards the young Joan were typical of those of so many girls who became Joan's devoted pupils—she had a sort of crush on her, and was in a kind of awe tinged with fear. Even then, Joan was businesslike and remote, but the girls expected adults to be like that. She gave the impression of being very 'refined'; in a rare class far higher than theirs, and they just would never have dreamed of being familiar with her. Although she was distant as a person, she was always very kind to her pupils. The airs and graces were directly from Glenapp and, like the old Earl, Joan acted out the role of the aristocratic, benevolent autocrat. As far as they were concerned, her red hair was lovely, her voice was lovely, and Miss Moriarty was lovely. Joan did not know how to form close personal relationships, or how to gossip. She felt comfortable with children, who were her obvious inferiors, and with people she could keep regimented, and at a distance.

In the same building, she started another class for Irish dancing. Perhaps she was advised that Irish dancing would catch on more quickly than ballet. She kept it going for a couple of years, but the classes between them didn't bring in enough money to justify renting the hall, which would also have been rather cold for dancing. Her solution was to try to get permission from Marion and the three adult males that she lived with, to completely clear their front room of furniture, and to install a barre along one wall for her pupils to hold on to during their exercises.

Once implemented, this plan would have meant that the family had only one small dining room at the back adjoining a tiny kitchen. This proposed solution would have been convenient for Joan, with no rent to pay, and a realistic possibility of heating the front room, but it would also have meant there would be no sitting room for her family, because there was nowhere in the little dining room to put a couch and two armchairs for the other four adults in the house. Marion and her three sons needed some time to think.

Meanwhile, Joan had quietly moved her class down near the riverbank, putting her pupils through their gymnastic paces in the fresh air. The terraced house that Marion had taken over had a large garden at the back, and the public riverbank itself was across the road, just outside the front door. It has been said that Joan Moriarty started her classes in a field on the edge of town. It was in this large garden, which would have been perceived by some children as a 'field', that Joan conducted her class. It is unlikely that she would have resorted to the riverbank field itself, but she may have. Perhaps some children stopped coming to her when the class moved down to the Broom Lane garden; maybe it was the weather, or perhaps Marion was shamed into agreement. Whatever the case, the field episode was short-lived, and Joan's blackmail worked. She won the battle and procured the front room.

Every year, Joan put on a show in the town hall. The children loved it, and all their parents came to see it. Joan danced the lead roles, and the children mainly danced around her star. Brenda's mother used to say there was one thing about Joan, you could always let any child go with her anywhere. It was fun for them. Jack had a car, and would take them to some other village if they needed to go. One day she got an invitation from some organisers in nearby Buttevant village to bring her Irish dancers and put on a show in the village hall. They all set out, costumes packed. When they got there, they found that some of the organisers were completely drunk behind the scenes. Whatever their motives were in hiring this novel little troupe, Joan didn't like the attitude, and herself and Jack whisked the children right back out again, and brought them all home. They hadn't even bothered unpacking their costumes.

When dancers work at communicating with their bodies, it is in the hope of attracting enough attention to inspire audiences towards some inner transcendence. Self-discipline is the price they pay in the process of working to invoke a psychological, emotional and/or spiritual transaction with viewing participants. Amongst people who crave audiences are those who have had severely fractured childhoods, and also those whose parents were abusive or indifferent to them. These obsessively and insatiably long for attention and, talented or not, will also drive themselves to extreme lengths, including the criminal, in order to shock people, impress them, or get noticed in some way.

What had happened with Joan Moriarty, was that dancing and piping had saved her. Losing herself in these had become the backbone of her life, the thing she could most rely on, her anchor. Thus they became hugely important to her. These are what gave her a sense of self, and of individuality, as well as a sense of worth. She had survived in her isolation by dreaming, and by living out dreams. Now a free agent in an unfamiliar land, she had to go to work. She was ready to work towards being watched and admired; ready to be noticed. The deep craving towards this was pathological. The loner's dreaming trancelike state was habitual.

She had to work with children because she felt safe with them, and she had to work at something that would get her noticed. Amongst the priorities on her agenda was a personal need to give young kids a better deal than she herself had known. She intuitively wanted to give them, through their own dreams, a means of survival through artistic expression. She said that she wanted to give young people something to dream about. She knew that whatever else was going on in their lives, the skills she could show them would enrich them. She was able to communicate vision, but her dance training had been patchy, and insufficient. The talent as a dancer and as an artist hadn't really been tried and tested. If it had been great, it is likely that Marie Rambert—assuming Joan's Rambert story was true—would have noticed.

Not all girls took to her. Some didn't like Miss Moriarty and her strict disciplines, and many dropped away. Still, she was able to keep going in this way for eight years, and would probably have remained in Mallow if circumstances had not pushed her towards the city of Cork. By the time she abandoned teaching in Mallow in 1940, she had around twenty pupils. It was on these young, impressionable pupils that she practised becoming Miss Moriarty. She saw the awe in their eyes when they watched her and when they listened to her made-up and exaggerated stories about how hard she had needed to work in order to become a dancer. One of the attributes that fired pupils, was the power of her imagination. To them, she was a wonderful teacher. They were aware that she had another life beyond the one in the dark little front room where as 'Miss Moriarty', she drilled them over and over again in simple exercises. They were aware that the people she played badminton with called her 'Joan', but these were high-class people, her friends.

6

Friends

Amongst the people the teenaged Joan counted as friends back in Mallow, were the upscale O'Connor family, who lived outside the town, in one of the elegant, spacious, 'big', houses built by Protestant settlers. She had been trying to get pupils without much success, when a friend suggested that the O'Connors might want to send their girls to her.

Of all the families she could have picked to be friends with in and around the little Cork town, she chose the most upmarket, fashionable liberals in the district. She would remain distant with other pupils, who were to call her 'Miss Moriarty' but with this family she made friends, and they knew her as 'Joan'. These were not the kind of people who would normally be on friendly terms with Clockhouse Bar people, absentee philanderers and smalltown, unambitious solicitors. They were country-house-party, tennis-set people. Although she lived in a working-class terraced house in town with little money of her own, Joan, as a penniless practitioner of art had the access to their privileged table. She was also a nobody who nurtured inside herself, the idea that she was a somebody. Two new factories had recently been set up in the town, and there were plenty of jobs going, but though she had been a waitress in England, Joan Moriarty was not interested in a factory job, or in any job.

At some stage, perhaps during her teens, certainly before she was twenty-five, Joan Moriarty had become aware of the identities of her father and mother. It is likely that Marion would have told her, but unlikely that she did it as early as their trip to England, even though she may have taken Joan there partly in order to seek these relatives out. Whenever Joan did find out, it was kept a strict secret, and she was never accepted into the Mackay family, except as a young cousin who spent a couple of holidays there. Neither was any knowledge of her passed down in the family. Aunt Joan was known as an aunt and Patricia as a cousin in any case. There is no evidence that Marguerite Moriarty ever made herself known to her daughter, and it is likely that she did not. Joan may even have known the truth during her visits to Glenapp, but after those early holidays, Joan herself never again contacted the people of Glenapp Castle.

The most likely occasion on which the whole of her history would have been reliably pieced together in front of Joan for the first time, was on the visit of a celebrity barrister-at-law, Eoin 'Pope' O'Mahoney, to Marion's house in Broom Lane in the 1930s. 'Pope' was a hereditary Knight of Malta, and an eccentric and flamboyant man whose real passion was genealogy. His work in this field led him to travel extensively, and his prodigious memory and extensive knowledge, combined with his charm and fluency, led to the making of popular radio programmes. People sought him out for his elevated brand of gossip all the time, and he knew 'everybody' in the UK, as well as in Ireland. He was generous with his money and his wine, and he attended, and threw, many parties. He was highly respected and admired for his ability to accumulate much information, forget nothing, and regurgitate everything directly from memory.

This barrister and media personality would have known the Cork and Dublin legal people, amongst whom Joan's secret grandfather, Justice Moriarty would have been well known. Pope would also have devoured all the gossip and scandal on the legal circuit, particularly if it was genealogical. He visited Marion's house during a visit to Mallow, possibly to attend a funeral, and had a long talk with her in the kitchen, tête-à-tête, and well out of earshot of the rest of the family.

A few years later, Pope divulged the secrets of Joan's real family tree, for the benefit of his friend, the composer, Aloys Fleischmann, who was a fellow Corkman, and Music Professor at University College Cork. Aloys then later made a tentative and probing reference to Joan herself, about piping, and Glenapp Castle. 'Oh, you've been talking to Pope,' she snapped, and flatly refused to talk further about piping and Glenapp.

From the moment she knew who she was, Joan Moriarty could start trying to map herself out. Before this, she'd had no way of knowing who she looked like, and what she herself was like. Before this, she had no points of reference that would show her what her talents were, how she was going to turn out, and nobody to ask. In the privacy of her own head, she had spent much time dreaming and wondering about it. Like many adoptees, she badly needed to know.

Her discovery of her background led her to think back. The idea of life in Dublin with a Chief Justice of Appeal for a grandfather meant nothing to Joan. She knew nothing of her mother's ways or her lifestyle, or her schooldays, or what sort of house she lived in. Everything about that was a blank. All Joan knew of her mother was the exotic name 'Marguerite', and that she had glamorously been born in France.

She was certainly not able to publicise it, but the Glenapp link, particularly on an unconscious level with 'grandfather', helped to stiffen her backbone. The lineage of the blood didn't go back further than the current Lord, but the lifestyle was sumptuous, and the Earl was a multi-millionaire. It did not occur to Joan to invoke the bitterness of the bastard without land or inheritance. She just affected an aloof sort of regalness.

Naturally, there would be some regret and brooding, but as half-aristocracy, however disgrace-ridden and shameful, she could feel that she had reason be be secretly elevated. She had a firm link with the castle, the Scottish-baronial style, the woods, and the sweeping lawns. Glenapp was part of her, by Scottish blood, by right. Piping was in her bones. Yet she was still an orphan. She would never forget that. And she was still in poverty.

There was one thing in all this that really worried her: the sadness and eventual suicide of her namesake. What if she took after Aunt Joan in this respect, too? Even as a young child, she had known the kind of despair that aunt Joan must have felt. Silently and instinctively, she had empathised with the soft, grey sadness that had overshadowed her aunt. It was understood that people took their own lives because they had become unbalanced or mentally disturbed. Suicide was a thing that was only done because the mind became distorted by despair. Joan worried about this aspect of her own genetic makeup. She never again wanted to feel that terrible unhappiness which she had felt when her isolation had for a few grey weeks after her illness, become so unbearable that she had turned her face to the wall. She could not afford to trust anyone. She was sure she couldn't trust herself.

Her Mallow friend, John O'Connor, was a Cork County Engineer, and famous for his construction of the Cork–Kerry Healy Pass over the mountains. He had married a Le Mesurier from Guernsey, who had died four days after giving birth to beautiful, gentle Madeline, their third child. The new wife he chose, to mother his two sons and baby daughter, was a lovely, cultured Austrian woman, whose father was the official portraitist in the court of Emperor Franz Josef.

Fun-loving, easy-going John and his Austrian second wife presided over a happy family on a seventeen-acre estate at Clydaville, on the outskirts of Mallow. The affluent John had bought one of the remaining Protestant big houses that had escaped the torches of the Irish freedom fighters and, as five more children appeared one by one, their mother took them on holiday to Austria, to have their portraits painted by her celebrated father.

In local Irish terms, seventeen acres of pure garden was the kind of luxury that few could afford. The wooded drive to the big house was long, and sweet-smelling woodsmoke curled to meet ancient, high treetops in a rising mist. Visitors arriving from their offices in Cork, never needed to leave the grounds. In the daytime, weekend visitors went on rambling walks over the grasslands, admired the flower gardens, and tramped through the woods. In the evenings they ate, played games and relaxed at the fireside in country house party fashion. The elegant but unpretentious mansion, hung with Austrian portraits of children, was full of a sense of history, and just as cluttered and lived-in as any family house.

The hospitable O'Connors loved life and freedom, and in their house, there was always plenty of food and room for everyone. The eight spacious bedrooms had log fires, wood panelling, and all sorts of nooks and crannies. It was a house of privilege in a very romantic setting. On a smaller scale, the genteel Clydaville was Glenapp all over again, and on her visits there from Broom Lane Joan felt poignantly at home.

John O'Connor had a weakness for women with red hair. He loved the striking, theatrical Joan at once. She responded gladly, and called him, 'Daddy' as his five daughters did. She attached herself to the family in these privileged surroundings, visited often, and the whole family teased him about his indulgent ways with her. John was a man who loved everyone, and it was nothing new for him to be tolerant with young people, and for everyone to love him. Joan was enchanted with his wife also and called her 'Mummy'. She played tennis with the O'Connors.

Clydaville meant gentility, unlimited hospitality, joy, love, and family life. Her contact with the O'Connors gave Joan a sense of stability, and resurrected memories of the only happy childhood times she'd had. The local importance of the family also fed her dreams of getting away from her poor orphan status, giving her a reflected social prestige and standing.

From experience she already knew that it couldn't possibly last. Part of her accepted it as a game.

The growing Joan had not always been dressed carefully or attractively, and her hair had been cut plainly, and too short. Towards the end of childhood, she had taken on the transitional ugly duckling guise, with unattractive, sloping shoulders, a long neck, and with a puddingy look about her. Her hands and feet were big. When other young women were wearing size five shoes, Joan was wearing an ungainly size seven, and eventually eight. Though she dreamed of and practised dancing, her legs were big, heavy and ungraceful, and she was rather tall. To anyone looking on, it might have seemed that she hadn't a hope. However, one of the reasons that she felt herself to be a dancer, was that she was comparatively flexible. Her body-awareness had begun with the pastime of contorting herself into postures, lying on her tummy on the floor, touching the back of her head with her foot.

As her adult self began to emerge, and she was free to let her auburn hair grow longer and more flattering to her features, her body slimmed down as it changed shape. When she had her own money and could do her hair herself, the way she pleased, as well as choose fashionable clothes, Joan was made aware of a most wonderful asset, a feature which suddenly emerged in startling fashion. She had become strikingly beautiful.

The long neck suddenly assumed a new gracefulness, to carry the shapely head with its growing mane. The skin was pale, creamy and free from blemishes. The tallness now spoke of elegance, and was no longer a drawback. The big mouth took on a new voluptuousness. She had small, neat breasts, offset by a small ribcage and a neat waist, from which her hips sloped gently in a pear shape, towards a full, rounded bottom. She had developed a glamour-girl, hourglass figure. The sloping shoulders were hardly noticeable, and as her poise and confidence increased, the heavy legs and big feet diminished in significance.

With her soft, auburn hair curling against her shoulders, her high cheekbones, and her big, heavily-lipsticked mouth smiling widely to reveal large, attractively-crooked white teeth, Joan noticed that people gaped at her. They were struck by her beauty. It was not surprising. Her attractiveness was not just physical. She was not any sheltered neighbourhood girl who had never been anywhere, or seen much of life. She was worldly. Quite a lot older than people thought, she had experienced a life abroad. She'd faced from infancy indescribable isolation and lack of love; serious illness and early depression; a nomadic lifestyle in testing circumstances, and had lived in many places, under the orders of people of all sorts. Her unhappy and various background now contributed to her pulling power.

In stark contrast, Joan's neglectful and unsupervised upbringing in another country, meant that she didn't know the rules. She was unschooled in the local social niceties that everyone else took for granted. Her background had given her fragments of social etiquette. She'd never had enough time in one place to assimilate a structure of manners that would stand to her anywhere. Naturally, she was nervous about it, but this was what gave her a strong individuality, tempered with a discreet quietness, that others admired. She'd had the freedom to create herself, and to choose how she would present herself. Joan still lived in Broom Lane with a grandmother-figure, and three much older men whom people thought were her uncles. Except for her friendship with the O'Connor girls, she was largely unable to form any bonds with her peers.

John O'Connor had a car. His office was in Cork. It was nothing to him to ferry young people about. If they wanted to go up to Cork, they could go up with him in the morning, and when he closed the office for the night, he could bring them down again. Naturally, the teenagers went up and down, Joan and the O'Connor boys and girls, exploring Cork with their pals.

Joan was already familiar with Cork. Her brother Jack also had a car and was always willing to ferry any of the gang up and down to the city, or to anywhere else. Joan was beginning to toy with the idea of performing in the city. The O'Connor family were all in favour. One of the sisters, Wendy O'Connor, was a dressmaker all ready and willing to make up new dancing costumes.

In the mid to late thirties, Joan got a spot in a variety show at the Opera House, and pupil Brenda Sexton went up with her to dance. Joan had taught Brenda a sword dance, and accompanied her on the pipes. This happened about three years in succession. The Director of Music in the Opera House was Tony Moffat. He was very interested in Joan. He used to come down to Mallow to see her shows, and she later took singing lessons with him. She was friends with him, but that's all. Four or five men came down from Cork to see her shows, and like a number of Mallow men, they were also keen on Joan. Solicitor James O'Donovan was one of them.

It was at Clydaville that Joan met a distant cousin of the O'Connors, Maureen Collins and her husband, George, who lived in Cork. Joan was to become lifelong friends with the Collins'. Another pal later brought down to stay for the weekend, who also became a lifelong friend, was Ethel Beare, a Jewess who lived in Cork.

By day, the young visitors mooched in the grounds, walked, tramped and laughed in a fun little gang. In the evenings, they danced to records in the big room, and stayed overnight. It was a good time. When Joan confided to her 'mother', Marion, that she was thinking of marrying James O'Donovan, the older woman was delighted. It is possible that Joan's easy relationship with Jamie was based on the fact that neither demanded sex or other demonstrations of intimacy from the other, but this idea came to nothing. Jamie was extremely keen on ballet, and on Joan as a propagator of it, but he was also homosexual. Perhaps his idea of marrying had been a matter of giving himself respectability. Perhaps not, because he did not seem to mind being seen over the years with a succession of male companions. Marion was disappointed when it all fell through, but Joan remained close friends with Jamie all her life. When people gossiped about them in later years, saying that Joan was Jamie's mistress, the pair did not mind a bit. Each by then had a secret agenda to protect.

Amongst the other friends she met during this period, was one who was to completely alter her life, and shape the future course of it. It was 1938, and time to meet the beautiful and powerful composer who would use her as his muse, control her existence, and ravish her soul. Though she could never have fully realised it any more than he did, the brilliant Aloys Fleischmann was to be the means that would bring her the success she craved. He was also to be the cause of the worst suffering and humiliation that she would ever be forced to endure. Her life under his influence was to be so much more arid than he could ever perceive, and at the end of it all, she would be a spent, dry husk. She was to embrace it all wholeheartedly, from exciting beginning to sad and lonely end. He was to create her, and though he loved her more than anything else in life, his work for her was eventually to lead to her destruction.

7
Soulmate

In his usual direct way, Aloys Fleischmann headed straight across the room, and offered his hand. The tall piper turned her red-lipped, open smile on him, the big white teeth agreeably crooked, the grey eyes softly veiling a vigilant gaze. How surprising it had been to see a girl playing such a difficult instrument, and so very well, the composer said gently, taking her cold fingers into his big, warm grip. It impressed him that she was so tall. She noted the cut-glass accent, the full, sensuous mouth. Bowing conspiratorially towards her, and brimming with admiration, he told Joan Moriarty, in his most gushing style, how much he approved of her performance. Then he told her what he was later to relate at interviews and public functions for the rest of his life—that he had found the sight of her in kilts, with her red hair flowing, a very striking figure indeed. What he didn't say, was what he hardly knew himself—that he had responded with exhilaration to her red hair, her height and her bearing; that he had found her mastery of the instrument strangely erotic, and that she herself excited him.

In a lazy, mellow voice that flowed seductively over him, she offered quiet thanks. The shy tones carefully mimicked his own accent, guardedly matching his own drawing-room timbre.

Joan Moriarty sounded genuinely flattered. She liked his paternal courtliness. She was used to men taking plenty of notice of her, but she was gratified that this time she had caught the distinguished-looking professor's attention. They chatted for a few moments, then she put down her teacup, and prepared to leave.

Hearing that she was leaving to catch her bus for Mallow, he impulsively offered to escort her to the bus stop. She shook her head. It was the very least he could do, he persisted, after she had given everyone such an edifying and dramatic display. He was at his charming best, and instinctively didn't want to let her go.

Seeing this flurry, Sean Neeson, the Irish music lecturer who had engaged Joan for the summer school concert at University College

Cork, immediately jumped to his feet. It was his responsibility, the lecturer told his head of department, to take Miss Moriarty to her bus. After all, it was he who had engaged her for the concert. As far as Sean Neeson knew, Joan Moriarty was under twenty-one. She had come to his notice after winning an All-Ireland piping championship in Killarney. Whilst she was under his care, he wanted to make sure she got safely on the bus and back to her home in Mallow. Joan left in the company of the Irish music lecturer, and Professor Aloys Fleischmann did not see her again for a while.

He was one of the privileged people, and he was very clever, but Aloys Fleischmann had not been a happy child. His gifted, beautiful and independent mother had little time for her only son. Tilly Swertz was born in Cork, to the organist at the North Cathedral, Hans Conrad Swertz, who had been recruited from Germany, and had built up a notable mixed choir in the cathedral. When Tilly was twenty, her German father sent her back to Munich to study under Bernhard Stavenhagen and Berthold Kellermann, both of whom had been students of Liszt. Kellerman had also been music master to the children of Wagner. In Munich, Tilly was a very hard worker, revelling in studying the technical secrets of the virtuoso master, and the recitals she gave as a student pointed towards success as a concert pianist in Europe. However, she met Aloys Georg Fleischmann, another music student, and fell in love with him. They married and returned to Cork, just as her father was on the brink of abandoning his job and emigrating to America. The reason Hans Swertz was leaving his post was that Pope Pius X had issued the *Moto Proprio*, banning women from church choirs and from church organs. This meant that the Swertz choir would have to be dissolved, and that Hans' accomplished daughter, if she should ever want to, would never be allowed to take over his job. Her father left for America in disgust at this barbarity, her husband conveniently took over her father's job, and Tilly Fleischmann went temporarily back home to Dachau, to be delivered of her baby son.

Immediately she returned to Cork with her new baby, the bright-eyed Tilly Fleischmann began dressing at twilight in embroidered evening gowns, sweeping up her thick, dark hair, and going out in her fur coat to give piano recitals. There was plenty for her to do in the cultural backwaters of Cork, and by the time Aloys was just one year old, his mother was away presenting, for the benefit of women in long dresses and men in bow ties, a special programme to mark the centenary of the birth of Liszt. She also started teaching piano, but hers was not ordinary teaching. She believed that the role of artist-teacher is vital in paving a path towards the creation of the soul of a work, by giving pupils, not just knowledge of technique, but inner understanding, and by the passing down of a great amount of musical tradition. She brought many allusions into her teachings, aimed at giving insight into the poetic qualities of the temperament of Liszt, and also of Chopin. She felt that it was crucial for a pianist to have an affinity of temperament with a composer, and she considered herself to be temperamentally qualified to play the music of both these romantic composers.

Aloys' father gave organ recitals, as well as playing in the cathedral, and was also hard at work directing the church choir, and a boys' choir. He also was too absorbed in his work to give his son any attention. Young Aloys' year of worst confusion and suffering, began when he was six years old. In 1916, his father, as an enemy alien, was removed to a succession of internment camps for the four years of the First World War, enduring prolonged privations of cold and hunger. Tilly, defiant and fully capable, illegally took over his job unseen in the organ loft. Determined to survive, she also kept her mind full with teaching and giving recitals. For Aloys there was always status and material security, but at such a young age, he found himself with neither mother nor father.

Whilst Tilly performed, practised and taught piano, her only child spent time alone in their large old house with the dark, heavy German furniture. When he did get some attention from his perfumed mother in the rustling gowns, it was never for himself. When he was allowed to enter her presence, it was only to be cruelly drilled at practising the piano. He loved his parents, and in later years the family got on very well together, but his mother was severe with him in the early days, and he must have picked up during those years, something of her internal emotional anxiety, as she threw herself into intensive work, waiting for the war to end, and for her husband to be released. Aloys remembered childhood as a time of feeling terribly rejected, wretchedly isolated, and timid.

Impotent to help, her young son's own emotional pain was expressed in the form of crying bitterly as he sat in rare closeness to his mother at practice times. He could smell her and feel her warmth. It was too much for him to bear, to stay away from her embrace, and he tried to hold her, and fall sobbing into her lap, but this display of weakness was ignored. She brushed him off, and sat him up straight on the stool again. Tilly herself worked hard all the time, expected her son to do the same, and never had another child.

Aloys was sent to St Ita's kindergarten, which was run by Mary and Anne McSwiney, where he gave vent to his rage by behaving very badly. He would disrupt the peace amongst the class, by bullying the little girls. He would take hold of handfuls of their hair, and pull so hard that they screamed loudly enough to attract the attention of the teachers. When Misses Mary and Anne told him to stop, he took no notice. Eventually, they found the behaviour of the angry little prince too disturbing to put up with. Telling his mother that they could no longer tolerate him in the kindergarten, they asked her to take him away. For the rest of his life, Aloys never quite knew how to behave towards women.

Even at the age of five or six he noticed that whatever he composed, his mother would take time out to write it down properly for him. The only other times he received any cursory approval, were when he studied very hard. Thus he learned to put his emotional needs to one side. He dried his tears, applied himself very diligently to his work, and he went on composing. His mother approved. Later, at the Christian Brothers College in Cork, schoolmasters supported his swotting. He could beat all his peers hands-down. He did it all the time, and they looked up to him. He was sent to St Finbarr's College, Farranferris, because his father taught music there, and he readily became an unpopular swot. A governess was later engaged to boost his French. What he saw going on around him at home, was hard work; hard work and much respect and acclaim for it. He became someone who worked hard.

When he was fifteen, his mother, who was on a Feis (festival) committee, proposed inviting the celebrated composer, Arnold Bax, Master of the Queen's Music, to come and adjudicate. When Bax agreed to come, the Fleischmanns invited him to stay at their house. Soon they were showing him their son's compositions, and the great man was clucking shy approval. Every year after that, Bax came over to Ireland for two weeks holiday, and stayed at the Fleischmann's home. He came to adore the country. Young Aloys used to drive him to their holiday cottage in West Cork, and on the way, Bax devised ways of relating everyday talk to musical themes. Roadsigns would spark off competitive games of linguistic associations. The admiring young Aloys used to sharpen his wits, trying to keep up with the clever conversation of the older man.

Aloys Fleischmann was useless at sport, did not bother socialising either with friends or with girls, he never drank alcohol, and he got first class grades in everything he did. He was not only top at his own school, but his marks for Music, German and History in the Leaving Certificate were top in the whole country. Intensely competitive, it was his brain power which gave him value, and it satisfied him to define himself in terms of this. He became someone who was brilliant. He became a first class academic, and at university, he organised a small student orchestra, as well as reviving the Art Society.

All the way through University College Cork, he took first class honours, with first place in all subjects. His BA was a first, and he won the Peel Memorial Prize. His BMus. the following year, was a first. His thesis for his MA degree, which was awarded with first class honours, was recommended for publication. His father then sent him to Germany for two years, to study at the State Academy of Music, and at Munich University. He wanted Aloys to succeed him as organist at the cathedral, but Aloys found that he was more interested in composing and conducting.

Aloys Fleischmann was twenty-two years old when he temporarily left his parent's home and went to Europe. In later years, he was to say that whilst all the young men around him in Munich were most interested in having a high time chasing women, he wasn't. He studied so hard in Germany, that he eventually developed total insomnia, and became unable to switch-off enough to go to sleep. His doctor gave him an injection which left him with a perpetual headache, and which he said remained with him for the next sixty years, day and night.

In 1934, he returned from Germany a big name. When he had written a movement for a string quartet, his father had engaged four Munich professional musicians to play it for him. A motet he had written, *Illumina Oculos Meos*, had been performed by the Munich Cathedral choir on the same programme as a Mass by Brückner, and had been written about in the newspaper. Such was his prestige that, the moment he got back, Merriman, the President of UCC, summoned him, to ask his advice on whom to appoint to lecture in Irish Music. Aloys himself had turned down the job, and, on being shown the applications, recommended Sean Neeson, who was given it. Professor St John Lacey, Head of the Music Department, which was staffed by only two, was due to retire. It was taken for granted

49

that the twenty-four-year-old Aloys Fleischmann would walk straight into his job. There were no other applicants, and as the new Acting Professor of Music, Aloys immediately founded the University Orchestra, which gave symphony concerts for the Art Society, and later became the Cork Symphony Orchestra. One thing his parents had taught him was that in the undeveloped second city of Cork, from where talent tended to depart, it was possible to wield power. He had a political mind. It was his taste for power, and his ready access to it, that facilitated him in his future climb. Such an egghead could only become a complete eccentric, and he did. For the rest of his life, as charming as he was, he was accepted by many ordinary mortals in other professions, as something of an oddity.

Aloys had just two students, more than enough money to live on, complete freedom to do exactly as he pleased, and plenty of time and energy to spare. He also lived in his parents' large house, where they had staff to take care of the cooking, the laundry, and the other mundanities of life.

Appointed to the Chair of Music the following year, he began a lifetime of charming his students with amusing stories of his own exploits, which he told over and over again. The first of these, was about the night he found that the Aula Maxima after library hours, was unsuitable as a base for his department. The porter had locked him and his two students into the building, and he'd jumped out of the window in his gown. The second story concerned his move, in 1937, to the tiny old Observatory, where he had a big concrete pillar removed from the centre of the room, so that he could get his piano in. The pillar he had so high-handedly destroyed turned out to be the main part of a seismograph which had been sunk thirty feet into bedrock. He had a schoolboy glee which never waned when he recounted these events.

Somewhere inside himself, he loved women very much, but his first expressions of this love ended with clumsy grabs. One of his very few intimate friends was the flamboyant writer Edward Sheehy. He was what Aloys termed a conqueror of women, and he was one of the first people who truly dazzled Aloys. Edward would boast that he could get any woman to fall for him immediately, and to say yes, even if she was a complete stranger. When Aloys looked sideways at this boast, Edward offered to give a demonstration in the theatre the same evening. With Aloys discreetly observing nearby, Edward sat directly behind his chosen prey—a young woman completely unknown to him—and began gently stroking her neck. He kept touching and stroking her throughout the performance, and at the end of the evening's attentions the couple left the theatre together. Edward later crowed that he had taken the swooning female back to his flat, and had made love to her. Aloys swore he'd seen the whole thing, right up to the couple's departure. He was impressed and thrilled by Sheehy, but never joined in. Mostly he was content to bask admiringly in the other man's successes with women.

At some point, Sheehy, no doubt feeling it would be only reasonable to include his friend in the adventures, arranged a foursome for a weekend trip to a country cottage. Immediately they arrived, Aloys tried to emulate the success of his friend, who was off tête-à-tête with the better-looking of the two young women they'd brought. Finding himself alone in a field with the other girl, Aloys made a sudden, unexpected grab for his quarry. Quickly pulling her down into the long grass, he began ferociously pawing at her body. She shrieked in terror, and struggled away from his clumsy assault. Running into the house, she headed for her room, slammed the door and totally avoided him for the rest of the weekend. Aloys was utterly mystified and at a loss. It was her behaviour that perplexed him, not his own. He wouldn't have known what else to do.

To Aloys, Sheehy probably represented an unexpressed part of himself; an alternative possible way of being. The red-haired, bearded Edward died young, and Aloys kept the mocking, devilish self-portrait of his friend over the fireplace in his own bedroom until the day he died.

Aloys later became superlatively charming to women, and kept his big hands off them. The gauche early fondling had been so crude partly from inexperience, but also because it was as yet alien to his nature, done mainly to keep up with his friend, and he was perfectly glad when it didn't work. He went back to what he knew; what he was most comfortable with. It was easier for him to worship the female from afar.

His mother had put stars in his eyes. She had provided him with an inaccessible, tantalising presence brimming with artistry, full of poetic vision, devastating with beauty. She was his first remote goddess. The clear message he had received, was that his mother was an awe-inspiring ideal. Her essence was unattainable; channelled through the keyboard towards some higher cause. Heady with scents, textures, colours and deep, flowing passions, Woman was lofty and untouchable.

All his life he adored women. He treated every one of them with a rare reverence, as though females were some precious species apart. In their presence, his manners, always respectful to the point of being courtly, became infused with new vigour, keenly conspiratorial. Over the years, he became adept at charming women; bowing ostentatiously, kissing their hands, praising, mocking, gently and insistently flirting. It was the sense of impeccable nobility about it all; the sense that his world was somehow elevated, even though archaic, that made women tolerate him from afar in return.

He was not lecherous. He was far too romantic to translate it all into mundane passions. He was also sexually unawakened, and hardly knew what he was doing. But there was something about his peculiar mix of German blood and Irish identity that meant he could not help but be at war with his own romanticism: He was literal-minded, dogmatic, obtuse, stubborn, prosaic. It was almost impossible for him to appreciate a viewpoint other than his own. He was full of vision and cocksure, yet at the same time blinkered, almost lacking in vision. He was what other men might at times have called a bloody fool.

When it came to choosing a wife, for him it was nothing at all to do with romance. He had never been in love, and didn't have any time for it. He made a cold, businesslike decision with his intellect, and unfortunately for Nancy Ann Madden, he chose her.

8

The Bad Years

In 1941, Joan had her first nervous breakdown. Shortly before Marion's death in 1940, she had moved to Cork, and taken a flat on Patrick Street, over Simcox's grocery shop, on the site of which now stands an AIB bank. She had a living room, two bedrooms, and a little kitchen. She turned the living room into a dance studio, advertised for pupils, and set off alone along the slippery slope of self-neglect. Joan had no idea how to look after herself, and she had insufficient social skills to cope alone in the city. Her instinct was to deprive and retreat into herself. She punished her body by exercising, she punished it by depriving it of food, and she swiftly sank into a deep and dangerous apathy.

According to her friend, Ethel Beare, Joan had moved to Cork around the late 1930s or during 1940, because her mother hadn't wanted her to be conscripted into the British war effort. This seems unlikely. Joan must have had her reasons for giving this story to Ethel, but in any case, it was nothing unusual for Joan to tell unlikely stories. In 1940, conscription was not an issue in any part of Ireland, but Marion could have been worried that Joan, who was a British subject, had been only informally adopted. Relations between Britain and Ireland were complicated at the time, but there could certainly have been some degree of paranoia on the part of the Irish.

Neighbours say that Joan never visited her mother after she moved from Cork. The conscription story would have conveniently explained this away, but it seems far-fetched, even allowing for a deep residual mistrust of the British, more than a decade after the Black and Tans reign of terror in Ireland.

Joan told Aloys Fleischmann that her life with Marion had been unhappy in the extreme, and that she had been excluded by the whole family in Mallow, and treated like a servant. Whatever her reason for being in Cork, Joan lived alone, and felt not only isolated, but very cut off from her home town. She also stopped going to see her best friends, the O'Connors.

It is certain that Joan stayed away from Marion's house before her breakdown, when the old woman was dying. On the face of it, this seems neglectful and uncaring to an old woman who was crippled with painful arthritis, but it is also likely that Joan partly stayed away from Marion for a reason that she herself was unaware of: she was deeply traumatised by signs that the old woman was dying, and was unable to face the prospect.

It was the neighbours who nursed the seventy-year-old woman during her brief, final illness in early February 1940. Joan appeared to have no sense whatever of belonging to Marion, or indeed to her Mallow family. After their mother died, the three bachelor brothers lived together quietly. Joan never came back in later years, except to visit briefly at Christmas time, on her way to see the O'Connors. Locals perceived her as being actressy, and a cut above.

Not very long after Marion's death, Joan took an overdose of tablets, and was rushed to hospital, on the brink of death. Ethel Beare spent time with her during her deep depressions in the flat in Patrick Street, and witnessed the onset of 'these awful breakdowns', at least twice.

The way Madeline O'Connor remembers it, Joan had a nervous breakdown because Marion had died, and the O'Connor family only found out when Joan no longer visited Clydaville. The nervous breakdown was also the reason given to Madeline O'Connor by her Austrian stepmother, for Joan's disappearance from the Clydaville scene. This argues that the depression had been going on for some time.

Pupil Brenda Sexton, who danced with Joan in Cork soon after she got her flat there, does not remember any visits to Cork from Marion, and believed Marion to be dead when Joan was in Cork. It is certain that before Joan had been in Cork very long, it was already apparent to others, that she was increasingly feeling she had failed. Her sadness was obvious to them. She needed support.

Joan eventually accumulated a very small class of six young women, including Ethel Beare. Ethel, who had the status of a friend, paid for her lessons in tapdancing. Though she lived in Cork, she often remained in the flat so late that she missed the last bus, and stayed over. They'd pull up a little ottoman against the couch, and both snuggle up together under Joan's blankets, talking all night. Whilst Joan was well, and in good spirits, this was exciting. When Joan was depressed, it was an ordeal that was difficult to cope with.

Ethel would go into the flat to find Joan lying despondent, unable to do the simplest, most basic of chores to keep herself alive. Ethel would find that Joan hadn't eaten anything, and that the idea of doing anything at all seemed pointless to her. She couldn't get enough pupils was the argument she used to explain her despondency, and she didn't have any money. Ethel looked after Joan as best she could, but the moment she was gone, Joan slipped back into apathy. Ethel struggled with her friend, but felt helpless and distressed, and with a clerical job to do in the daytime, couldn't be there with her all the time. There were other friends closer to Joan, who spent time looking after her. George and Maureen Collins were two of the people she depended on.

Pretty Maureen was the daughter of a colonel who had spent many years in India and was related to the O'Connors of Mallow. Maureen's husband, George, was manager of the Cork and Kerry Creamery Company. He was handsome, fun-loving and shrewd, and they were an integral component of this off-beat crowd that was forming.

Ethel arrived at the flat one day to find Joan gone. She started asking around, wondering what had become of her friend. She was told that Joan was in hospital with depression, but few other people were told. There was a stigma attached to mental illness, and Joan's supporters covered up for her. Ethel went to stay in the flat whilst Joan was away, and found everything arranged just as though Joan had popped out, and would be coming back at any moment. No plans had been made by Joan to go into hospital. It had been an emergency.

In an interview she gave three years before her death, Joan Moriarty gave some indication of her real state of health at the time. She had been so short of money, she said, that she had lived on just one dinner roll per day for a whole year, along with cups of cocoa without milk or sugar. Eventually she was rushed to the Bons Secours hospital by ambulance, where she was given the last sacrament in anticipation of her death. She was kept in hospital for two months, she said, and her heart was affected. This, she volunteered, happened twice, and on both occasions she had nearly died. The reason she gave for all this, was that she had no money, and had become severely anaemic.

Some of those facts are correct, but there are crucial omissions. If she was rushed to hospital, as she said, it was not for the reason she gave. Nobody is rushed to hospital by ambulance with severe anaemia, and given the last sacrament, unless they are haemorrhaging for some reason. Joan was not. She was weak, yes, and probably half-starved. But the reason she was rushed to hospital was that she had succumbed to her own worst fear, the possibility that she had inherited the same tendencies as her Aunt Joan, and she had tried to commit suicide. She later said that her heart was affected. These sketchy details related by Joan herself, suggest that she had taken, as her chosen method of suicide, an overdose of drugs, probably aspirin, which would affect the heart. Nobody is kept in hospital for two months with anaemia. She was kept in hospital for such a long time because she needed rest for her heart, and because she was receiving psychiatric treatment.

Her friends visited her in hospital, where they photographed her, and did their best to cheer her up. Her brother, Jack, also came up to visit. Her sadness made them feel helpless and protective towards her. Two months is a long time to be in hospital, and a large bill had to be faced when the penniless Joan was due to be discharged. This was taken care of by the affluent and generous 'Mummy' O'Connor. Joan came out of hospital, gaunt and haunted-looking, with deep shadows under her eyes. She was immediately taken to Clydaville. Though Joan convalesced with the O'Connors for six months, Madeline was never told that Joan had actually been in hospital. She was told the truth about Joan's mental state, because of Joan's haggard appearance, and because her fragile state of mind was apparent. Over time, 'Mummy' got Joan going again, encouraging her to be active, and to play tennis again, like the old days. She also paid the rent which kept Joan's flat on.

As well as the death of Marion, another psychological and emotional factor that contributed to Joan's depression, was that 'Daddy' O'Connor, who was an extremely important part of Joan's life, also died in 1940. 'Daddy' had been her ally, her link with Clydaville. In the absence of any real father, 'Daddy' had been her benign, fond father-figure, and after his death, she stopped going to Clydaville altogether.

Joan's self-destructive behaviour at the time of the deaths of Marion and 'Daddy', was not a coincidence. It was a pathetic response to the loss of these two key parent figures, and shows her psychological dependence on them, and her sense that they were irreplaceable. These sudden and unexpected life-events plunged

Joan into a response-pattern that had been waiting to happen. She lost all heart to go on, and once again, there was no help available to her, that would address the underlying causes of her reaction. Her internal sense of isolation was excruciating. She did not value herself.

That she became seriously depressed several times, also argues that she had an underlying conflict which she could not resolve. Her own idea of herself was shaky. She was very insecure about who she was, and how she fitted in. In addition to this, teaching dance to adults, and trying to dance in the big city of Cork, was very different from trying it all out under Gus' wing in Mallow, and teaching little girls. Now she would have to re-invent herself, alone in the city, and she didn't know how to go on. A void yawned in front of her.

Brenda Sexton felt that Joan would never have left home whilst Marion was alive, since she understood them to be very close. She believed that Marion really adored Joan, and that Joan felt the same about Marion. Madeline O'Connor also believed them to be very close. Yet after Marion's death, Joan continued to tell her closest confidante how Marion had neglected her when she was a child, how she had been treated like a kitchen maid in Mallow, and how the only time she was ever happy, was when she walked her dog down by the Blackwater River.

Joan also went on to confide that her brothers had all treated her like a kitchen servant, too, and had never included her in any family discussions. Observers felt that she was closest to Jack, who helped her quite a lot, and often came to see her little shows. She herself related that the only compassionate filial gesture ever made to her, was by Denis, who brought up the couch on which she slept to her sparsely-furnished flat in Patrick Street.

When Denis became terminally ill in 1947, the year during which Joan was enabled to put on her first evening of ballet at the Opera House in Cork, the brothers were in a state perceived by neighbours as neglect. It was Myra Greaney from next door who brought Denis the newspaper, and looked after him. Three years after the death of Denis in 1947, Gus married a woman called Nellie Murphy. She moved in with the two brothers, and took in lodgers after their deaths in the 1960s. The last time neighbours remembered seeing Joan Moriarty in public in Mallow, was at Nellie's funeral in 1979.

The family of Joan's 'father', Michael Augustus Moriarty, do not have their own family grave in Mallow. Marion Moriarty and her sons, Gus, Jack and Sid, are buried against the East wall in the graveyard of St Mary's in Mallow, in Marion's own family grave, that of the McCarthys. Gus' wife Nellie is also buried here. All they have for a tombstone, are two small, plain, loose tablets, propped up, one on top of the other, against the imposing high cross and tombstone which bears the name of Marion's father, Denis McCarthy, and his immediate family. Of Marion's husband, Michael Augustus Moriarty, there is no mention. Neither is there mention of Joan Denise Moriarty, who is buried in Cork.

When Joan eventually went back to Cork, following her long convalescence at Clydaville, it was seen to that she was not left alone. Wendy O'Connor, the dressmaker, took off to Cork with her, moved into the second bedroom, and set up her sewing machine in a corner. Wendy gave her a fresh incentive by being on hand to make all the costumes, and do all the alterations. She made Joan a beautiful long black velvet evening dress, with a full skirt, and big green and white flowers attached to the shoulder. With Joan's red hair and her slim waist, it made her look stunning, and she wore it for years. Wendy stayed with Joan for about a year and a half.

Soon after Joan's return to Cork she managed to get a spot dancing in a show at Queenstown, now Cobh, a port near Cork. On the first time out she fell onstage and broke her leg. With Joan unable to get up and dance on the curtain was brought down. Everyone wanted to know how she seemed so sure it had broken. Oh, yes, she answered. She'd heard it crack. After such a long time away from her exercise regime, she could not possibly have been fit enough, or exercised enough to resume dancing immediately, and no dancer who knew anything about the body would have gone straight back to performing. Joan continued to teach with her leg in plaster.

There were also happy times during the early forties. Joan started hosting fancy dress parties at the flat, and attracted a fashionable young crowd. She and the girls used to go over to the coffee bar across the road for a chat, and to meet up with their friends.

A 1942 picture shows her wearing dark glasses, and a little summer suit with a short skirt. With her shoulders back, her bosom forward, and her legs attractively wound round each other, she looks very self-aware, and glamorous.

In 1943, Joan spent summer weekends cycling out of town with her friends. At the end of July, she set out on her bicycle in a fine, misty rain, towards a memorable weekend at George and Maureen's timber bungalow near the harbour village of Crosshaven. She went with Ethel Beare, and with Marion's nephew A.T. Lucas and his wife, Cassie. They pulled up steep hills on their way towards French's Bay on the coast, and freewheeled down the other side. Pictures taken at the time show that this was a very happy and carefree time for Joan.

Joan stayed lifelong friends with the Collins', and was particularly close with Maureen. In the pictures taken at this time, which Joan kept in her album, she looks confident, flirtatious and full of fun, but George always seemed noticeably intense, brooding and abstracted. Tucked inside a white envelope at the back of one of her photograph albums, Joan kept a series of pictures of herself and one of George, obviously taken by each other, on a woodland path, and on a beach. In contrast to her vivacious appearance in July 1943, she is looking thin and a little haggard in these pictures. Both look intense and serious. Handwritten on this envelope, is the caption, 'Should auld acquaintance be forgot and never brought to mind?'

During a press interview given by Joan Moriarty in 1988, during which she talked about her hospitalisation, she made reference to another occasion during these early forties, when she again nearly died, and again was hospitalised, and given the last sacrament. This was her second suicide attempt.

She had plenty of stress. One difficult saga of the early forties, which threatened her livelihood, was a court action taken out by her closest neighbour against her. She had started her adult tapdancing class in the evenings, for young women who were at work during the day. One evening, the tenant of the flat overhead, Mrs O'Sullivan, appeared at the door of the studio, and said that she could no longer stand the constant music being played over and over, and the terrible clattering of feet coming up to her rooms day and night. Joan refused to make any concession to the woman, and went on trying to earn her living. While Mrs O'Sullivan kept up a stream of complaints about the din she could not escape, Joan kept right on with the evening tapdancing class. Unable to get any change at all from Joan, the tenant upstairs finally brought a court action, asking for a judgement debarring Joan from holding any classes, on the grounds that the noise was unbearable. Rather than back down, Joan hired legal representation, and went to court. Cork solicitor, Gerald Goldberg, argued for her, that Patrick Street was a business area, and anyone renting rooms there should not be debarred from working in it. He suggested that Mrs O'Sullivan find another flat in a residential part of the city. The case was dismissed, but along the way Joan modified the noise by switching to a ballet class, rather than tap.

It wasn't classical ballet. Variety shows were the sort of entertainment that attracted people, and so Joan duly worked up a variety act for herself and her few dancers. But money was still impossible to get. Two free meals a day was as much as she was offered, and for that, she had to appear three times a day, and present a twenty-minute, mixed variety show. The manager of the Savoy Cinema in Patrick Street fed her and her dancers lunch and dinner, and in exchange the girls did folk dances, jazz dances, and anything that Joan thought might interest people, and fill in the time. Fred Bridgeman played the organ, and the performances were stretched across the day, and well into the evening. The first was at two o'clock in the afternoon, the second at five, and the third show was at nine o'clock at night. The costumes were a mixture of the hired and the makeshift. After all that, they were expected to vary the routine for the next week. This came to an end after a few months, either because the dancers were too tired to keep going, or because they had exhausted their repertoire and people had seen it all.

Unable to get paid work performing, Joan started taking part in charity concerts, just for the experience. It was at one of these, in the Savoy Cinema on St Stephen's night, that she tried a little classical ballet. The story she later told the press, was that the ballet extract was met with boos and jeers. As unlikely as some of her anecdotes were about her early life, in this case, it is highly likely that a Cork audience looking for a variety show, might boo and jeer at ballet. Amidst the cacophony, Joan stopped the dance and moved to the front of the stage. She silently stared the audience down, until they became silent. Then in a loud voice, she commanded Fred Bridgeman to begin again, and as she danced, they remained silent. She later gave this event mystical status, by saying that at the moment when they applauded at the end, she resolved to break down the barriers of prejudice against the dance.

It is also highly likely that Joan would already be accustomed to boos and jeers. City cinemas were always anarchic places during afternoon performances, and Joan had plenty of experience of being a fill-in act. Variety shows could be rowdy. Noisy children talking, shuffling and stamping their feet, rustling sweet papers and generally getting involved with the acts, would have been part of her experience. On the occasion of the charity concert, however, things were different. It was an evening performance, which would have featured a number of city acts, and would have been organised and staffed by responsible people. Perhaps it was the organisers who instigated the demand for hush, and the grateful Joan was thus able to go on dancing.

In 1944, Joan taught a class of little girls, which included eight-year-olds Mary Conran and Margaret Barry, and ten-year-old Patricia O'Gorman. George Collins was helping her out generally, and knew enough about her falls, faints and breaking bones, to issue a warning to the children. If anything happened to Miss Moriarty, he told them, if she should twist her ankle, or fall, or anything, they were to keep on dancing regardless, and simply ignore the fall. On the face of it, to ignore a fall seems like an alarming instruction to give to children.

Because of her background, Joan Moriarty may have had osteoporosis at an early age, due to calcium deficiency, which was making her bones likely to break. A true bone-breaking fall would have been serious enough to stop any show, and could not have been ignored. It wasn't that which was making her fall and faint. She could have had low blood pressure, but it is more likely that the fainting and falling were side-effects of the medication she was on. This would explain why George was so sanguine about it to the children. George expected her to faint, and so did she. Some people around her considered her 'accident prone'. This all suggests that at this time, she was quite well used to taking an antidepressant drug, of which dizziness and fainting were the expected side-effects.

It would be perfectly usual for someone who had been as depressed as Joan had, to be subsequently prescribed an antidepressant. There is also strong evidence from her habits, her predispositions, and from the nature of her responses throughout the course of her life, to suggest that she was a long-term user of antidepressant drugs. Use of prescribed drugs explains otherwise unaccountably mysterious behaviour. Joan was an acknowledged insomniac. Triptofan, which she was taking after she was deposed from the Irish National Ballet, and at the time of her death, is a combination of an antidepressant and an antipsychotic. It is used for the long-term treatment of depression which is accompanied by insomnia and anxiety. Dizziness is a possible side-effect of this drug.

In later life, she developed Parkinsonism, also a side effect of the long-term use of antipsychotic drugs. She readily acknowledged that she was a long-term insomniac, and at the end of her life, she was prescribed sleeping tablets, as well as anti-anxiety drugs, and tranquilisers. Of the other illnesses which surfaced later in life, some of them were stress-related, and others were serious side-effects of other long-term medication. Her use of corticosteroids, prescribed for emphysema, was the probable cause of her peptic ulcer.

The most misunderstood features that were apparent in her makeup, and which probably resulted from long-term use of anti-depressants, were the results which onlookers mistakenly perceived as character strengths. People thought she showed superhuman self-sacrifice, asceticism, and iron will, all in dedication to her art. The sad truth about this, was that her heroic self-neglect was manipulation, and that her libido had been suppressed.

The idea that starvation and self-neglect became a manipulative tool in Joan's mind during her first depression following scarlet-fever, has already been discussed. Throughout the course of her life, Joan used this method of control over others.

The suppression of Joan's libido first occurred after she moved to Cork. At a certain point in early adulthood, Joan seemed to develop a sexy bloom. After this brief period, it appears that her libido suddenly subsided. Whilst her life, over time, suggests that her libido was almost non-existent, there was no evidence whatever from her actual work, that she had chosen—as artists can—to sublimate her sex drive into a grand passion. It was as though she went through the motions of pretending that she had.

Ballet is a grand passion. There is no such thing as a ballerina without internal fire, and there is no such thing as a decent choreographer without a spark. Joan Moriarty did not have fire. She was committed but cool. There was no indication that she was having a major relationship with her art. She did not even have an arrogant belief in herself or what she was doing, which would have carried her. In terms of passionate expression, she was as dry as a twig. Her choreography was always anodyne, her interpretation asexual. When any reference was made to gender or sexuality, as it was in *Reputations*, a ballet full of romantic couples, which she choreographed in the 1970s, it suggested a sterile, pre-pubescent approach to sexuality. Her choreography in the work of which she was most proud, *The Playboy of the Western World*, was dull and monotonous.

In Ireland, it was neccessary for Joan to ensure that her ballet performances appeared respectable and safe, but she would have been incapable of anything more.

Lack of libido and emotional coldness is a feature of a personality which deeply fears letting go of control. Lack of libido is also caused by depression, and by the taking of drugs, with the possibility that these two causes can be linked and intertwined. Her low libido was caused both by a desperate need to keep control at all times, and also by depression. These drugs then further lowered her libido, and her sense of creativity, thereby extinguishing the vital spark that she so badly needed.

Public opinion in Ireland, which highly values the ascetic, the nun, the renouncer of the world, and the self-sacrificer, approved of her aridity. She became much more acceptable to society because of her apparent frigidity. People expressed deep awe of her daily life, with its punishing exercise regime, precisely because it was inhuman. She shrewdly made a virtue out of her rigid asceticism and perfectionism, and over time, details of her sterile existence were considered indications of her dedication to her art. In a traditionally Catholic Ireland which emphasises worship of the sinless female, the ultimate saint on earth is the totally sexless being, and Joan Denise Moriarty increasingly qualified.

Joan was not just deceiving others; she was deceiving herself. Vital sparks are dangerous to those who fear them. Joan never wanted to see the void that was so close to her, so she embarked on a journey of stripping herself of life's emotion, life's turmoil, life's pounding insecurities that she had seen too much of, and she did it through her work. She needed to feel safe, so she settled for a fake, stylised world that dared not attempt integration. She could not bear the darkness, so she created a false veneer of light.

9

Aloys' Life with Ann Madden

Aloys Fleischmann did not get on with his wife. All that interested him when he first met Ann Madden, was her organisational skill. A medical student of mediocre physical attractiveness, Ann—who was also known by her nickname, Nancy—made an effective student secretary of the Art Society at UCC, which Aloys had founded. It was not even himself who noticed her. A colleague pointed out to him that she would probably make Aloys a good wife, since she was rather good at packing halls. This was a quality that Aloys was likely to admire, since it was something he wanted for his performances, but it was hardly a basis for a good marital relationship. He bantered with her about this great flair she had, and provoked her into boasting that she could certainly fill a hall for him. He challenged her to do it for him, and she did.

His decision to marry her was based on nothing more than his appreciation of this gift, plus a realisation that she would make him a decent personal secretary. She was also in the process of training as a doctor, but that went unnoticed, and eventually unused. His rationale was that she would help him in the extra-curricular workload of organising the Cork Symphony Orchestra, and the budding Cork Orchestral Society, thus helping to develop the music department. He also had the usual expectation of the time, that a man must have a wife to attend to all his day-to-day personal needs. It was time for this. As far as romantic love was concerned, he was utterly unawakened, and it is doubtful whether he had any feelings for her at all. It was an intellectual decision.

Whatever her expectations in 1940 of marriage to Aloys Fleischmann, things went disastrously wrong for Ann during the first week of her married life. She must have been under the impression when agreeing to help with his correspondence, that she would also be involved in the decision-making process. Aloys' grasp of English was outstanding, and his approach to language was sophisticated. He used words accurately, with flair, and he used grammar rather more in the English way, which he would have considered preferable to the Irish styles. His facility for words surpassed that of many of his peers, and he could effortlessly impress politicians and newspaper people with his skills on paper and in argument. Her Cork-based English could not match his. So when the first letters appeared before him, which Ann had typed during that very first week, he was aghast to find that she had made her own alterations. In his blunt, uncompromising way, he tried telling her that in no circumstances does the typist alter any letter dictated by someone else. No doubt she felt that she was more editor —or at least helpmate—than typist. A woman of very strong, deep feelings, she was horrified and stung. Dismayed to find that he would allow her no power, and feeling rejected and humiliated, she stopped typing his letters almost as soon as she'd started. He felt that she was being very difficult, but it was not in his nature to placate.

She packed the hall repeatedly for him, appropriating power in her own sphere by making up strict rules. One of Aloys' colleagues, arriving late for a lunchtime concert, found the door closed against him. He turned the handle and pushed a little, but it did not give. Ann had her back against the door, determined to exclude any latecomers. He pushed, and she pushed back. The male professor won the battle, and heaving her bodily out of the way, got into the concert. She later complained to Aloys that his colleague was a 'dreadful man', but Aloys only took his part. He also noticed that she hated the man bitterly for ever afterwards.

Also very early during their adjustment period in marriage, he greeted her one morning by handing her a sweater which had come unravelled at the sleeve, asking her to please mend it for him. Her response was to snatch the sweater and angrily throw it in his face. She obviously felt she was being taken for a servant, but he had no time at all for violent behaviour of this sort. Shocked and bewildered, he withdrew, and stopped asking her to do things for him. She kept house, cooked, and bore five children for him, but Ann Madden never practised medicine after she married.

Not long after the couple married, his parents announced their intention to move house. It was decided that if Aloys and his wife moved in with Herr Aloys Georg and Frau Tilly Fleischmann, they could share the expenses, and afford to buy a bigger, grander house. Ann agreed to this, and the four bought the big house and proceeded to set up home together. Ann soon found that she did not like Tilly

Fleischmann, her new husband's mother, and did not get on with her at all. At the end of just one week in the new house, Aloys arrived home from college one evening to find, instead of supper, Ann with her bags packed, ready to leave. She would not, and could not spend one more night in the house with that woman, she said, and marched out. He felt he had no alternative but to hang the expense and follow his wife.

He never saw his wife naked. This would not have been all that unusual in Ireland in the 1930s. Whether she loved him or not, he certainly did not love her. Ann wasn't terribly interested in sex, and Aloys wasn't particularly interested in her physically, either. Both were disillusioned with marriage, and disappointed in each other. Real communication was non-existent, but they slept together in a double bed, and made the best they could of it, soon starting a family.

Ann Madden hated ballet. It was ballet and music that came between them. She made no secret of her resentment, when night after night he went out to rehearse, when he should, she felt, have been home with her and the children. He was almost never home, but when he was, he was upstairs in his study, marking papers, composing, replying to requests from students for help, or writing endless political letters to newspapers. She made plenty of noise about his prolonged absences, and he ignored it all.

She never let their differences show publicly. Social norms of the day meant it was necessary to keep up appearances. There was to be no public acknowledgement that anything was wrong with their relationship. For him, there was no question, ever, of him leaving her. With children to raise, he never considered it as a possibility. That was the Irish way. Ann emerged on first nights, to be seen attending the ballet as the wife of the composer and orchestra conductor. Since opening nights usually involved not just the usual dressing up and fuss, but also admiration and applause for her husband's collaboration with the beautiful, slim choreographer, this may well have been a very miserable ordeal for the unacclaimed graduate wife who had never practiced her own profession. Aloys insensitively felt that she emerged purely to bask in the limelight.

Her pathetic revenge was to denigrate and insult him in front of the children, when she had him at bay round the big dining room table at home. He felt he had no alternative but to accept her insults quietly. He had no intention of coming out into the open. He would not discuss his habits, or modify his too-frequent absences. He intended to do as he pleased. His marriage was a write-off, and what little he saw of Ann Madden must be borne. He already had an inherent tendency towards 'tunnel vision', and he easily reconciled himself to estrangement, simply excluding her from his life. To her fury, he made no attempt to reconcile with her, or to placate her. Quite the reverse—his collaboration with Joan Denise Moriarty, included inviting her into the house for dinner on Christmas Day.

Whenever Ann talked to anyone about him in passing, the comments were derogatory. One day, in the centre of town, she found one of his batons lying in the street, which Aloys must have dropped from the battered briefcase he carried on the back of the scooter he drove in the 1960s. 'It's bad enough having to clean up after him at home,' she complained to Beatrice Hunt, one of his ballet colleagues, 'without having to clean up Patrick Street.' This was taken merely as a piece of Cork wit, but it could also be seen as biting sarcasm. 'He only ever had one friend,' she remarked bitterly to one of her husband's music colleagues, 'and he died.' She was referring to the writer, Edward Sheehy. The gallows humour here, implied that Edward's friendship with her husband contributed to his early death.

By the time their fifth and last child, Alan, was born in 1952, Aloys Fleischmann was gone from his wife's bed, never to return. After little more than a decade of marriage, Ann could take no more, and was ready to leave him. There was a showdown which resulted in his banishment to sleep alone in a single bed, in the tiny attic room at the top of the house.

Culturally in Ireland, divorce was illegal, and separation was extremely bad form. Marriages had to be perceived to endure, no matter what, and when relationships did break down, trapped couples often led totally separate lives under the same roof, pretending to the public that they were happily married and cohabiting. Outsiders thought Ann appeared fond of Joan Denise Moriarty. Aloys' children were certainly very fond of Joan, but Ann tolerated her, mainly to save face. Joan was known, after all, to have nobody in the world, and Aloys was busy whipping up public sympathy for her.

There were very few people that Ann Madden tolerated in her home. She was not one of the professor's wives who gave dinner parties, and she would not allow graduating students to gather for farewell evenings. Nothing was allowed, and the gregarious, fun-loving Aloys grew resigned to having all his parties and functions elsewhere.

In later life, Ann became increasingly deaf, and increasingly reclusive. She withdrew into herself, and took to reading 'trashy novels', as he called them. Since there was no evidence of these in the house, she must have borrowed the books from the library. She politely answered the phone for him right up to the end of her life, and attended his eightieth birthday party at the Metropole Hotel in Cork, at which he danced with laughing female students. As usual, people almost ignored her, and gasped in admiration at the aged music professor's energetic dancing prowess as he spun the young girls round, one after another.

Soon after this, following a very short and dignified illness in her early eighties, Ann Madden died. She was buried, at her own request, in a black evening dress. 'To watch someone die alters your whole perspective on life,' Aloys mused, the day his wife died. She was buried in St Finbarr's Cemetery in Cork, but not in the plot she thought was originally intended for her. She was buried in accordance with a scheme her husband had worked out when buying the grave, in order to accommodate Joan Denise Moriarty.

There was a Fleischmann family grave, in which Ann Madden refused to consider eventual burial, because Aloys' mother was in it, whom she hated. She fretted about wanting another plot, so when Aloys bought a large one adjacent to the family grave, she assumed it was for her. It was not, but he let her think it was. When Ann Madden arrived at the funeral of Charles Lynch, a colleague of Aloys, who had been pianist for Joan Denise Moriarty's Irish Theatre Ballet, she discovered with a shock, that he was being buried, under Aloys' direction, in the new plot—her grave. Charles Lynch was a man she hated even more than she hated Aloys' mother. She then refused, as Aloys had known she would, to be buried in the same plot as Lynch, and decided she'd rather be interred in the family grave when she died after all. This left space in the new grave for Aloys to make eventual provision for Joan Denise Moriarty, which is what he had intended all along. It would have been unthinkable socially, for his wife to have agreed to be buried in the new plot with Charles Lynch, alongside the Fleischmann family grave, and equally unthinkable for her to have made a fuss at her husband's provisions for the impoverished but aristocratic Lynch.

After Ann's death, Aloys immediately moved back from his single bed in the attic, into the double bed in the master bedroom, and went on with life as though she had never been there. Bereaved spouses, no matter how bad their marriages have been, usually recover memories of the early, happy days, and acknowledge these, partly as a route to acceptance and reconciliation in death. Not only did Aloys not grieve, or show any regret or compassion, he did not even seem to be aware that he was bereaved. Asked whether he ever missed his wife, he looked at first blank, then astonished. 'Not at all,' he snorted softly, as though the very question were ridiculous. He got on with his work, as though too busy for regret, or even the expression of relief. But he made just one reflection: At the end of his life, Aloys Fleischmann, who was a very gentle man, said sadly that he'd made a great mistake with Ann. What he ought to have done right at the start, he came to believe, was to have refused to tolerate her insults and her difficult behaviour. Instead, he said, he should have taken his wife, and beaten her.

All along, he had been convinced that his wife was impossible to live with. This may have been true, but he could not have been easy to live with, either. They were alike in some ways. Both were strong-willed and stubborn. Both felt deep, incommunicable, irreconcilable hurts—but they had many differences. She was a dull, middle-class Irish woman constrained by Irish society of the 1930s. She had no job or social standing to speak of, and was a mere appendage to her publicly successful husband. He was a star of the Opera House, accustomed to much applause and admiration. He was one of the people with power, and because of his education, he had influence amongst those of higher and more powerful social, educational and political standing.

He was eccentric enough, and self-absorbed enough to ignore his wife and her needs most of the time, but ironically, there was one crucial benefit that a loveless and difficult marriage to Ann brought him. It met most of his own basic needs in life, and confined the mundanities neatly. He was an oddball and a romantic. His tendency was towards idealism to the point of otherworldliness. The ivory tower of the splendid university suited him perfectly. He was conservative, but as thinkers tend to be, he was deeply unconventional. He may have subscribed to old values like chivalry and decency, but only out of a sense of personal honour and pride. His courtly manners were anachronistic. He was out of touch with what others might call reality, but most of what was best in this man, was lost on Ann. And whatever good there may have been in her, was extinguished for him under the crushing oppression of her regime. Relief came for her, in the conventional savagery of the private vendetta. Whatever was left of her, after bearing children, she threw her substance away on the passion of hatred.

It is doubtful whether Aloys ever tried to get to know his wife, and equally doubtful whether he partnered her through the kind of day-to-day emotional routines and life-changing events that usually bind partners together. Ann lived in an everyday world that was distasteful to him. He was also unable to deal with her disillusionment. So he paid all the bills for the running of the house, and abandoned her in almost every sense except the visible one. But he didn't count on her bitterness.

In her own domestic domain, with no relief and no understanding, she started on the long, lonely road of withdrawing into herself. For him it was different. Unaware and still utterly unawakened, his unsatisfied soul remained wide open.

As he went his way about his musical business in Cork, he began to notice that increasingly on the circuit, was the beautiful red-haired young woman who played the pipes in the university.

10
Collaboration

J oan emerged on the circuit in Cork, with bright red lips, curled hair, high heels, fitted little jackets and short skirts. Glamorous and sexy, she was noticeable, and whenever she signed her name, it was 'Joan Denise' rather than 'Joan'. She did not want to be like her Aunt Joan, and 'Joan Denise' had a similar ring to 'Marguerite', the name of her real mother, similarly exotic and different. The quality it was most obvious for her to develop—and in her situation, the most prudent—was her easy power of seduction. When she remembered to move carefully, paying attention to her walk, her heavy legs lost their clumsiness, and her looks impressed people. This became one of her most powerful weapons, and she was to use it with dedication. Another asset was her lovely, mellow voice.

Her work was a grind, and far beneath the kind of dancing she felt she deserved to be doing. A hand-to-mouth struggle would have been bad enough. Plenty of people were involved in that, but to have to do variety fill-ins at cinema matinees just for food, and without pay, was demeaning. She wanted more.

She couldn't help being unfathomable to the average Irish mind. She was an unknowable, exotic creature. The message with no words was, that this strange woman in the big black brimmed hat, was keeping something back, and intended to go on doing so. She did not belong anywhere, or to anybody. She was ready to become a calculating, classic dark woman of mystery.

Aloys Fleischmann did not perceive her as a strange misfit who played the pipes as a novelty act in pantomime, accompanying her pupils as they sword-danced. He saw her as a musician who had performed at UCC, and who could play the unusual warpipes well enough to make an impact. As a woman musician, she had never seen any university or drawing room disciplines, and this made her very different from the scholarly female musicians he'd seen all around him. In some ways, she was like his unusual outsider mother, and she excited him.

Sean Neeson had whisked her away from him the first time, but now Aloys had the field to himself. He was in a position to recruit and display musical talent, and he had a greedy personal appetite for it. He was well aware that his own brand of music had limited popular appeal, and felt that Joan's unorthodox, hit-or-miss approach to entertaining had a charisma that his well-ordered musical world needed. Since he had been an infant, kissed at bedtime by his mother as she rustled away towards the concert hall, he had been powerfully seduced by the idea of perfumed glamour. What he wanted, was not just to reproduce the impression that Joan had made on him, but to harness it, enlarge on it and enhance it, so that his next work would sparkle with popular impact. He also wanted to capture whatever Joan had, and control it in the way that he had not been able to capture his darling mother Tilly. His sixth sense told him that Joan was ripe for the plucking.

He decided that central to his next work would be, not the war pipes for their own sake, but the war pipes for the sake of this particular woman piper and the impression he felt her appearance would make on the audience. It was a totally selfish decision, but it turned out to be a gift for her, and it changed both their lives. He approached her with respect.

Cork, the second city of Ireland, with a cathedral and a liberal university reputedly built on the site of St Finbarr's ancient seat of learning, has always been said to have delusions that it really is the capital city. Cork people have always been known to be cute, to be clannish, to be constantly on the lookout for secretly getting one up on their rivals in Dublin. As in Ireland generally, society was rigidly demarcated, and if you belonged amongst the top people, fine, if not, you were nowhere.

With her secretive cuteness and her delusions of grandeur, Joan might have been said to possess a Corkonian mentality, but she also was socially nowhere. In his numerous musical and academic capacities, Aloys could appear as of right at any top table in the city. The position, prestige and power that he treated very casually and more or less took for granted, made him very attractive to Joan.

In 1944, Aloys Fleischmann had been commissioned by Radio Éireann to write one of the works for a concert which was to mark the centenary of the death of Thomas Davis, chief poet of the Young Ireland movement. He had chosen to work on Davis' poem *Clare's Dragoons*. His idea now, was to write a piece for baritone solo with

72

mixed choir and orchestra, and to add the war pipes and Joan Moriarty to the score. She jumped at it.

Only the year before, Aloys had removed his small classes from the little Observatory in the grounds of the university, where he had not so long before destroyed the seismograph in order to get the piano in. Despite his earlier complaints he now decided that this poky, noisy, detached little stone Observatory with the high slits of windows, would be a perfect venue for himself and Joan to study the grace notes of the war pipes for *Clare's Dragoons*. Though she needed space to march up and down in order to play properly, he also decided that it would be a grand place for her to practise in. When they were not working in the Observatory, they were together in her studio in Patrick Street.

At the end of their lives, they gave a joint interview, in which they talked about their first collaboration in the Observatory. They both remembered with amusement that it was hot and cramped in the stuffy little room. She remembered the students craning to look in, to see what mad things were going on in there, and said that she and Aloys had been kindred spirits, both trying to do the same thing, which was to overcome prejudice and start something in Cork. He agreed, adding that at the same time as she was struggling to establish a ballet company, he was trying to start an orchestra.

This 'both starting off' idea doesn't fit the facts, because at the time he wrote *Clare's Dragoons* the orchestra was well established, having been in existence, in one vigorous form or another, for about thirteen years. It was fourteen years since he had founded the flourishing Art Society, he founded the Cork Orchestral Society in 1939, and had revived the University Choral Society in 1943. The latter's first rollicking concert took place in the spring of 1944.

Kindred spirits, maybe, but there was no comparison whatever between their respective situations. She herself did not formulate the concept of breaking down prejudice until later, and even then, not by herself. All she was doing at that time, was simply trying to find somewhere to perform; trying to find a way to survive, and she was doing it by taking classes and performing in variety shows. What actually happened, was that he took her on as a protégé, at great risk to his reputation. At great risk to his marriage, he also fell in love with her.

Collaborating closely with Joan, he completed the work within a year, and the first performance in 1945, which included a huge choir from the Royal Irish Academy of Music, and the RTE Symphony Orchestra, was held at the Capitol Theatre in Dublin. The invited audience included the President, the Taoiseach, Eamonn de Valera, and assorted members of the cabinet, the Senate, the Dáil, judiciary and Civil Service. 'Probably,' Aloys later had cause to write bitterly, 'the most Philistine audience ever assembled in Dublin, most of whom had never been at an orchestral concert before, so that a less receptive audience could hardly be imagined.'

Early on in the work, the war pipes, accompanied by strings, were played off-stage. At the end, as the male voices of the choir sang vigorously, the war pipes struck up at the back of the theatre, and the piper marched up through the audience. On reaching the stage, the piper joined the whole ensemble in what was intended to be a rousing climax. His judgement completely blinded by the rosy flush of his first experience of love, Aloys had expected that the appearance of Joan Moriarty would have the same *coup-de-foudre* effect on everyone else, as it had on him. He had thought that her appearance marching up through the audience would have been riveting. But it wasn't. The audience did not seem to like the work.

'Even the tall lady piper,' he lamented many times afterwards, 'with her green kilts and her shock of red hair marching through the auditorium, failed to rouse the apathetic audience from their torpor.' He never forgave Dublin, and often repeated this story in condemnation of the capital city, completely unaware that it was self-revelatory of his excessive admiration for his piper. The follow-up, told with equal relish, was that when the spectacular work was performed at City Hall in Cork shortly afterwards, it received, he said, a tumultuous reception. Subsequent performances ranged from adequate to disastrous.

As for Joan Denise, she didn't take too much notice of whatever torpor there might have been amongst the audience. There had been no noise as she marched through the audience, no boos and no jeers, no heckling. For the first time in her performing life, the men and women in the audience were the kind of company she'd craved; the kind of people she'd secretly gazed on in dumb fascination from the stairwell at Glenapp Castle. She had been introduced to the President and the Taoiseach, and to cabinet ministers and their wives. On top of that, she had performed in the capital city at a prestigious event, she had been paid well, and she had travelled. Joan was well satisfied.

The worst part of the evening was meeting the big names from the audience. Aloys knew who people were; she didn't. She was terrified, wondering what they'd say to her. Previously always perceived as the unwanted poor relation, she was afraid she might say the wrong thing; afraid her accent was the wrong one; afraid her lack of education might show; afraid people would see right through her. Instead, people readily accepted her as a performer introduced by the well-known, well-respected Aloys Fleischmann, and thought her enigmatic and beautiful, with a regal bearing.

It was probably when they were together in Dublin for the first time, and having dinner in the hotel where they were staying, in separate rooms, that she poured out her unhappy story to her protector. She'd been dragged round from school to school, she confessed, and had been given no education at all. She also told him that she was an orphan, that she had no money, and that her whole adopted family in Mallow had treated her like a servant. Prior to this, Aloys had been told only that she had been a pupil of various ballet schools and of Marie Rambert, and that Joan had learned to play the pipes on holiday in Scotland. As he got to know her, he had been unable to see how she could be so lacking in confidence, and how it was that she felt so very shy in company. His experience had been limited to mixing with educated people who had decent bank balances, and decent houses, and it had puzzled him that she could be so devoid of elementary *savoir faire*.

Now he knew the reasons, and his response was to gallantly offer his support to this lonely woman. This was luck beyond her wildest dreams. She snatched at it with a sense of *déjà vu*. For Joan, here once again was the kind king; here was the benevolent autocrat; here was the rich, indulgent father-man; here was the gentle, aristocratic man of influence dangling a fairytale in front of her. On the surface she took his declaration of allegiance with a level-headed pinch of salt, but her mute impassivity was not the rejection he feared. It was her guarded inability to leave herself vulnerable to any further hurts. It had the effect of goading him to offer more help. He effortlessly took over with the post-performance pleasantries, leaving her to look demure, mysterious, and silent.

Aloys immediately started promoting her. She sat back and watched. His first thought was that Joan Denise might perform in the presence of Sir Arnold Bax, the keeper of the Queen's music, the next time the composer came over to stay on holiday at Oileán Rua, the big house in Rochestown that Aloys and his parents had bought together. His parents, who entertained many visiting composers and musicians, as well as writers and poets, readily agreed to this new piper being invited to perform in their salon. Once Bax was installed, a small, private party was arranged. The guests were to be entertained on the lawn, and it was a hot summer evening.

Into the house that Aloys' wife had stormed out of, never to return, now walked Joan the beauty, Joan the sensitive, sad, needy creature. After tuning her pipes out of earshot, she emerged into the garden marching slowly, the wail of the pipes filling the humid air above the mown grass thronged with clouds of midges. Her strangely loud, piercing piping made an impact amongst the guests in the garden. The sensitive skin on her face, her hands and her bare legs was bitten again and again by midges, but she played on. Tilly and Aloys Georg were enchanted by this novel talent, and also noticed their son's sudden new animation in this woman's presence. Their only son was married, and he had children, their grandchildren. But they immediately befriended Joan. Her reaction to the evening was an allergic one. She was, she later recalled, in bed for a week, plastered in calamine lotion after all the midge bites.

It wasn't long before Joan was back at Oileán Rua, this time to perform some of her ballet steps, posing *en pointe* in a tutu on top of the gatepost; leaping exhuberantly for the camera across the lawn in some other bright little costume. Here, at his parents' house was a private chance for Aloys to get to know Joan. It was a happy time and a fun time, and it was not long before he was acknowledging more than just friendship, and she was realising that this composer of influence, who claimed he wanted to help her, had a whole orchestra at his command. It was an amateur orchestra, but he was energetic, and drawn to new challenges. From then it was but a short romantic step to his placing the whole outfit at her disposal.

He could see her problem clearly, he thought. She wanted to perform, but she knew nobody, had no money, and didn't have a clue about arranging things. He knew everyone, money for him had never been a problem, and he was very experienced in organising from behind the scenes. What she needed if she wanted to get anywhere, he told her, was a strong committee of people with pull. Then she'd also need sponsorship. She couldn't talk to people and she couldn't write letters, she confessed, and wouldn't know who to approach. He could talk to lots of people with clout, he answered, he could write letters easily, and he could type. Taking on the arranging of the life of this woman who was completely unable to speak or write a sentence with confidence, came very easily to him.

The plan was that they would put on a performance somewhere together using her amateur dancers and his amateur orchestra. Her job was to muster enough dancers to form a troupe big enough to fill the stage for a whole performance, and to arrange some dances. Word started to go around the Cork upper-classes and children began turning up at the studio for lessons. The incentive was that all dancers would have a chance to perform in this proposed show if they reached the given standard. He was to orchestrate it all, and oversee it, because it had to be good enough to fill a whole evening, and unlike him, she had never done anything like it.

This meant for her, that instead of being a novelty item in someone else's show, she would have the prestige of putting on her own performance herself, with her dancers. For him, it meant bringing his orchestra into a place where he could attract more support.

More importantly for both of them, that first evening of ballet in 1947, was to be a symbolic cementing of their romantic liaison. He had whispered persuasively the outline of a new mythology, and she had listened. Artistic unity and personal unity could coincide, he argued, mutually nurturing each of them, and the fruit of their union was to be the ballet. He suggested that Smetana's symphonic poem *Vltava*, which traces the progress of the chief river of Bohemia, would be ideal as the grande finale of the evening. Joan was to dance the part of the river goddess. She set to work, and a series of tableaux were arranged, illustrating the various scenes past which the river wended. A hunting scene, a peasants' wedding festival, water nymphs dancing in the moonlight, and ancient castles were arranged. To Joan and Aloys, the river, finally passing tumultuous rapids as it flows toward the sea, was an image of their love. *Vltava*, was for them a potent symbol of their secret union.

'To My Dearest One,' he wrote on a card which he slipped into her first-night bouquet, exactly thirty years later, as he had put so many others into the bouquets he sent her down the years:

'As we journey on, after thirty happy years together, like Vltava, to our ultimate goal—the sea.'

Using the beautiful logo of the Orchestral Society for the first performance in 1947, as he would continue doing for many years into the future, Aloys wrote the elegant programme notes himself:

BALLET PERFORMANCE
BY THE
CORK BALLET GROUP
AND
CORK SYMPHONY ORCHESTRA

A novel venture in the artistic life of Cork city, sponsored by the management of the Capitol Cinema Theatre, is to take place at the Opera House, Cork, on Sunday night, June 1st, at 8–15 pm, when for the first time a full-length performance of Ballet will be given by a local company, in co-operation with the Cork Symphony Orchestra. The Cork Ballet Group, consisting of some forty dancers directed by Miss Joan Denise Moriarty, who has studied choreography in London and Paris and is herself a distinguished dancer, have been undergoing intensive training for some months past in the preparation of a number of interesting ballets...

She had his logo, her dancers had the sponsorship of his orchestra, and were given the title, the Cork Ballet Group. The name by which she would henceforth be known, thanks to Aloys, was now down in black and white. It was also now down in black and white, and was to remain unquestioned, that Joan had studied in Paris and London, and that she herself was a 'distinguished' dancer. The great collaboration had begun.

Old stage sets were repainted, courtesy of the Opera House, by Marshall Hutson and Frank Sanquest. Aloys' political mind had been at work. Foremost amongst the organising committee was the influential Jane (Jenny) Dowdall, a close friend of the then Taoiseach, Eamonn de Valera, who was godfather to her son. She was a happy recruit to the ballet, and was extremely helpful when she became the first female Lord Mayor of Cork, a Senator, and a member of the Council of State.

Patrick Farrell, manager of the Capitol Cinema Theatre, was persuaded to sponsor the evening at his place, but when it was discovered that the concrete stage was not suitable for dancing, he stayed committed, and the show moved to the Opera House. The Minister for Posts and Telegraphs, Mr P. J. Little, was not only invited to the performance; he was asked to address the audience from the stage. He was glad to oblige. Two eminent musicians, the composer E. J. Moeran, and the pianist Charles Lynch, both colleagues of Aloys at UCC, publicly endorsed the Minister's view that the standard was 'astonishingly good'.

The press gave not just good reviews, but reviews that were uncritical. Public kindness was a great virtue, and Cork was in the habit of being good to its own. Aloys and Joan gaily leapt on these positive write-ups as proof of their own prowess, but the truth was that almost nobody had seen any other ballet company before, and even if they had, there was no tradition of critical reviewing in the press. The rave reviews the ballet got, were used down the years as a stick to beat potential sponsors with, as well as the Arts Council, and as evidence that would bring in grants, costumes, and everything else that was needed. He was political enough to use anything that came to hand, and courted newspaper writers with his eloquence. He clipped out everything that was written by the press about the ballet in Cork, and pasted it all into huge scrapbooks. He may have believed them. Joan, however, suspected in her own heart, that many were not worth the paper they were written on.

'Gloriously successful,' gushed *The Cork Examiner* reviewer, on Monday, 2nd June 1947. 'A pleasure it truly is to watch graceful movement or to have the imagination stimulated by flitting steps and sweet music, but those who feast upon such pleasures can surely look forward to the future with confident anticipation...without the closest co-operation and understanding between these two important personages, success could never have been attained...the ballet was polished and well-nigh flawless.'

Even the stagehands knew better. Having watched professionals rehearsing they could see that Joan Denise Moriarty hadn't a clue. She knew nothing at all about working on stage and, as a dancer, she had little technique. They could tell she was an amateur, and so could many others. People rather pitied Joan, and indulged her in the same way that they indulged their own cute children performing enthusiastically on stage with her for the first time.

Irish people would never come right out and say anything derogatory about a performance anyway. They would make soothing, diplomatic noises, and keep the truth to themselves. Nobody would have been cruel enough to criticise this woman who was trying so hard. People could see she was doing her best, and realising that things would improve, they straightened their bow ties, they saw and were seen, they took their seats, and unwittingly entered the glittering conspiracy.

The Cork Examiner reviewer picked out the two dances that had particular significance for the couple. *Vltava*, he wrote, 'had a fluid interpretive quality, deeply symbolic and stirring in its rhythmic grace. *La Calinda* possessed this same quality, and this dance, too, was to impress greatly.' What he really meant without knowing it, was that there was a chemistry between Joan and Aloys which they had communicated to the audience.

Also at the first performance, Aloys, who had known Cork's most famous disgruntled exile, Sean O'Faolain, set the tone of his own personal political agenda:

> 'Prof. Fleischmann thanked Mr Little for his remarks and said the Minister was transforming musical life in Dublin. It was encouraging to find him so interested in the 'under-nourished' capital of the South. Before this work was staged, they had been told that such an ambitious performance could not be given in Cork, the history of which was strewn with corpses of movements such as this. He felt that Miss Moriarty and her young dancers would give many performances such as this and gain a reputation for the Cork Ballet Group.'

Aloys not only wanted Joan to gain a reputation. He wanted himself to cut a swathe through Irish cultural life. He wanted to find acclaim in propagating an esoteric art form, as well as all sorts of other musical ventures, in a backwoods arena where great figures before him had spectacularly failed to achieve. O'Faolain took every opportunity to insist that Cork was merely a place to get out of. The hugely popular actor, Micheal MacLiammoir, whom it was believed at the time was a Corkman, spent his time in Dublin. Aloys Fleischmann, who years later had the opportunity to take over the retiring Professor Larchet's chair of music at UCD, chose not to do so. Larchet was not only surprised, but deeply hurt. Fleischmann could hardly explain that he preferred, not just to be a big fish in a small pond, but to remain in the second city as the champion of Joan Moriarty.

Their first event ran at a small loss of £43.00, which Patrick Farrell paid. The original intention was to put on a performance every week, but this idea was scrapped, and the couple worked towards doing something the following year.

On that first night, as she performed the solo dance *La Calinda* from the Delius opera, *Koanga,* in which she acted the part of a slave girl passionately breaking out of her chains, her mesmerised little pupils wept. Joan was symbolically liberating dance from the shackles of ignorance and prejudice. Showing no sign of the artistic restraint personified by powdered concert pianist Tilly Fleischmann, the barefoot woman dancing to the accompaniment of her paramour's full orchestra, appeared ecstatic.

11
Showdowns

As Aloys spent more time with Joan, he spent less at home. His wife went on having his babies. Ann already felt she had plenty of grounds to complain about the prodigious workload that kept him away from the family. When he was home, he spent a lot of time in his study, writing music. In addition to his teaching and orchestral society work, he had written *The Four Masters*, an overture of 14 minutes duration in 1944, and, in 1946, *Elizabeth McDermott Roe*, a lament for strings, as well as *The Fountain of Magic*, a cycle of four songs for soprano and orchestra.

He also obtained an Arts Council grant for Joan, and offered to combine his Orchestral Society with her Ballet Group, for joint ventures. A merger would mean that they could pool resources, as well as spend time together. They combined for a December 1947 production of Milton's masque, *Comus*, complete with splendid costumes, but the Arts Council immediately threatened to cut off the grant to both the Orchestral Society, and to the Ballet Group if they amalgamated. So they reluctantly separated again, but continued their partnership more strongly than ever. Completely under his control, the Orchestral Society sponsored all ballet performances in which the orchestra participated.

Aloys proposed doing things in a big way for their next production. The idea was to put on a full week of ballet, and to introduce a brand new ballet to Cork. Joan was to choreograph the story of an old legend, and he was to write the music specially. The full orchestra would support her; the choir was ready to do his bidding; the sponsorship money was there; the committee was doing its job; he would again write the brochure—and it was all for her.

As the time drew near, they sometimes practised six nights a week. She may have felt that this was all too much, too soon, but it was too good a chance to miss. It was a heady time. Joan knew that the show and the publicity would bring in more paying pupils to her day classes. She set to work, arranging the choreography to suit the

Showdowns

limited skills of her awed little dancers. Well-dressed, happy children don't need much technique. Her dancers were always cute.

Joan rechoreographed *Puck Fair*, written by Irish composer Elizabeth Maconchy, which had been staged by the Dublin Ballet Club at the Gaiety Theatre. Aloys wrote the music for *The Golden Bell of Ko*, based on the Chinese legend which tells of the willing sacrificial death of three women.

Also on the team in 1948, was the talented Leslie Horne, in charge of lighting. Leslie, an insurance manager, served the company devotedly and brilliantly always, but when money was provided by the government years later, to form a professional company, Leslie was not given a place on the board. The reason Joan gave for unfairly treating the man, was that she did not get on with him. Aloys pleaded on his behalf, but she would not budge. Leslie was extremely hurt, and later confided to Aloys, that when she dropped him, he had been on the brink of willing his entire estate to the company after the death of his wife.

In December of 1948, the Cork Ballet Group co-operated with the University and Aeolian Choirs and the Cork Symphony Orchestra to put on another masque, this time Henry Purcell's *The Fairy Queen*. In 1949 another week of ballet was delivered, and again the press issued glowing reports. The young people danced well, in formation, and Joan often took the male parts. Aloys was interested in Irish legends, and *The Children of Lir*, with libretto by Patricia O'Reilly and music by Eamonn O'Gallchobhair, appeared for the first time, in the Ballet Week of 1950, attended by the Taoiseach, John A. Costello, and his wife.

By this time, the pair were being seen, flushed and blooming, at opening-night parties. The 1950 opening-night party was held at the house of the President of the Orchestral Society, Seamus Fitzgerald, who was also Chairman of the Cork Harbour Commissioners, and a prominent member of the Fianna Fáil political party in Cork. Next day a picture appeared in the paper of Joan Moriarty and the Fine Gael Taoiseach, cutting a magnificent cake together. The rank and file of the Fianna Fáil party complained, because it was unthinkable, at the time, for a prominent Fianna Fáil person to entertain a prominent Fine Gael person.

People began to talk for another reason. They were talking about the two glamour individuals who were out practising, performing, and partying together whilst Aloys' wife stayed home having babies.

82

Eric Cross, author of the bawdy *The Tailor and Ansty* weighed in with a letter to the newspaper, arguing that the citizens of Cork ought to be proud of Ballet Week, since it had established the city as the artistic capital of Ireland. Yet this talk of art did nothing to defuse more earthy gossip, and cut no ice with the clergy. When Joan Moriarty attended Saints Peter and Paul Church on the Sunday morning after the final performance of Ballet Week in 1951, the preacher denounced the scandalous scenes that had been onstage at the Cork Opera House, of a semi-nude female figure which offended all normal codes of decency.

Both Joan and Aloys took the priest's outburst as a sign of philistinism; an indication that the tutu, tights and leotard of the high art of ballet were still regarded as indecent by the super-religious, the ignorant and the uncultured. But prior to this, no Cork priest had taken any opportunity to denounce ballet, even though the couple and their supporters had been promoting and performing it in Cork for the past few years. It was not costume which was at issue. It would have been more realistic for Joan and Aloys to realise that what had really offended the priest was their apparent relationship, and the threat it appeared to pose to marriage and the family. Some people didn't like the idea of this couple being seen to be celebrated, fêted, and hobnobbing with high-ranking government members, whilst at the same time, their apparent liaison could be seen to be, whether it was or not, issuing a flagrant disregard of morality. Neither of them realised, until Aloys' wife forced a showdown.

Since she married Aloys in 1940, Ann Fleischmann had given birth to four children. She had never liked the devotion that Aloys seemed to have for his work, which kept him away from her and the children, all day, every day, and long into most evenings. Her husband had argued that he had no more spare time to spend at home, but he had taken on this whole extra ballet workload, and was becoming more committed to it, and more excited and absorbed by it as the days, the weeks, the months, the years went by, and he was spending less and less time with his wife.

Ann usually appeared at opening nights as the wife of the conductor, but in May 1952 Ann Fleischmann was heavily pregnant, within a few weeks of giving birth to their fifth child. Her husband's workload must have been crushing at the time, for other composers were invited to write some music for this occasion, during which they planned a change of programme on alternate nights. Sean O'Riada, a gifted composer who later attained much higher musical standing in Ireland than Aloys, for his inspired traditional work, and who was a music student of Aloys at the time, scored Schumann's music for *Papillons*. Composer Eamonn O'Gallchobhair produced *The Singer*, based on Padraic Pearse's play of the same name. For this last theme, about a poet who abandons the writing of patriotic songs, in favour of joining active combatants in an uprising against an occupying power, the fired-up audience at the closing performance in Cork, gave an ovation.

Ann's last baby, a second son, was born on Monday the 23rd of June. By the weekend, Aloys was packing his bags for a jaunt. On Saturday, 28th of June, just five days after the birth of his son, he took the entire orchestra and all their instruments, and Joan took her entire company and all their costumes, and they all went off for their first adventure outside Cork, to bring on Sunday the 29th, a ballet programme to the Savoy Cinema in Limerick.

The picture taken in Limerick testifies to their apparent health and happiness at the time, but the Limerick performance was important not just because it was a way they could spend time together in relative freedom. The painter, Cecil Salkeld, also executive officer of the cultural activities of An Tóstal, was in the audience, as well as author Sean O'Faolain, writer of *She Had To Do Something*, a satirical play about ballet and philistinism in Cork. An Tóstal (literally 'assembly'), was the innovation of Sean Lemass, Minister for Industry and Commerce at the time. As Aloys wrote, 'he had come to the conclusion that the country was half asleep, and to arouse it from its lethargy he conceived the idea of stimulating every city, town and even village to have its own Tóstal or festival.'

Aloys wanted to be in on that.

Ann had told her husband repeatedly that she was not happy about his going out to the ballet and to Joan night after night. She told him that she didn't like his involvement in all that, and heartily wished he would stop. His response was to keep right on going. He either cared little for her feelings and convention, or the momentum was such that he seemed unable to take any notice of her.

There was a rumour going round that Aloys and Joan were more than just friends, followed by another that Ann was on the brink of leaving him, and of going away to join the missions. One story which was current, but which was greeted with disbelief by some who heard it, was that the couple had actually been seen in an intimate embrace. The first-floor windows of Joan's Emmet Place studio were half-opaque. People on tiptoe could see out, but people on the first floor across the road—in the public bar of the Opera House, for example—could not see in. It was said that from the players' bar on the second floor, a person could look across and see down into Joan's studio, through the clear upper half of her first-floor window. It was from such a distant vantage point, that some storyteller claimed to have seen lovemaking between Joan and Aloys.

When the rumours started, Ann confronted him. It is unlikely that she would actually have heard the 'intimate embrace' story, but she was not blind. As one onlooker of the time said, Ann would have been crazy not to have been extremely upset by her husband's behaviour, and crazy not to have at the least threatened to play her ultimate card—to leave him.

His response, as an Irishman, and in the face of being presented with a full-scale scandal which would have brought them all down, was to deny everything, and to reassure her that for him, there was absolutely no question of his deserting her in any way, for Joan Moriarty or for anyone else. He had taken on the responsibility of a wife and five children, and he fully intended to go on providing for them to the best of his ability. The real question of what he was going to do about Joan Moriarty was not addressed. His blank, astonished face argued his deep distaste for the question, as well as pompous denial, but she'd had enough. Unable to get through to him, she played her last card. She told him that she wanted absolutely nothing more to do with him. In traditional Irish solution to their marital problems, he left his wife's bed without a backward glance, and took over a small attic room at the top of the house, where he slept alone in a single bed for the next forty years.

Then he invited Joan Denise Moriarty to be godmother to his newborn little son, Alan. From now on, he was to make sure to address her in public and to refer to her as 'Miss Moriarty and she was to address him in public and refer to him as 'Professor Fleischmann'. For good measure, each was extremely, ostentatiously reserved and polite to the other in public, and all these maneouvres served, not only to convince people that there was no romance between them, but to add spice to their little game.

Aloys' idealistic nature had reserved a pedestal for a goddess— one that was extraordinary. His goddess would have to be someone much like his mother—beautiful, perfumed, exotic, dressed in evening gowns, and a performing artist. Joan Denise Moriarty would do very nicely. She would be his muse. Joan was emotionally unavailable to anyone, but he already took it for granted that such a goddess would be unattainable, and his whisperings encouraged Joan Moriarty to climb onto the pedestal. She was not as excellent as he imagined her to be, but because his memories of the talent of his high-class mother were projected onto Joan, she didn't need to be. He had a blind spot where Joan's artistic worth was concerned.

The arrangement added more stress to Joan's existence. She'd never had anybody, and she still had nobody. That was unsatisfactory. It was one thing to fall in love with someone. She was not Irish. The next move for an unhappily married person who had found someone else, in the English culture she knew best, was to obtain a divorce. In the culture she was now part of, this was impossible. In any case, Joan was not in the slightest bit interested in cooking, in sewing, or in fixing things up for a man. She was not a giver in that sense, she was a taker. Whenever there was any cooking or sewing done, someone else was usually doing it for Joan. She was far from traditional wife material. It did not seem to be an imperative in her makeup to need a man in her bed, and he seemed more than perfectly happy not to get domestically entangled with a woman again. They kept going ahead with their mutually convenient arrangement.

Anyone who remains in a secret triangle of this sort whilst children are being born and whilst a semblance of family life goes on, experiences serious inner conflict. Joan accepted that along with the package. She could have chosen to get out at any point, but she did not. She preferred the role of the other woman.

He was many things to her, and she was deeply grateful. He looked after her—he was the father she'd never had. He was her teacher—he taught her about Ireland, about myths, about poetry, about using words. He was her crutch—whatever she could not do, he took over and did it. And whatever else he represented for her, Aloys Fleischmann was extremely useful to her—more useful, kind and generous, than anyone had ever been. She trusted him, and she kept going. But she was also under stress from the work she was involved in, which some of the time, was way above her head.

He spent days in a university full of intelligent adults, and could go home at night to a house full of family company. She spent days exercising little children, and retreated at night to an empty flat on the main street of the city. Aloys had a very strong sense of responsibility towards her, and was working on her behalf. He had taken his cue to fill the void. In 1953, he arranged for her to move into the big house with Aloys Georg (known to the family as Faw Faw), and Tilly Fleischmann. In this way he marked her out, claimed her for himself, as well as taking care of her. Implying that the lovely Joan would be available to nobody else, this ploy warned other men away.

She had changed her solicitor from Gerald Goldberg to James O'Donovan, the man who once said he wanted to marry her, and Jamie helped her to get a better studio opposite the Opera House, in Emmet Place. This was for business use, and, so, in vacating the studio in Patrick Street, she left her bedsitting room life behind forever.

Installed in the Fleischmann household, she immediately adopted the Fleischmanns as honorary parents, and was welcomed as the daughter they'd never had. Here she was safe, looked-after, and happy. Aloys could come and visit her at the house he was to inherit any time he felt like calling on his mother, and nobody could object. Joan came to love Herr Georg, and the dignified, ageing woman in the black lace dresses, and they both loved her, just as 'Daddy' O'Connor and his Austrian wife had loved her.

In here, too, was the sense of scale, the sense of order and of rightness that she craved. Here was a place where people did not go hungry; a place where people who had the security of money lived; here was a place of culture. Aloys discreetly visited her whenever he legitimately visited his parents, and his wife had no option but to tolerate it. Ann managed this, partly because she had written him off as a lover and as a companion, also because she was trapped, but mainly because she was Irish.

The Cork programme for the first Tóstal in 1953, consisted of High Mass in the Catholic Cathedral, a military parade through the town, exhibitions, recitals, lectures and sporting fixtures. Handel's *Messiah*, with Our Lady's Choral Society, was played by the Halle Orchestra, conducted by Sir John Barbirolli. In the centre of all this came Ballet Week, and Joan devised *Tableau for An Tóstal* as a salute to what was to become, over the next seven years, the large-scale Festival of Cork. After the tableau, they revived most of their previous ballet pieces, and then took the whole production to Killarney, to help out with the Tóstal in Kerry.

Joan's troupe with the lease on the three-storey large premises in town, now changed its title to the Cork Ballet Company, and 'Miss Moriarty', became its Artistic Director. 'Professor Fleischmann' became Chairman, and both the Artistic Director and the Chairman, addressed each other in the most respectful tones, each giving the impression that they were totally in awe, as well as in the debt of the other. The charade was almost Chinese in politeness, almost upper-crust Elizabethan in style. Leslie Horne was Manager, and Dame Marie Rambert and Dame Alicia Markova were first patrons. A later patron was Dame Ninette de Valois, an Irishwoman from Wicklow and founder of the British Royal Ballet. They also set up an Advisory Board which Senator Mrs Dowdall headed.

The board of the Cork Ballet Company fluctuated over the years, but included several supporters who remained until the end. Amongst these were Beatrice Hunt, Maeve Coakley, Lavinia Anderson, George Collins, Patrick Murray, Patrick Fleming, Patrick Leonard and James O'Donovan.

For the 1955 Tóstal, a full three-act *Coppelia* was staged before President and Mrs O'Kelly. Aloys noted with relish that, 'the entire house was in evening dress, and during the final bars of the ballet, the applause was so thunderous that the dancers could not hear the orchestra'. It was always important to him to be able to report that houses were packed and that applause was deafening, but the truth was that standards were unavoidably low, and the ballet often played to houses that were less than half-empty.

He only liked to remember packed opening nights, and so did she. Opening night was special, because so many complimentary tickets were given out and so many sponsoring firms and schools were allowed blocks, that the house was usually packed. Parents always love to see their children performing, and this was a big venue, with a big night out for the family, and there was a general atmosphere of indulgence. In any case, middle-class people of the city welcomed the opportunity to wear evening dress for the special occasion.

An answer to the problem about standards was to import guest dancers and, in 1956, Domini Callaghan, a member of Mona Ingoldsby's International Ballet, came to play Odette, in the second act of *Swan Lake*. Peter Darrell, of Sadler's Wells, came both to direct and to play Siegfried. In the same programme, Joan mounted her first large-scale work, *The Seal Woman,* to Hamilton Harty's Irish Symphony. Cherry Hutson played the lead. Some of the children danced barefoot. Watching these professionals in rehearsal gave Joan some valuable lessons in dance, in direction and in stagecraft. The following year, Domini came again, to dance *Giselle.* This time, the imported director was Swiss dancer and choreographer, Michel de Lutry, Domini Callaghan's husband. Joan Moriarty played Queen of the Wilis, and she watched the professional dancers at work.

In 1958 Michel de Lutry produced *The Sleeping Princess* and his wife danced Aurora, in the company of five other professional dancers. Norris Davidson, a ballet and opera buff who was making a television documentary which was to include scenes from the ballet, asked Joan Moriarty in advance, whether *The Sleeping Princess* was a bit too ambitious. She said, no, that she had a plan. In an interview during one of the performances, he said he wondered how it was, that they had ever thought of attempting this difficult work. She was silent. Aloys Fleischmann replied that the answer was the same as when Sir Edmund Hillary was asked why he attempted to climb Mount Everest—because it was there. Their answers did not dispel the scepticism of onlookers. It may have seemed noteworthy to some that a whole team of professional dancers were being drafted in to dance amongst rank amateurs, in a work produced by a guest artist, and all under the heading of the Cork Ballet Company.

Bringing professional dancers in cost money. The Arts Council gave special grants to bring Patricia Mulholland's Belfast company to Cork, and Father Aherne's Siamsa Tire group from Tralee. Marina Svetlova was brought in soon after.

Next Joan Moriarty switched to folk dancing and formed a little offshoot folk dance group of twelve members of her company. This time there were no children involved, just young men and women, and Joan and Aloys took this group to the International Dance Festival of Wewelsburg in central Germany. She danced as the central pivot of the group and played the war pipes, whilst Aloys, fluent in German, did the talking. Her style of dancing, which was a loose adaptation of Irish step-dancing and ballet steps, attracted criticism from traditionalists because, although the dancers wore costumes adapted from traditional garments, like Aran sweaters, tweed trousers, red skirts and shawls, it was not purely traditional Irish dancing that they were doing.

This trip, a rare holiday in comparative freedom, gave Joan and Aloys an opportunity to spend some time together, but relations between them deteriorated. In pictures they took at the time, both look serious, strained, and brimming with emotional pain. In one picture, she is looking anxiously and almost apologetically up at him, patting her hair, and trying to gauge his mood. In a picture of Aloys, taken by her on a woodland path, and later mounted in her photograph album, he looks handsome and attractive in a good dark suit, but also angry and disappointed. The equivalent picture of Joan in Highland uniform on the same path, taken by Aloys, shows her looking thin, headachy, disappointed, defiant, and slightly apologetic. Perhaps they were both extremely tired. Maybe abroad in a hotel together, with opportunity and anonymity, they discovered that they were not totally in tune with each other's needs. Perhaps this was the moment when Joan made the decision that she did not like sex.

In 1959, The Festival of Cork began with the London Symphony Orchestra and Sir Malcolm Sargent at the Savoy Cinema, when Claudio Arrau played Brahms 2nd Piano Concerto. Joan Moriarty was still looking thin and strained, and the ballet programme was crowded with guests on every level. Marina Svetlova, prima ballerina of the Metropolitan Opera, New York, was guest artist with the Cork Ballet Company, along with Kenneth Melville, one of the principal dancers with Sadler's Wells and London Festival Ballet. For them, Peter Darrell specially created *Aegean Caprice*. For these dancers, Joan Moriarty did not dare choreograph on her own. To the rescue came Stanley Judson, a member of Anna Pavlova's company, as guest producer and choreographer. He also co-operated with Peter Darrell in the choreography of *Aegean Caprice*. Joan Moriarty was completely out of her depth and embarrassed, but Aloys insisted that everything was going smoothly. The huge disparity between the level of her own dancers and that of the imported, well-paid professionals had convinced her of one thing. She wanted to start up a totally professional company. All it needed was money.

12
Poetry

I f Aloys did not realise the extent to which the whole thing depended on himself, Joan did. A note she sent to him in December, 1955, which she playfully folded into a little paper aeroplane, was headed 'In Praise of him'. It may not be a wonderful poem, but it gives a powerful indication of how she really felt:

'Strong in Mind,
Strong in Will,
Strong in deed,
Strong in body,
Strong four times over!
The second stronger than the others
Yes! Will
That word which gives this City
beauty of Sound, Movement
Ideas, Ideals,
Take that word away
and the pack of cards
tumbles! Collapses!
and falls into dust!.'

Here, in green ink, she was praising Aloys for his strength of will, on which the ballet completely depended, and comparing the ballet with all it represented, to a pack of cards, and also to dust. To compare her own work to dust is just about the most extremely negative image she could have found, and it not only gives the immediate impression of the sadness, futility, and depression of her own feelings, but it is almost chilling in its accuracy. She is saying that she felt weak to the point of total inability, and utterly dependent on his support, without which, the 'pack of cards' would 'tumble', 'collapse', and 'fall'.

The inappropriately playful aspect—folding it into a paper aeroplane, shows her pathetically lacking in confidence. By wrapping such a powerful insight as a joke, she was also negating the power of her own valuable prescience. If she had taken notice of what her own soul was telling her, life may have turned out differently. As it was, she chose to follow the path of promise that Aloys was marking out for her.

This kind of poetry was her instinctive, intimate way of expressing herself, and she often used green ink. She wrote like this partly because she could not rely enough on her mastery of language to communicate articulately in prose. It was also her intuitive way of giving half-acknowledged feelings some revealed form. Apart from her most private, behind-closed-doors self, it was here in strangled little poems and playful word games that she was at her most genuine.

1955 was the year in which they'd had an eerie scare during Ballet Week. During the third act of *Coppelia* the lights in the orchestra pit failed completely and the music stopped. The dancers froze onstage, and as the time went on and the lights had not been restored, Aloys himself addressed the audience, explaining that the musicians below were in total darkness. The power came on again after a few minutes, but some of the company were spooked, believing the blackout to be a portent. The company were never again to perform in the old Opera House because soon after that it burned down.

Without the Opera House, Joan was under serious stress. She could not now dream of going back to one of the cinemas to perform, even if that had been her inclination. Cinemas had already been outgrown, partly because of the unsprung stages, and also because they were popular venues that he would have considered down-market. There was now an orchestra to fit in, as well as the composer's bigger ideas. In accordance with his social standing, his status as university professor and his work as composer, conductor and sometimes organist, he was quite used to grand and imposing venues. Comfortable and on top of things in his own city, he thought the massive, stone-pillared City Hall an obvious choice.

For her it was different. She was intimidated by the prospect. On one hand, she knew that, even though Aloys was doing a great deal of work for the company, she would not be able to keep her side of things going solely on the basis of her own skills. On the other, she felt she couldn't go back to the kind of work she was doing before she met Aloys. Every effort he made to help her, only put more strain on her own resources. Her own dancing technique was not good enough for the glittering possibilities held out by him, and amongst her amateur dancers, there was nobody really competent. That she had no confidence in her choreography was no less than realistic.

One of Aloys Fleischmann's blind spots with people was that he could never really see how anyone could hold some point of view different from his own. He could always see a way around the most considered objection, and stay right on course. Any fears that Joan expressed, he countered with upbeat answers, and big ideas. Another of his blind spots was that he had no real insight into people and their motivations. Even if he had been interested, he was not equipped to fully understand exactly how Joan had been shaped and how she felt.

As well as being deeply out of touch with herself and her own feelings, Joan also held back on information. Because she could not tell him absolutely everything about herself, he could never fully understand the basis of her worries. Thus his answers to problems often aggravated her deepest fears.

He threw himself forwards into the fray. Her stress levels silently increased, but she was used to suffering. Winters were very hard for her. The Christmas card she had sent him in 1953 was unseasonably bleak. It showed a picture of a lone, bare tree on a riverbank, battered by the wind, and leaning away from it. Bare blue mountains shone in thin winter sun in the background, and large white boulders were strewn in the foreground. The words she wrote inside, seem incomprehensible at first glance:

'Xmas 1953
Bathe me in thy Coolness
Oh stormy waters,
Pave thy stony surface with moss
brown and green,
Wind blow tree and blue mountains
watching over me,
Waking in the sunlight from
dreams serene—
Oh! stormy water's (sic) envelop me deep
in thy mysteries waking not from such dreams'

Aloys folded the unsigned card, and kept it in his breast pocket. Later, he put it away in his study, and kept it always.

It is clear from this card that although she had not told him everything about her background and lack of training, Joan was telling Aloys something about herself. She was saying that she was willing to be enveloped deep in the stormy waters, with the wind blowing, and only the cold mountains to watch over her, for the sake of the mysteries. In her dreams there was to be found, under those conditions, coolness and a kind of serenity. She was, in some way, being washed—i.e. cleansed, by the stormy water. She was also saying that she felt herself to be alone. In this, there is no specific mention of the beloved. She is not writing in praise of the beloved; she is welcoming a dark personal experience that involves only herself and the elements, but the implication is, that he in some way represents these elements, that he is in a sense her guide. That she did not want to wake up, indicates her deep yearning for mystical experience, but altogether, this is the extreme approach of the ascetic, and it is laden with guilt.

Joan had a lot of guilt that she needed to deal with, and she was very anxious, and in need of reassurance. She had guilt about being illegitimate, guilt about her orphanage upbringing, guilt about her lack of qualifications, guilt about her lack of education, and guilt about misleading the public. She also had deep conflict about having socially upmarket and aristocratic genes, yet having to consort fraudulently as some sort of impostor, with the rich and cultured. She had the inevitable guilt and inner conflict about her part-public, part-secret association with a man who belonged to another woman. Some of these feelings were misplaced, but she was hardly aware that she had deep, underlying guilt, and far less aware that there was little justification for a good deal of it. Like many others who feel they deserve to experience pain, she found some release, some ease for her inner conflict, in suffering. Aloys was both the means by which she was reassured, and the means by which she was enabled to suffer.

Part of the dynamic of their relationship was the steeping of their lives in nature, and in images of nature. Whenever they could, they would get out of Cork together into the rugged hillsides of West Cork and Kerry, where they could lie undisturbed on the banks of streams, looking at the birds and the water. They were strongly attracted to waterfalls, where they liked to listen to the incessant roaring, and watch the foaming turbulence. As part of the quest for freedom to be together, they sought out high cliffs and wild waters.

And all the time, in an ardour of crooning commentary, he was likening themselves and their lives to the forces of nature. Aloys was extremely good with words, and was gifted with a superb speaking voice. His poetic nature was constantly invoking imagery from literature, myth, art, and religion. To suit the moment, he could twine the most unlikely themes together, and make them seem just right. And he did all this in the most seductive, spellbinding way. She was his dearest one, his Queen, and his darling, and with deep, hypnotic intonations, he opened up a whole new world to her, seducing her with words.

Two things had happened to Joan Moriarty. When she had first entitled herself 'Miss Moriarty' it was for use with pupils. Lots of friends had known her as 'Joan'. Now, because of the ostentatious public politeness that Joan and Aloys displayed in order to defuse gossip about their relationship, Joan was treated by Aloys in public with exaggerated respect. It was seen as a game some of the time, particularly by him, but the 'Miss Moriarty' that Aloys created was a far more formidable and remote figure than the one created by herself.

The second change that she had undergone was her re-creation as 'Artistic Director' of the Ballet Group. She was about to take on almost a whole troupe of high-ranking, professional dancers from abroad and she knew that she was completely unqualified. She had always discouraged familiarity with her pupils, but now that she had so much more dread of being found out, and with so much more at stake, she retreated further from the dancers. The only workable solution, in the circumstances, was for her to withdraw further into herself and become even more isolated and less knowable than she had ever been before.

She had to arrange things, particularly with the guest artists, so that nobody would dare ask questions. To protect herself from exposure, she had to become unapproachable, and the instrument she used to deliberately intimidate people was a forbidding exterior.

The queen walked into the ivory tower that the king had made for her.

In private with Aloys, she made it clear that she felt she was just not good enough, that she was not able to train her dancers up to the standard she would have liked, and that she was never satisfied with what she had been able to achieve. She also made no secret that she felt herself unworthy, and unfit for the job.

His response was not to think she was being ungrateful for what had fallen into her lap, but to gush torrents of lavish praise on her, and to fight with increasing ferocity for greater status for the ballet, greater standing for her, and more recognition. He seemed to be trying to prove his love for her by taking the world on, but that was not what she really wanted. The fact that nothing impressed her commonsense and depressed nature, fuelled his determination. But he did it because he wanted to. Basically, he was doing it for himself.

If she had been left to herself, she would have been content to stay with her amateur company and her little school, where the only standards expected of her would have been within her scope. In tandem, this is precisely what she did. No matter how big the edifice of the ballet became—and it eventually became massive and unwieldy—she also hung on to her own little company, and remained inside the loving circle of a few close and faithful friends. The people from the early days were those who loved her, and these were the people who were ready to protect her, and to stay with her.

In public she made it clear that she was dissatisfied with the standard of ballet she was producing, but she transferred the blame. Safely beyond scrutiny for her own dancing technique, now that her own dancing days were over, she criticised dancers, goading them with tales about her own supposedly gruelling days at the barre. The message the public got was that she herself was completely dedicated to this high art, but that to her disappointment, few others were.

She had once been full of fun, at the same time as being dogged by serious depression. She'd had plenty of laughs with Ethel Beare, and she'd had fun with the Collins' at Crosshaven. She'd been exuberant when she first met Aloys, dancing on top of his gatepost, leaping across the lawn, and she'd danced in an extremity of emotion in *La Calinda*. There was a time when she could playfully find a word beginning with every letter of the alphabet to describe Aloys, and what he meant to her. She wrote to him:

'I know of one who is most
Adventurous
Beguiling
Captivating
Danshing (sic)
Enduring
Fearless

96

Generous
Heartsome
Inguestitive (sic)
Jaunty
Knightly
Loveable
Manly
Naughty
Optimistic
Passionate
Quelling
Righteous
Sympathetic
Thrustworthy (sic)
Unselfish
Victorious
Wholesome
Xanthous
Yielding
Zealous

Which of these do I most admire?—All of them—Why?
Because they all go to make a whole—And why do I like the whole?—Because—
but then I'll have to start all over again.'

But her life lost the sense of playful highs and sad lows, or even of normal up-and-down reactions to everyday events. These responses were replaced by a serene-seeming sameness that was to become her unchanging hallmark. Her faraway steadiness and grey-eyed equilibrium was noticeable to those who came into contact with her. Although the control was strangely unfamiliar by normal standards, and the equilibrium perceptibly inappropriate, people around her were nudged into misinterpreting this unhealthy sense of balance, as evidence of an inbuilt ability to ignore the temporal baubles of success.

In this, they were egged on by her equally uncomprehending champion, who glorified her to the point of near-sainthood. She was most unlikely to explain to him, or to anyone else, that her unusual composure was chemically induced.

By December of 1966, she was entrenched in a grief of the soul. She sent a message to her lover about it. Her Christmas card to him was a postcard of the Cork Art Gallery picture *Off the Donegal Coast* by Jack B. Yeats. This is a grim painting of four men and a woman in a long rowing boat on a very high sea, who have shipped oars, and are being thrown a rescuing line from a big ship, of which only the rail is visible at the edge of the picture. The woman's face is visible only partially from behind, but she is wearing black clothes, and with her high cheekbones, she resembles Joan. She wrote:

> The Rough Seas of Life,
> The dividing waves,
> The Rope of Hope
> being caught with
> both hands and arms
> open
> The face of worry,
> woman tense, but
> Guilty sits, waiting
> as always, alone
> and composed
> Strong muscels (sic) holding
> the weight of heavy
> water
> The Rail of a Ship and home turf blazing.'

Here Joan is trying to communicate a deep and private pain. She is saying that on the rough seas of life, she is aware of divisions created by the waves. This is a reference to her sense of alienation, both from her work, and from her lover, who is separated from her not only by his marriage to someone else, and by his superior education and culture, but by his different agenda. But the 'rope of hope' being caught with both hands, is Joan taking the opportunities that come. Then comes the result—the worrying. The tense woman is Joan herself. She is guilty, alone and waiting as always. Hers is the passive role, but she is composed.

In the picture, there is every indication of tension in the woman's body posture, but no apparent guilt. Joan is projecting her own professional and personal guilt, onto the woman in the picture, and possibly implying that she is alone because of it. Here, more than a decade after her 1953 note 'In Praise of Him', Joan is continuing her attempts to tell Aloys that she feels herself to be alone, and that she does not like it. The 'heavy water', is how she sees the difficulties she is surrounded by, and the strong muscles holding the weight of the sodden rope, are those of Aloys. The rail of the big ship represents a gateway to safety, and right at the end, Joan inserts an apparently irrelevant image which is not in the picture—home turf blazing. This most primitive of images—suggested to her by the big ship's rail—is one of the few clues Joan ever gave, of what she really wanted.

Joan Moriarty felt that the little rowboat of lies which her and Aloys were in, together with a few friends, was in great danger of being overwhelmed. What she hoped would happen, would be that they would somehow be rescued, and go on from there, not to bigger adventures on the high seas, but grounded back at the simple heart of things. Joan wanted to go home. She wanted to start all over again, safe and warm at some metaphorical hearth she belonged to, and could relate to. The home soil she craved to find some footing on, was a guiltless base. Since 'turf' also means peat, a fuel used in Ireland, she was making a reference to her deep craving to be Irish, which she was not. She wanted roots, but she had none that she could claim.

There are other significances of the idea of home turf blazing, but in any case, Aloys did not understand her messages. Full of brio as always, he was not in need of being rescued in the way that deep down, she was. Her unconscious distress calls went unanswered. Even if it had been possible that she could have been saved and taken home, he was intent on going on to greater glories.

Joan was the apparatus he needed to bring himself into production. Whether she was the choreographer who made the dance work, or merely the figurehead, didn't matter. What did matter, was that he was able to harness her relationship with performing, for his own work. That their own relationship was, or later became, non-sexual made this bond between them stronger and clearer. One great attraction for Joan was that the love he gave her was an ongoing healing experience. And in receiving this gift of healing, she could also be sure that she was needed by him. Huge energies went into the ballet.

Aloys was also clearly being used as Joan's muse. It was his mediating presence that drew from her soul these authentic cries of anguish, and she presented them—her real works—to him as gifts. He kept her few handwritten, unsigned poems, but he destroyed most of her letters to him.

13
Irish Theatre Ballet

J ennie Dowdall, Senator, Lord Mayor, frequenter of top tables, and patron of the ballet in Cork, had a catch-phrase. 'When de Valera comes to Cork, he sleeps with me,' she used to joke, meaning that the Taoiseach habitually stayed at her house. Corkman Jack Lynch, at the time a government Minister, later to be Taoiseach, and his wife, Mairin, who liked ballet, were on familiar terms with her. Not only did she have the ear of the leader of the Irish government, but she had a great deal of influence with other top people who ruled purse strings. She was also someone to whom her friend, Aloys Fleischmann, could send a draft of a letter, seeking support for the ballet in Dublin, or in some other quarter where Jennie had pull. She would have her secretary copy out the letter, word for word, and then sign it as Lord Mayor.

Much correspondence passed from Aloys to Jennie in the Lord Mayor's office during 1959 and 1960, and from there on to people of influence, requesting sponsorship from companies and individuals, and offering invitations. Aloys worked out diplomatic and flattering letters, and passed them on to Jennie, who had them copied out without amendment. Sometimes Aloys drafted a letter for Chairman Jamie O'Donovan to sign.

With the help of Jamie, Aloys, Joan and Jennie formed a company, The Irish Theatre Ballet, and then set about looking for money. They thought nothing of travelling up to Dublin in a deputation, often with Jamie, to argue for sponsorship with the managing directors of firms like Arthur Guinness and Irish Dunlop Co., and they were very often successful. In 1960 the trio approached the Taoiseach of the day, Sean Lemass, who was not as co-operative as Jennie's friend, de Valera, whom he had succeeded.

'Dear Mr Lemass,' the letter of 25th April ran,

'Re: Lack of adequate support for artistic enterprises in Ireland, due to shortage of Arts Council Funds.

'I wonder if you could kindly agree to receive a small deputation from Cork with regard to above. The deputation will be Professor A. Fleischmann, Miss Joan Denise Moriarty, Mr James O'Donovan and myself. We promise to make our case concisely and to take as little time as possible.

'As you know we have established a small Professional Ballet Company here in Cork which needs financial support and this can only remain in existence if given that support by the Arts Council.

'If it is suitable to you we could come to Dublin on Thursday, May 5th at any hour convenient to you and if this does not suit please let me know when you could see us.

'Trusting you are keeping well.

Kind regards,

'yours sincerely,

LORD MAYOR.'

It was slapped down. 'Dear Lord Mayor,' Sean Lemass wrote from the Taoiseach's office, on 28th April.

'As I feel sure you will appreciate, the general question of the adequacy of the State grant to the Council is one which it would be best to leave to the Council to deal with....

'As the particular question....the purposes for which the council may expend the moneys placed at their disposal are for determination by them in their own discretion. I would, therefore, not wish to intervene by pressing them....

'In the circumstances, I feel that there would be no point in putting you and your colleagues to the trouble and expense of coming to Dublin for a discussion with me....'

Undeterred, Aloys composed an immediate reply.

'Our hope was that we might influence the Government through you to give the money to the Arts Council. Their problem is they are not in a position financially to give us the support we need but if they had a greater allowance they are most sympathetic to the work we are doing and would help us.'

As far as invitations to see performances and hospitality in Cork were concerned, ambassadors in Dublin were never neglected. The commanding officer of the Southern Command in Cork was invited in 1955, and personally received at the Imperial Hotel. Catherine Beit was invited to travel from Wicklow and have a delicious supper afterwards.

The company had American friends. Mrs Kermit 'Belle' Roosevelt sent a donation, along with co-signatories, Mabel Blum, Margaret Curtis and Kathleen Raikes.

Jennie was invited to dine with Sir Charles Harvey, of Guinness's, his daughter, Mrs Lawson-Tancred, and managing director, Sir Hugh Beaver, at the Metropole Hotel, on one of their visits to Cork.

'May I remind you,' she wrote afterwards, 'of our little discussion about the Ballet and I enclose a Memo to make you aware of our progress and our needs....'

The courting of Dame Ninette de Valois began in 1960. Aloys drafted the letter of invitation for the Royal Ballet head to visit the Festival of Cork, as a guest of the newly-formed ITB. He gave it to Jennie Dowdall to copy out, and she sent it to Covent Garden on official notepaper, signing it as Lord Mayor. But Dame Ninette couldn't come. She had visited Ireland privately several weeks previously, and was due to return to Dublin for two weeks in May with the Royal Ballet. A third visit, she wrote, could not be managed in so short a time.

Big money was raised fast. As always, Aloys mapped everything out in advance. An Arts Council Grant of £1,200 was easily secured for the first season. Then Aloys, Joan Denise and Jennie all travelled to Dublin to interview the directors of Arthur Guinness and Co., at their headquarters. They were entertained to a sumptuous lunch and given a cheque for £500. The Irish Dunlop Co. and The Irish Refining Co. were approached, and pledged support, and the fund-raising team got another fourteen companies to contribute. Thirteen people took out life membership for decent sums, and thirty-four people put their names down as annual subscribers. They soon raised a total of £8,000, a large amount in 1959, and held a press conference on September 16th at Joan's studio, to launch Irish Theatre Ballet.

Miss Moriarty was Director. Marie Rambert and Alicia Markova were patrons, as well as Senator Mrs Dowdall. Since between Aloys and Joan, it was felt that it would be wiser for Aloys to take a more behind-the-scenes role, it was Jamie O'Donovan, Joan's solicitor and friend of them both, whom they elected as puppet Chairman.

James was useful in another way. He was close to Joan, and she liked him a lot. But the closeness he achieved with her, was a non-threatening intimacy, devoid of sexual complications. This was the sort of attachment Joan encouraged, and when people started talking around the town, and kept on talking over several years, that Joan was Jamie's mistress, nobody in the inner-circle of the inner-circle particularly minded. They could not completely prevent gossip, but all the Joan–Jamie talk at least meant that the heat was off on the Joan–Aloys speculation. People in the street at that time would not have read anything into sightings of Jamie with menfriends.

Also at the top end of the new ballet company was Stanley Judson, of the Pavlova company, who already had pioneering experience with the Vic Wells Ballet in England. He agreed to join Joan Denise as Associate Director in this new enterprise. The enthusiastic and talented Leslie Horne was given the job of manager, and Mrs Maeve Coakley was wardrobe mistress.

Charles Lynch, an upper-class Cork man, was appointed pianist to the company. His father had been a high-ranking member of the British Army, and the family lived in a huge mansion called Park Gareth on what eventually became Monkstown golf club. His maternal grandfather was Sir Abraham Sutton, one of the original, so-called Merchant Princes of Cork, a group of rich upper-class people who lived a life apart from the rest of the city.

Charles had been disinherited because he was an artist. A pianist of note, Charles Lynch was said to have helped Rachmaninov to finish a piano concerto, and to have played the first performance of it. He also played first performances of Bax, Moeran, and Hamilton Harty scores. Charles imagined he was still living in his mansion, and was only happy in huge rooms. He felt comfortable in hotel lounges. He never drank, but constantly smoked. The lounge of the old Hibernian Hotel in Dublin was one of his drawing rooms. Wherever he went he held court, and usually ended up telling stories about the ghost that used to walk the cobble-stoned courtyard of Park Gareth.

Joan found this eccentric musician wayward and difficult to work with, and he used to deliberately behave badly in front of the class. 'We'll start now, Charles,' she would say, but instead he would light up a cigarette in the studio, which she hated and did not allow. Ignoring this she would wait but he then might send out for a bottle of milk and a packet of cotton wool and quietly wait smoking.

The call, 'will you start, Charles,' fell again and again on deaf ears. When the shopping arrived, he would slowly begin to clean the piano keys in cotton wool dipped in milk. She could do nothing to tame him, and neither could anyone else, but one reason she had agreed to hire him, and that she put up with him, was that he was a talented musician of high, almost legendary, social standing. A further, irresistible reason she wanted him, was that he had worked

103

as pianist with the famous Rambert, and being a compulsive storyteller, he was a rich source of information and lore about the temperamental Dame.

Eight girls were picked out from the Cork Ballet Company, to continue as professionals, and at the same time to be trained. These were Lavinia Anderson, Julia Cotter, Madeline Moore, Patricia O'Brien, Maureen Weldon, Susan Featherstone-Haugh, Juanita Smale, and Sheila Miller. Stanley Judson invited dancers Jaqueline Johnson and Leo Senn, from an Australian ballet company to join. Other dancers were Paul Sanquest from Cork, Victor Maynard from London, Kay McLaughlin, Alun Jones, Sandra Torode and Gilde Proudley. The dancers were paid an average wage of £5.00.

Eleven short ballets were choreographed for the coming season, and seven were chosen for the opening. Of these, three were choreographed by Miss Moriarty—*Sugrai Sraide* (Street Games), to music by T.C. Kelly and E.J. Moeran; *Peter and the Wolf*, to music by Prokofiev; and *Voice in The Wilderness*, to music by Bloch. Four short ballets were choreographed by Stanley Judson—*Springtime in Vienna*, to music by Johann Strauss; *Crown Diamonds*, to music by Auber; *Pas de Quatre*, to music by Chopin; and a reproduction of *La Spectre de la Rose*, to music by Weber.

As many distinguished people were invited as they could think of, to the new company's first night at the Palace Theatre three months later, and a rave press followed. It was coming up to Christmas, and Seamus Kelly, who wrote the column *Quidnunc*, for *The Irish Times*, added his own fairy-tale insights:

'Cork was specially illuminated by a brilliant frosty moon for the debut of ITB,' he wrote. 'The artificial Christmas illuminations along Patrick Street added to the festive air that the Leeside city assumes so gracefully and gratefully on any occasion of this kind. The 62-year-old Palace had had a face-lift for the occasion, too, and with its red, pale blue, and gold decor and its new amenities, it looked once more like a real theatre, part Covent Garden in miniature, partly a Baroque and friendly Brighton Pavilion, with Byzantine boxes added. It was a gala night, and the audience lived up to its mood as they chattered in the foyer, watching the distinguished visitors arrive, with Marina Svetlova conspicuous among them in a magnificent blue mink.'

Seamus Kelly had his own agenda. He liked, in his sometimes overwritten reports, to display his erudition in matters of art, and to issue unsubtle reminders that he was also well-travelled and well-read. Though he knew almost nothing of the actualities of it, he remained an admirer of Miss Moriarty's work and almost never missed any golden opportunity to add his own poetic embellishments in support of everything that was produced.

What he probably didn't realise, was that he was an influential conspirator in creating the myth of the work and the person of Joan Moriarty, whom he nicknamed, 'the red-haired de Valois of the South'. Other unwitting conspirators, were a Cork press whose transgression, when presented with this artform, and with perfumed foyers crammed with tuxedos and evening gowns, was only that they were perpetually kind and, in typical Irish fashion, always found something to praise.

Joan's ongoing amateur group, the Cork Ballet Company, was kept on. It was thus given the opportunity of performing, by joining in with the professional company, when they put on shows at the Opera House. The amateurs were glad to swell the numbers of performers, by providing a supporting cast for crowd scenes and other subordinate roles.

Sean Cunningham, who joined the ITB in 1960, was paid ten pounds a week, which was quite a lot at the age of seventeen. Sean, also known as John, the English version of his name, was a student dancer. He had been working as a trainee manager at Roches Stores department store in Cork, and his only experience of ballet had been when a friend asked him to come over and help out at the amateur ballet where they were short of young men. He had joined in as a favour and his steps and stances were based purely on impromptu imitation of the other dancers.

In 1960 'Miss Moriarty' asked him to come and see her, and asked to see what he could do. He showed her the few steps he'd copied from the amateurs. 'He's alright, he can do it,' she announced, and asked him whether he would like to be the first-ever male dancer to be trained in Ireland. At ten pounds a week payment for being trained as a student dancer Sean accepted. One of his strengths was characterisation, and he was eventually to join the Irish National Ballet, and become Christy Mahon, the playboy in her ballet *The Playboy of The Western World*.

It was always said of Joan Denise Moriarty that she knew right away on meeting people whether she could or could not trust them; that she went on gut feeling, and that she was usually right. It is true that her intuition was finely-tuned. She had developed what might be called a manipulative personality. Getting her own way by indirect means was just her way of going about things. For her own reasons Joan Denise tended to respond to people who had their own agendas, when they fitted in with hers. She demanded to be looked up to, but she did not want to be put on the spot. She liked creative people, people with some spark of their own, people who would be willing to get on with it and adapt to her; those who would rally round and make something of what the company had. She favoured people who either could not see, or who were willing to blind themselves to her own faults and defects, and for the sake of what was possible, to forge something out of their own personal creative resources.

She never said as much. The clue to her relationships was that acolytes had to be smart enough to stay back; to develop a silent, distant rapport with her, by way of their own commonsense. The company was new. She knew, and they knew, that for those who were ready to take the chances and the opportunities there were reputations to be made.

She felt at ease with confident people who didn't ask questions, and who wanted to ride the wave for their own sakes. There were good fees and salaries for those who were to be given the chance of pioneering with her, and the unspoken trade-off, was that they would go along with and accommodate her style and her position as the boss.

She was obsessively private and worked hard at invoking loyalty in people; getting them to maintain the wall of protective secrecy she never ceased building around herself. (Her personal telephone number was ex-directory—unusual in Ireland, even amongst very well-known personalities. The one or two people who did have her number, had it written down in code.) They were generous people of vision, who were happily seduced into her increasingly mythologised orbit, and she motivated them, manipulated them, and in her own condescending way, cherished them.

Whatever it was she responded to in his own character, Joan Denise Morarty took to Sean Cunningham. He got to know her style, and he got to know her as a person. Rapport was a big ingredient in her relationships, and Sean came to know how to help out with actions without anything being spelled out in words. At a time when he knew she'd be watching, and at a time when he knew she was trying to create something, he'd start inventing steps. Sometimes they'd be crazy, improvised movements. 'Oh, John,' she'd call out, casually, in her seductive voice, with its polished Northern English accent that sounded upper-class in Cork. 'Keep that. We'll use it tomorrow.' Next day, at rehearsal, she would imperiously command certain male dancers to watch him. 'What was that step you were doing yesterday, John? Er, David, John will tell you that. Just learn that step, and then teach so and so, and so and so, the same step as well.'

Having spoken with spurious authority, she then vanished, and they got on with perfecting their own improvised steps, by themselves. She would later apply the new steps intelligently, sometimes incorporating them into some combination.

Her part in it was to add characterisation. Once the technical bit was over, she would tell them how to play it. She would describe the character and try to get them to inhabit it. Then she would let someone like Sean go on and on for about a week, letting him overplay the part. Then she'd drive him back, and 'square the character off' as he put it. He never felt dominated by her at first, he felt that there was a rapport, a sense of heading towards the work, and developing. He was exhilarated by it.

She was well known for never letting the dancers feel appreciated for their gifts. She never came right out and admitted that they were contributing, or thanked them, or said, 'well done, that was brilliant'. Dancers interpreted this as perfectionism, and felt it was a matter of her always wanting a bit more out of them. The reality of it was that a lot of the time they were doing the creating, and that she was feeling her way all the time. In her efforts to create the illusion that she was in control of everything, she pretended she was the instigator of everything and hoped they wouldn't notice.

Some guessed, but since the dancers were deliberately kept in the dark at all times about everything, nobody ever got the full picture. Her treatment of dancers throughout her career bordered on insulting their intelligence. Only once did she ever say to Sean, 'That is exactly what I wanted', and that was in 1979, in Dublin, when Sean played Christy Mahon with the INB in *The Playboy of The Western World*. It was the most magical night of his career. In retrospect, Sean felt she had seen Christy in him from the very first. As close to her as any male member of the dance company got, he was never a friend.

Amongst those who made their appearance in this first professional company, were the people who remained her lifelong friends and suppporters. Designer Patrick Murray was one of them. Pat Murray was a talented young Corkman who had at first worked with designer Frank Sanquest at the Opera House. Miss Moriarty gave Pat the opportunity to design sets for the new professional company, to travel with them everywhere they went, and to be given a decent salary. From then on, his work dominated theatrical design in Cork. Jokey, and easy to get along with, his expansive Jupiterian nature did not put Joan under threat, and he easily produced fairytale set designs which accommodated her ideas in ways which delighted her, and enchanted audiences. Pat was a member of her inner circle.

Plenty of people had reason to be grateful to Joan, and to be loyal to her. It was through her that quite a number of reputations were made, and in the same way, it was through their work, that her own reputation was made. A good deal of very strong artistic bonding took place, and many of these bonds were first formed in Irish Theatre Ballet.

The Irish Theatre Ballet company was enabled to tour Ireland when, in 1962, the Gulbenkian Foundation donated a van for the transportation of sets, props and costumes, and Motor Distributors supplied a small Volkswagen bus for the company to travel in. Beatrice Hunt, whose mother was a close friend of Joan, was invited to be tour manager at eight pounds a week. Beatrice, also known as 'Billie', was eventually to become matron and part owner of Shanakiel Hospital, and one of Joan's dearest friends.

Her mother had been close to Joan since the first production in 1947. It was to Mrs Hunt that Joan had first gone with yards of butter muslin, looking for someone to dye it green for a sea scene. The butter muslin ended up in Mrs Hunt's garage, dripping green dye. And it was to Mrs Hunt that Joan wandered with yards and yards of pink tulle, looking for someone to make pink roses, to sew onto the dresses of the little dancers. Mrs Hunt obligingly made hundreds of little rosebuds, and sewed them all onto the dresses, adding trailing pink ribbons. Mrs Hunt was one of the few friends that Joan would ask directly to do her a favour. It was Joan's more usual form to wonder aloud, half in despair, in her best cut-glass tones, just who she could find that would be able to do such and such a job. The people to whom these comments were aimed usually then offered.

Mrs Hunt's house in Douglas was Joan's second home. For almost the whole of the fifty years she spent in Cork, Joan never cooked Sunday lunch. Every week, she was invited over to Mrs Hunt's for Sunday dinner, and she'd stretch out on the couch for a couple of hours afterwards, chatting, or watching something on television. Then around four she would start to get agitated and getting up, would say that she had work to prepare for tomorrow, and leave. After Mrs Hunt died, Joan kept coming over to Billie for Sunday lunch.

With the ballets they'd organised for the season, the company took to the road. In 1963, the Irish Theatre Ballet travelled to more than sixty different venues throughout Ireland. The scenery went in the van and the people went in the minibus driven by the ballet master. They plugged into the Irish Countrywomen's Association. All around the country, a network of ICA members would feed the company, and put them up for the night. Then these marvellous hostesses would send their families to the draughty halls where the ballet was being performed. The company would also go to convents and give educational matinees for students.

Money was short and the company, a group of exuberant young amateurs learning to be professionals, did everything themselves, including making costumes and posters. Joan would try to teach them to be careful with spending. In theatres, they sometimes slept in costume skips. Billie was the electrician, and a total greenhorn. Money from the Gulbenkian bought a sound system consisting of a large tape recorder and big speaker nicknamed Charles. They carried lighting, and had their own old, shabby dimmer board, which invariably packed up at the wrong times. With four floodlights and two spotlights included in the eight five-hundred-watt bulbs they carried, the ordinary domestic wiring in the town halls often made the dimmer blow, but they were young and they didn't give a damn.

Usually they'd set off at ten in the morning, set up stage on arrival, and try and do a class. Friends would take them in and give them a meal. They always seemed to manage to get people to welcome them. If the company were anywhere near home they came home at night. If they'd performed in Kerry they would land home at Emmet Place at about two in the morning. There was a dirty little fish and chip shop round the corner. They'd go and wake the woman up, and she'd consider it worthwhile to get out of her bed for such a big order, and come down to make them all fish and chips.

Joan Denise Moriarty didn't always go out with ITB. She did her best to go, but everyone knew she had her schools to run. As well the school attached to her amateur company in Emmet Place, she had, without any fanfare, also opened a school in the nearby town of Clonmel, and one in Waterford. She charged fees by the term, and installed young teachers who had passed RADA exams. When she did go out with ITB she would go to a matinee and give a talk to the children. She always had a ten-minute lecture for the children, with everything explained and described. She'd tell little Irish stories with characters in them, like stone breakers and farmers in the field, and she would tell children how important it was to do the right sort of ballet training, and how good it was for young children. When she was not there, the ballet master would give the talk.

Irish Theatre Ballet did *Cinderella* just after Christmas, and had the Cork Ballet Company to perform with them. A young Israeli dancer called Domy Reiter-Soffer played the Prince. More than a decade later, when she could again offer decent fees, Joan was to depend heavily on the choreography skills of Domy.

On the day of any dress rehearsal, it was an early start, and rehearsals would go on through the day. Everybody would bring food with them because they knew they'd be in for a long, hard day. Joan never brought food, or anything to drink. She would commence work and people in the company got the impression that it was her intention to work right through the whole day without stopping to eat at all. They imagined that she would never think of eating.

She didn't have to. At three o'clock, Mrs Hunt and a friend would arrive in the theatre, laden with flasks and sandwiches. They'd call Joan away from her work, and get her to sit down with them in the back of the theatre and eat. It was their belief that they had to make her sit down, and they loved playing their roles, but she needed no persuading and happily ate anything that they gave her. This routine was an established pattern of her life over many years, and her apparently negligent attitude to her own nutrition was taken as a sign that she was an ascetic and a saint. What she was really doing, was manipulating the supportive women around her.

She had told people certain bits of her history. The reason she had been hospitalised twice in the early forties, she told everyone rather proudly, was because, having no money, she had been undernourished. When company members complained to 'the Professor', that she was penny-pinching, and objecting to their spending, Aloys had an answer. He had duly disseminated for her the romantic story that she had starved for her art in the early days, and he told them never to be angry with her. If a dog has once been starved, he would say, it never forgets. The story that she had starved for her art entered folklore as evidence of her superhuman dedication to ballet.

Her close friends thought they knew her well, and imagined that they were responding to an alarming tendency in Joan Denise to be so dedicated to her work that she forgot to feed herself. It was for them a privilege to feed her. They were wrong. It did not occur to anyone that she was manipulating them into doing the job for her. Joan was unable to forget the lessons she had learned in her depression after scarlet fever, and in the depression of her early twenties—people took notice of her when she failed to eat. Instinctively, she couldn't help incorporating this pattern into her strategy for survival.

The end of Irish Theatre Ballet came when the Arts Council asked the company to amalgamate with the Patricia Ryan Company in Dublin, in order to qualify for a joint grant. This they did, but things did not work out at all. The two companies did not mesh and in the summer of 1964 the money ran out and everything stopped. The company dispersed, and Sean Cunningham went to train in London. Many of the core people who had been with Joan in ITB remained with her in the original amateur company. With more children in the country getting to know about ballet through ITB there were more offshoot schools that belonged to Joan. Her shrewd business mind did not miss a beat. The year after ITB folded Joan's amateur Cork Ballet Company received guarantees from the Arts Council, for performances in Cork, Limerick, Waterford, and Clonmel, towns where she had established ballet schools.

14

Dijon

The first Dijon experience is forever remembered amongst some from the folk group days as the one and only time the teetotal Joan Moriarty got drunk. It was remembered by Aloys Fleischmann as the time of the onset of her emphysema.

In 1961 the Folk Dance Group of the Cork Ballet Company flew to Dijon to take part in a competition as part of the wine festival. Aloys, Joan, and Maeve Coakley checked in to l'Hotel La Cloche, overlooking Le Parc Darcy.

The company members paid their own fares and stayed in terrible boarding school dormitories where they washed in cold water.

One of their first appointments on arrival was a grand welcoming reception. Canon Kir, a local hero of the resistance movement, was Mayor of Dijon. The drink, kir, a mixture of wine and cassis, was named after him. At the reception, all the guests were introduced to kir, and to kir royale, a cocktail of champagne and cassis.

In keeping with the tradition amongst Irish people of letting their hair down, the Irish group got busy becoming connoisseurs of kir royale. Aloys did not drink the kir, preferring his usual apple or orange juice. Joan thought she was drinking blackcurrant juice, and enjoyed it. She began to giggle, appearing tipsy, at the age of at least forty-five, for the first time in her life. When she became alarmingly flighty her nearby compatriots closed in.

'Mind the pipes,' she said to Pat Murray, bundling her war pipes into his hands, as they tried to get her to stand up. 'I'm going,' she laughed, head spinning. 'I'm going.' Aloys held her up on one side, and Pat Murray on the other, and together they got her out of the building, and down the steps. She was bundled back to the hotel and into bed for a short while. However, the bus waiting to take them to the venue where they had to perform had arrived. They brought her back perfectly composed, kept her near an open window on the bus, and she was later able to perform.

Joan's sudden reaction to the drink came as a surprise to others in the company. Nobody else seemed to be suffering the same effects so soon. Some might have been keen drinkers, but there doesn't seem to have been time enough for anyone else to get drunk. It may have been, not that Joan had drunk too much, but that the alcohol reacted with tablets she was taking. She never drank again but it was said that once in about every five years she would take a glass of pink champagne.

At Le Parc Darcy, Joan and Aloys sat on a bench by the lake, and watched the swans feeding. Joan went to Mass at the splendid Renaissance church of Saint Michel. Aloys was not a believer in God. Joan bought some postcards and addressed one depicting the church to Mr and Mrs Leslie Horne. 'Greetings,' she wrote briefly in red ink. 'Arrived safely, Joan.' She did not send the card.

When several heats had been run during the event the competing countries were to take part in a grand parade. Joan, dressed in full highland kilt with a jacket made of wool tartan and thick woollen kneesocks, began tuning the bagpipes for the long, three-mile march through the town. It was a boiling hot afternoon, and the tweed-clad Irish were totally out-of-place in the continental heatwave. The men were wearing specially-made trousers of traditional, heavy Irish tweed, and traditional, heavy, hand-knitted Aran sweaters with woollen caps to match. The women were wearing long, full, heavy skirts and shawls.

The group did not give all that much for their chances against the Yugoslav and Russian teams, who were considered to be at the pinnacle of folk-dancing. The Polish team were impressive and jolly. As the groups from the different countries were marching under the blistering sun performers began to drop away along the route, overcome by the heat, and by the effects of the wine.

A contact of Aloys, who had possibly enjoyed Irish conviviality the night before, and who knew what judges might be looking for, gave him a friendly word of advice. 'Keep her playing at all costs,' he murmured earnestly, pointing to Joan. 'That is what matters.' Aloys made his way over to Joan, and instructed her that whatever else might happen in the heatwave, under no circumstances was she to stop playing. They were in with a good chance, he told her, and it was imperative to hold on to the advantage.

She nodded, and set off. Three miles along streets thickly lined with sightseers was gruelling. Accordionists and pipers struggled.

People waving flags laboured. As they marched, peoples' stamina flagged, and several girls literally fainted. Joan kept going. At the head of the Irish procession, head high, reed in mouth, she marched through to the very end, piping constantly. Through the heavy reed of the bagpipes her breath was failing, but she did as Aloys had told her, and she kept playing. They won second prize, and brought home a bronze medallion on a heavy chain.

Joan began to look ill. The years of strain and her plethora of illnesses were taking their toll. Aloys later remembered that she had developed emphysema in 1961, but she was pictured still playing the pipes when she returned to Dijon in 1965. He thought that the pipes had caused the emphysema, but healthcare professionals contend that playing the pipes would not 'cause' it as such. Anyway, when she did develop emphysema she was in her early fifties and she had stopped piping altogether.

Making her way across the darkness backstage in the Opera House one night, Joan neglected to put on the pilot light. She ran straight into some taut wires, and cracked her sternum. Her bones were brittle. In a convent in Monaghan she walked onto the stage and immediately slipped. The nuns had polished it. She dreaded convent stages. The company threw bathroom scouring powder onto the floor, but it wouldn't work. They used to pour Coca-Cola onto the floors and let it dry, and then put scouring powder on top of that.

As ill as she was, and as often, she never allowed anyone other than Aloys and Beatrice to know any details. Nobody was allowed to sympathise, or to get in any way close to her through these weaknesses. She never commented on her illnesses, or made any reference to them. Even from a hospital bed she kept her distance, and instilled a form of reverence in visitors that precluded questions. She simply would not allow people to be on those terms with her. If anyone ever asked her how she was, she would always say she was fine.

She hated what she called 'small talk'. She did not want to be out in the open during conversations, where any topic might be touched on, such as, 'didn't so and so go to school with you in Mallow?' In addition, her background was so alien that she felt out of her depth in casual, informal relationships. All exchanges had to be given a framework—even a cup of coffee in a café had to have a topic.

In 1964 George Fleischmann died, and in the winter of 1967 Tilly Fleischmann died. The house, inherited by Aloys, was immediately put on the market to be sold. Joan moved all her things out and took up residence at her flat in the studio. With her she brought the high, polished, wooden, single bed she had slept in, and the big chest of drawers that she had used in Wellesley Place. She also brought Tilly's piano stool with her and some photographs, mainly of Aloys.

Not too long after that, Joan's asthmatic chest became so bad that the doctor told her to leave the city centre—which is in a bowl-like depression, surrounded on all sides by hills. She took a flat high up the hill in fashionable Montenotte. It wasn't enough. One night, she called Beatrice from her flat, in the early hours of the morning, to ask her to please come over. She couldn't breathe at all, she said. Beatrice called a doctor on her way and by the time they got there, Joan was practically unconscious. The doctor gave her an injection and Beatrice sat up all night with her. At seven o'clock in the morning, she started making arrangements to take Joan over to her house for a few days.

It was the beginning of steroids and cortisone for Joan and she was on them for the rest of her life. Her bones became even more brittle, and over time, she would develop two awful side-effects: Cataracts would develop on both eyes, and her thin, shapely face would be cruelly transformed by the long-term use of corticosteroids, and become a flat, moon face.

15
Schools

Joan Denise Moriarty was at her most comfortable when working on ways of prospering her schools, and she did this without reference to anyone else. School was not just home ground to her; it was home. Her own little school was where she started, by herself, without help, and where she owed nothing to anyone. And it was with her own school, decades later, that she was to finish. From her start in a Mallow field, in a parochial hall, and in a poky sitting room in a small, terraced house, this semi-illiterate woman had built up her own business, and she never let it go.

In her schools she taught the things she herself knew well enough—movement at its most elementary level, with some other very basic additions like limbering and deportment. When she became in the public perception the 'First Lady of Ballet in Ireland' there were so many 'achievements' attributed to her, that it wasn't really quite the thing for her to dwell on the true personal significance of these schools, if she was even conscious of it. But in her heart, this private woman was most proud of, and most attached to one achievement that could rightly be credited to her: she was a teacher of dance to lots of little children. She could no more renounce being that than she could stop being an orphan.

She enjoyed being with children, and was happiest when telling them stories and lecturing them. Imagination interested her, and she was gifted in drawing out the imagination of young people. Those who came in contact with her, never forgot that she had been interested enough for them to work at valuing their own imaginations. Some ex-pupils talking about her hardly knew quite in what way she had touched them. They had found her to be fair, strict, remote—and they had loved her. For many pupils to have remembered her so fondly, argues that she had a gift as an inspiring teacher.

In reality, her forte was character. She instinctively, if crudely, made people understand how, by the use of their bodies, they could become some other character; she showed them how to act. She also saw potential. With an imposing bearing, and with the simple confidence of one who has visited the terrain, she helped them to dream their own dreams. When she herself was a dreaming child and most needed validation the response she had found around her, was at best indifference at worst, scorn. 'Your imagination will be the death of you,' she was told, as she watched pictures forming in the firelight.

As soon as the Cork Ballet Company was running smoothly, she went out with a troupe of chosen dancers to other towns, and quite easily seduced local children into wanting to go to ballet class. This was always important to her. She wanted little ones to see ballet being performed. The little ones onstage, dressed as frothy fairies, multicolored elves, and painted dolls, always looked cute under the lights. Children in the audience were entranced, and parents were always enthusiastic. When ITB was formed it was also pressed into service round the village halls.

Joan was in the habit of giving an astute pep-talk which mentioned that, just in case any of the children watching might be interested in performing on stage like this, in sugar-pink tutus, she was planning to start a local class. In this way, one by one, parents were persuaded, and she gradually opened schools in other towns.

It was all strictly village-hall, kid's stuff, and in community terms, none-the-less commendable for that. The trips out to draughty halls would not have been every dance teacher's cup of tea, and sometimes the dancers complained bitterly about the conditions they found around the country. The dressing room facilities varied, and it was always a matter of making do. Halls were often cold, drab and cheerless. Toilets were not particularly clean. Sweet papers and discarded soft drinks cans littered some floors before the performance even began. There were rattlings and rustlings and scraping of chairs. Voices echoed discordantly. Sibilant ssshhhhhing made things worse. Music issued from a too-small tape-recorder.

There was the thick makeup, the transforming costumes, and Miss Moriarty's rigid back and amused, raised eyebrow, breezily goading them all to be stoical, pooh-poohing them all to get on with it for goodness sake, and smoothly reminding them that they'd better know their steps, because they'd been given this chance to perform, and all these people—there may have been just a handful of people in the audience—had left their homes especially to see Miss

Moriarty's Ballet, and that of course she knew dancers weren't going to let herself and the audience down. The show must go on, and that was that.

The truth was that she felt at home in these draughty halls. She felt most comfortable enduring a spartan experience in which she could go back to something familiar, and she felt validated. Conditions of privation were part of her currency. It was home base, and she needed to keep returning to it. She was strongly drawn to the plush, moneyed, cocktail party side of things, but deep down, it left her alienated and keening inside, like a frightened, trapped animal yearning for the wild.

One girl stayed away from class one day, and explained why. 'A cold?' Miss Moriarty demanded, her incredulous lips drawn back in horrified scorn—'a cold?' A feeble, everyday cold, was simply not enough excuse to stay away. She managed to convince the child that, in future, nobody could miss rehearsals unless they were literally dying. All other illnesses didn't count. You got on with it, and there was nothing more to be said. She herself got on with it, ran her often repeated refrain, and had seen worse, much worse. Dancers these days, she always snorted, didn't know what hard work was. Then she would appear onstage, regal, calm, full of grace and smiles, and give a honey-voiced talk that could somehow be heard in the rafters, charming the audience, smiling her wide, big-toothed smile at them, holding herself like a queen. That she always demanded more of people, and never, ever praised anyone, impressed a lot of her pupils.

As well as her school in Emmet Place, she sent her young teachers to Clonmel, Mallow, and Bandon, and somehow managed to find girls to teach in Limerick and Waterford.

Classes were held each afternoon and evening after school hours, for children from three years up. She charged fees according to age. There were two terms in the year, and she charged by the term. This meant that if pupils didn't bother coming, she still had the money, and could pay her employed teachers.

Term fees in a lump sum also meant that only higher-income people could enrol. There were leotards and ballet shoes to buy right away, and then costumes would have to be paid for by pupils. Low income people would not have been able to afford her ballet lessons. Classes were from three to five years of age, from six to eight years, from nine to eleven years, and from twelve years upwards. The teachers who staffed her little schools were enthusiastic girls that she herself had trained.

Class venues changed to suit changing conditions. Sometimes day schools were used, and halls of all sorts were found. Her school in Limerick was held at one time in the Franciscan Hall in Henry Street, and at another in the Royal George Hotel. There were classes some of the time in Youghal in the League of the Cross Hall, and in Fermoy in the YMCS Hall. In Bandon, at one point, a class was held in the Devonshire Arms Hotel, and in Waterford at the Bishop Foy School. Miss Moriarty herself held all the interviews and did all the enrolling on opening day, but her chosen young teacher would then take the classes the following week, and forever after.

Under the heading, 'SCHOOL OF BALLET AND MODERN DANCE LIMERICK' her typed, duplicated leaflet said:

'Ballet as an educational subject is of great value and importance to young people, not alone do students develop poise, good posture, a graceful walk, but a knowledge and insight of one of the most beautiful arts, an art which covers all the arts, movement, music, drama, painting.'

The grammar may be shaky, but the idea is clear. It went on:

'It is Joan Denis (sic) Moriarty's ambition, to establish as many centres as possible with CORRECT Ballet tuition, under proper supervision. Many parents do not realise that bad Ballet training can be most harmful physically and mentally.'

It didn't matter at all that the whole lot of them were amateurs. Nobody could have expected anything else. It worked, and it was her successful business. Her claims were modest and realistic. When she wrote that she would teach students to develop poise, good posture and a graceful walk, she was perfectly genuine. People only had to look at her to realise that she herself had wonderful poise, a terrific posture, and an extremely graceful walk. Not only was she slim and beautiful, she was a walking advertisement for what she was offering to do. If people would only follow her instruction, her own presence suggested, they too could look as well as she did.

The wording on the circular is extremely careful from a legal viewpoint. As well as making meaningless statements like 'Ballet as an educational subject is of great value,' Joan is not making big claims to teach ballet. Rather she states that good posture, poise and a graceful walk may be expected. Also she does not claim to teach the classes herself instead she uses the words 'under proper supervision'. This kind of safe writing and safe claim-making could not have been learnt by accident and it is unlikely that Joan developed these skills herself. It is likely that her life-long friend solicitor Jamie O'Donovan educated Joan over time in these arts.

Many dancers went through her hands, particularly in her own school, and they were grateful for her fairness. In Irish society at the time people often claimed that the doctors' and the teachers' daughters got preferential treatment at schools. In Joan Moriarty's class there were never any favourites. There were those, however, who never got as far as the ballet class, and these were the dirty children from the working-class tenements nearby who sometimes crowded surreptitiously in through the open door of the Emmet Place studio, and crept up the stairs to have a peep at the glossy middle-class girls in their expensive pink ballet shoes. 'Get away!' Miss Moriarty would shout. 'Get away!' and they would all go tumbling back down the stairs, as she emerged dramatically from the studio, and shooed them out onto the street. The children with dirty knees and dirty dresses were tantalised by the sight of the clean kids arriving at the studio and they often all trooped up after them just for the fun of being shooed out again by Miss Moriarty. Although very rare, it was not totally unknown for the odd one of these children, to manage to go to classes.

To find costumes, Miss Moriarty would invade their territory. She would regularly visit the shawl ladies at the old market in Caol Quay, where second-hand clothes were heaped on barrows, and ask in her gentle, honeyed way, for Victoriana, velvet curtains, scarves, fringes, shawls, men's tweed jackets, men's boots, trousers, and anything else that had any theatrical possibilities. She became a familiar sight down amongst the shawl ladies and the women became fond of her.

They would keep back heaps of things they thought she might like and she handed over the five pound note without bargaining. Then, with her usual, purposeful stride, she'd carry the lot quickly to her old car and disappear. Her extensive and oddly-assorted personal wardrobe, which was far from consistent in taste, suggested that perhaps she was in the thrifty habit of keeping an assortment of these second-hand garments and shoes, for her own use.

She would stand quietly watching these same tenement children at play near the railings at the side of the old Opera House. At the same time as knowing that they hadn't a hope of affording the leotards for the classes she'd neatly priced them out of, she opted to observe their behaviour, and made up a short ballet based on their street games. To dance such works her middle-class dancers would then put on the clothes she'd bought from the working-class women, and act the parts of street children.

It never seems to have occurred to Joan, that there was some paradox in this, just as it doesn't seem to have occurred to her to facilitate the imaginations of poor children. Perhaps they were too close to her own childhood condition for comfort. Or perhaps she felt that she had risen in the world, by virtue of her blue blood, or her own efforts, and now was merely occupying her rightful place amongst the middle-classes. Whatever it was, for the most part, and for all her contact with them, it never occurred to the children playing outside in the street, that ballet was for them. Maybe the bottom line was simply that first and foremost, Miss Moriarty was a businesswoman, and that money was the name of the game.

It can't be overlooked that, in her relationships with children, she put the middle class children through punishing schedules, at the same time as deriding them for not being made of the stuff that she was made of. In childhood she herself had been very like one of those unkempt little children on the street, the sector that she now deliberately denied any opportunity to dance.

There is no doubt that she could have helped the children on the street, in all sorts of ways, but she didn't. Whatever her reasons, her brand of ballet was not available to everyone. It was for the glossy-haired, moneyed set.

At a certain point, the Royal Academy of Dancing rules tightened up and Joan Moriarty had to change tack. Prior to this new rule change, anyone could hold classes in the front rooms of their homes, and call themselves teachers of dance, whether they had any training or not, and they could enter their pupils for the RAD examinations at all levels. Under the new rules, teachers of dance themselves had to satisfy RAD of their fitness, not just to dance, but also to teach. Anyone not examined by RAD, and approved by them, was henceforth not allowed to enter pupils for any RAD examination whatsoever. Joan Denise Moriarty had a big problem.

In August 1963, at the said age of forty-seven (she was popularly believed to be forty-one at this time), she applied to the Royal Academy of Dancing to enter for an elementary examination in London. This was an executant examination and not a teachers exam and would only have qualified her to apply for a teaching examination. In the event, she never took the exam. She was not able to attend, she explained to RAD, because of illness. The illness was not specified.

RAD records only include major executant examinations, but it is unlikely that she entered for any teaching qualification at a later date, because she would first have needed to take the executant examination.

So, unqualified to teach, she changed her approach, and she did it with flair. The syllabus of the Royal Academy of Dancing was taught in her schools by younger ex-pupils who *had* taken their exams, and it was easy for her to claim to be too busy to teach. Instead, she would inspect each school periodically, correcting any flagging postures she discovered, and adjusting stray hand movements on a regal walk around a class. It was a golden relief to her to leave the main bulk of the teaching to others, and to act out a grande-dame display of fixing the fiddly bits. Classes included mime and character dancing, but as far as real teaching went, she was careful not to stray into unknown territory. Students interpreted these occasional but routine displays of adjusting the fine points of gesture, as perfectionism, and felt privileged to be singled out for individual attention to the detail of their postures by this icon who had made a rare, and discreetly theatrical entrance into their class. In reality, wool was being regally pulled over their eyes.

In the sixties, she also held classes in Cork for working women and students on keep-fit, posture and dance. By this time she was genuinely too busy to take class herself, but since she had become by this time something of a legend in Cork, the young women didn't mind if they didn't see much of her—and they didn't. Ballerina stories were by this time part of the comic-book and literary diet of young girls, and it meant quite a lot just to get into her studio with the plain wood floor, the barre and the wall mirrors, exactly as they'd seen it in stories. For these young women, black polo-necked jumpers and thick black tights were compulsory uniform, but the little black ballet pumps with elastic at the instep, were optional.

Miss Moriarty would briskly climb the stairs in her flat shoes, carrying a bag, and wearing her usual headscarf tied gypsy style. Increasingly, people did not see her hair. She kept it pulled back, like a nun, with the severe middle parting. By now it was brownish, and not red any more. She might be wearing big, hooped earrings, but her face was severe. Almost fifty, she seemed ageless. Her youthful, flexible figure would be covered in a long coat. She was always well-protected against the elements. Underneath she would wear a dark, high-necked jumper, and either slacks or a full, floral skirt that swished when she walked. They knew her by her walk.

The people in the class would stiffen up the moment she appeared. A certain hush would descend. She would stand watching the whole thing in progress for a while, her chin up. Then she'd go round speaking with people. She'd ask them what job they did. If they were doing a certain hand movement, she might straighten an arm, or bend it. If fingers were tense, she would run her hand over the person. She was not friendly, but she was kind. If they groaned she'd smile kindly. She'd tell them they were doing very well, and they'd be secretly thrilled. Her presence was enough for them to feel blessed, and it was all part of the act. Women kept their ballet shoes in their wardrobes for years afterwards, and remembered the reverence they'd had for Miss Moriarty.

The very good dancers were up at the front. The novices were along by the barres. There were a lot of floor exercises for tummy, legs and thighs, all done to tape recordings of piano music. She was concerned, she told them, that working girls were not getting enough exercise. She, and the teacher she appointed, talked to the class about the posture hazards of working at desks and in offices. The girls learned how to sit down properly, and how to stand properly. They spent a lot of time exercising. Then the more competent girls would be asked to do a dance. There was something of the ballerina about the more competent girls. The others loved to see it. They found it all very soothing, relaxing, and restful.

When she talked to people, or instructed them, she never trusted herself to ad-lib. She could only ever pronounce maxims that were well-rehearsed, and that she thought would be acceptably worthy. She dealt in unyielding absolutes. Whatever seemed to have a fine ring to it, she would regurgitate at every opportunity. When she got a chance to moralise, she would come out with stiff, half-baked ideas about getting young people off the streets, into the ballet studio, and away from unhappiness and crime; ideas which were incredibly naive. She seemed to believe in her own ideas. She could never understand, she would say simplistically, how people could go round killing each other. People felt that she had a tendency to become preachy, and she did, but she did it mainly with captive audiences, most of whom would not have dared to correct her, or argue. People were used to being preached at from school and from the pulpit, but they were also too polite and in awe of her to highlight the flaws in her arguments, if they saw any.

People thought she was a fighter. She wasn't. She was a survivor. Aloys was the fighter. Her temperament, background and early experiences had given her the ability and the endurance to survive whatever life might throw at her. All her efforts were towards surviving, not achieving. Her childhood had made her hard inside, more resilient than a person should be. She would not come out fighting, as he would. That would have been too risky. She was not that sort of risk-taker. She was a responder. She would sit and wait, and when life and people presented themselves, she would then seek the advantage. She could use situations to her own advantage; she was a manipulator.

The reason people thought she was a brilliant fighter for her art, was that Aloys spent many years telling them exactly this. It was he who told anyone who would listen, that she was a true fighter, a terrible battler, and a great sufferer. He never knew how wrong he was. He acted as though he was unaware of the schools she was running; as though they did not really matter. To her it wasn't the 'battles' that counted. It was the schools that were her lifeblood. The schools meant everything to her. They and her own Cork Ballet Company represented something that he could never be part of. If everything else failed, she knew the schools would save her. The battles they fought in public had an intimate significance for them as lovers.

16
Legend

The foundations of the Irish Ballet Company were not just shaky, they were mythical. Guided by Aloys, who, like his mentor, Sir Arnold Bax, was very influenced by Celtic literature and art, a secret epic drama took place behind the scenes over forty-five years. To act it out, he and Joan Moriarty adopted names, and to some extent, personas from principal characters of Irish mythology.

The auburn-haired Joan took the name of the legendary, red-haired Queen Maeve, powerful warrior wife of the legendary Ailill, king of Connacht. Maeve, or Medb, also appears in the pre-Christian Irish sagas and myths, as the wife of many other high kings. She was overtly lustful and had many sexual affairs. She was a goddess of sovereignty; kings were not legitimate unless symbolically wed to her. The battling, ruthless and fiery Maeve remains a symbol in Ireland of fiercely independent womanhood.

There were many references fed by Aloys to the press down the years, of the 'battles' that Joan had taken on. The idea of the unstoppable, single-handed battler, Miss Moriarty, was a product of his deeply infatuated imagination. The secret meaning of battling, and of the 'battles', was a loose parallel of the mythical battles chronicled in Irish legends.

The famous Táin epic, which came out of a long oral pre-Christian tradition has, as its centre, a cattle raid, in which Queen Maeve appears as a strong ruler. The 'pillow talk' story at the outset, consists of a conversation in bed between Maeve and her consort, Ailill, in which each lover brags that they have a more magnificent bull than the other. The implication each makes, is that the other has married extremely well. Maeve discovers that her best white bull has strayed into Ailill's herd, having decided against remaining in the herd of a woman. She discovers the existence of a brown bull in Ulster, an equal of the white one, and goes to war to capture it. Much blood is shed in the protracted expedition of the Cattle Raid of

Cooley, in which the chief defender in Maeve's war against Ulster is Cuchullain.

Aloys did not take the name of Maeve's legendary husband, Ailill, king of Connacht, probably partly because Ailill was a weak king, and perished as a result of being influenced by the ambitious Maeve against his better judgement. The archaic name would also not have been suitable for Aloys to be signing on postcards, or even for using just the initial, which was the same as his own.

Instead, he took the more heroic name of 'Colm', legendary poet, prophet, composer of hymns, and eventually saint of the sixth century. Also known as Colm Cille (dove of the church), and Columbanus, many stories concern this monk who established a Christian monastery off the isle of Iona, in Scotland.

In their personal correspondence, the couple would sign these names, and occasionally refer to 'Etain'. The mythical name of 'Etain' was the codename chosen by Joan and Aloys to represent the fruit of their union, the ballet. There are several Etains in Irish legends, the most probable here being the beautiful Etain Echraidhe, with whom the god Midir fell in love, and who, through jealousy, lived an enchanted existence in several forms other than her human female one, amongst them a pool of water, and a fly.

Any student of Aloys would admit that he had a hypnotic and dramatic way of telling a story; it was one of his great delights. Part of his courtship of Joan involved giving her a sense of the legends that these mythic characters appeared in, which she had never heard before. He educated her, then he mythologised their own dramatic episodes as they went along, and she drank it in. It was a game of two gods busy constructing their own history.

The context was the Cork Ballet Company, which they had started together, as a vital part of their love affair. The kingdom was Ireland; the booty was sponsorship, acclaim, and millions of pounds in government funding; the battle arena was the stage with scores of players, and the 'battles' were each new production for the annual Ballet Week in Cork. It was gigantic, exciting, and private. The ballet epic was played out in front of the nation for decades, and he did it, he said at the end of his life, 'for fun'.

Ballet 'battles' played out in Cork by Aloys and Joan as Colm and Maeve, were not just performances and productions, but years of protracted struggling to bring up 'little Etain', their 'child' the ballet.

That was the vision, and for more than forty years he commemorated every battle.

On opening nights, his bouquets to her were always accompanied by a small sealed envelope containing a plain gift card. A prim and discreet 'Miss Moriarty' would be written on the outside of the envelope. Inside, he would gush praise. As she was about to include in the Ballet Week programme her new short ballet *West Cork Ballad* with music by West Cork composer, Sean O'Riada, Aloys wrote:

> 'To a Queen of the Celts, a warioress (sic) who is victor of a hundred battles, and the greatest of all from 2–7/10/70 in love and admiration—Colm.'

Aloys' handwriting was full of barely legible words, he tended to write hastily in capital letters with a thick nibbed black felt-tipped pen. Like Joan, who favoured green ink, and sometimes red, he never used blue ink. Whenever his letters were typed, which for business they most often were, he always typed them himself.

He tended to count the battles:

> 'To my darling, on the eve of our 24th battle—and may she be as triumphant as ever before! Colm.'

She logged the date on this note 'Nov. 8th 1971'. It was Ballet Week in Cork, exactly twenty-four years since 1947, when they had presented their first performance of ballet. She believed that she was living out one of the great love affairs: when his notes and letters were undated, she often logged on the date or date of arrival, usually in green ink, and inserted the initials of the ballet company.

As well as counting the anniversary 'battles' of the Cork Ballet Company when he sent opening-night bouquets, he sometimes gave performances more heroic status:

> 'On the eve of the Battle of Leinster' with continuing admiration and love from Colm.'

Occasionally, he was unable to be with her, but usually managed to scribble a fond note with the flowers:

> 'To my love
> Heartfelt wishes for tonight! Desolate I can't be with you. Colm.'

But there were other bouquets at other times. 'The first laburnum!', he wrote on a yellow page, 'Looking towards our summer and the Fleascin.'

The first laburnum was a ritual offering to his 'goddess', and he cut her the first bunch from a tree in his own garden every year. The Fleascin, means 'little festival', and refers to their secret, brief summer holiday together. On a Christmas card showing ponies in snowy fields he wrote:

'To my darling with things at the darkest time of year to the brightest and lightest, leaping seven months ahead to when our Fleisean Ceol will be snugly sited, by high cliffs and wild waters. Colm.'

Here he is using the term 'Fleisean Ceol', which means 'little music festival', to refer to their private time together in a little caravan. This was to be towed by her in summer, to a remote, anonymous spot in the West of Kerry.

They were both recognisable to the public, and therefore they could not be seen much together. Aloys usually celebrated Joan's birthday with her. They went to a place he called 'our pool' which could have been a municipal or hotel swimming pool, but is likely to have been a river pool somewhere around the outskirts of Cork city.

Gifts were accompanied by encouragements:

'To my darling—

and may the fifty bulbs sprout in the spring, as have her visions and her high deeds! Colm.'

She sent him a postcard of four sculpted figures by Henry Moore depicting a seated mother with a child in her lap, together with a father and another child. On the other side of the card, Joan was her usual, cryptic self. She wrote simply,

'Colm, Maeve, Etain, Dreangha.'

'Dreangha' was Joan's initial attempt at spelling their codename 'Dreena', which later became 'Dreenagh'. This name represented another of their offspring—the professional company they dreamed of.

By the early 1970s, Aloys had been honoured for his other work, both in Ireland and in Germany. In 1964, he was awarded an honorary doctorate of Dublin University. In 1966 he received the Order of Merit of the German Federal Republic, and was elected a member of the Royal Irish Academy in the same year. He had been appointed to the Irish National Commission for UNESCO in 1962, and from 1955, he was a member of the Advisory Committee of Cultural Relations, in the Irish Department of Foreign Affairs.

In 1957, he had begun work on his massive thirty-year work, the thematic index to the published collections of Irish folk music, and had composed his *Songs of Colmcille* in 1964. In 1965, he composed *Song of the Provinces.* As the commissions came up, there were many other compositions. His own views on many topics had appeared in many academic publications down the years, as well as in the popular press. Whilst he loved the limelight for himself, he wanted more for Joan. Apart from doing a series of TV programmes with her folk group for RTE, Joan had received no real recognition. In his mind, it was time this was changed.

As one of his friends and allies, Corkman Jack Lynch was most influential when he became Taoiseach. Jack perceived Joan as most reticent, and not at all active in promoting herself. He was a very warm, very approachable and friendly man, but it was Jennie Dowdall and Aloys who would do what Joan was not capable of doing. They would approach Jack.

Jack's wife, Mairin, had always been very interested in ballet, and had brought her husband along to performances. In 1947, when her relationship with Jack was in the very early stages, Mairin had been holidaying at Glengarriff in West Cork, and had travelled the seventy miles to Cork city to spend the evening with Jack Lynch. The passionate, very first performance of ballet was about to take place, with the chemistry between Joan and Aloys at its first flood, and Mairin got Jack to take her to see it.

Jack went along for the sake of duty, but the infectious performing rapport between Joan and Aloys had appeal for the lovers. The romance of the ballet immediately became part of Jack and Mairin's own bonding process. He came to enjoy it, and he developed a very lively interest in the Cork Ballet Company. All four of them became good friends, and down the years, Jack and Mairin were happy to attend functions connected with the ballet. Jack tended to be in Cork and available to attend opening nights with Mairin on Mondays, because the working week at the Dáil in Dublin began on Tuesdays.

Jack Lynch already knew and respected Aloys Fleischmann. He had been an altar boy at the Cathedral when Aloys' father, Herr Georg Fleischmann, was organist and choirmaster, brought by the Bishop from Munich. Later, when he went to UCC, Jack knew Aloys as a professor. Jack was a barrister, and was a friend of solicitor John Coakley, whose wife, Maeve, was a tremendous help to Joan in the costume-designing and making department. He also knew solicitor,

James O'Donovan, who was on the board of the Cork Ballet Company. James was one of the people close to Joan, who would make representations to Jack about the company.

Jack also moved in the same top-table circles in Dublin and Cork as Senator and Lord Mayor, Mrs Jennie Dowdall, one of the early vocal champions of the ballet in Cork. There were a lot of other socially-interlinked people who were influential and ambitious for their city and who welcomed the ballet.

Coming and going in the city for years, Jack Lynch was aware that forming a professional company was an ongoing desire, and also that standards had to be raised to the right level.

He knew that years were spent getting the company ready, and when the time was judged to be right to attempt a move on it, Jack was asking people who knew more about ballet than he did, whether in their opinion, the quality of the company justified making it professional.

The tight little inner circle that Aloys and Joan cultivated consisted of roughly two sorts of people. There were ballet people and power people. When she recruited people to work in her ballet branch of the inner circle, she went on gut feeling. Aloys had no intuition or expertise in all that, and went along with her. His arena was the power-broking, political side of things, of which she knew little, and he presided behind the scenes over every move.

Having worked out a strategy for getting money from the government and the Arts Council to establish a professional company, they had put on a first performance at the small Gate Theatre in Dublin, and were trying to make an impact at the large Abbey Theatre. He wrote to Joan from Chicago on 8th March, 1971, during a lecture tour he was doing in USA, and enclosed a postcard of a Picasso from one of the American galleries.

Referring here to Joan as the mother of, 'darling Etain', he reassures her by rubbishing ballet in New York, and to encourage her, he uses the codename 'Dreena'. He then instructs her regarding the next move in their strategy, including his draft of a letter, which he says she is to send on the matter to the West Cork composer Sean O'Riada:

'My darling,

Have been thinking and worrying a great deal about you— whether you've got rid of that bad cold and are able to cope, whether the Abbey is on or off, and so on....

Saw a second ballet show in New York City Center Nikoleis Co. with quite fantastic lighting. Costume-changes for each dancer effected by lighting only! Ugly electronic tape throughout. Frightening scenes of mob violence and hysteria. Dancers wept and moaned in chorus, or exploded into gales of laughter, or shrieked in terror or babbled incomprehensibly. A mirror of our time, it seems, was the intention.

Greetings to darling Etain, for whom and mother this Picasso intended. Do hope you're surviving every adversity, as I am.

Remember Dreena!

Love— Colm.'

On a separate page, he dealt with the business, composing a letter for her about the ballet to composer Sean O'Riada.

'So sorry to give you this bother,' he concluded, 'but it would be best coming from you. He won't reply, but that doesn't matter!'

The codename 'Dreena', was also referred to by him in other notes as 'Dreenagh'. It represented an aspect of the love transaction between them, which they hoped to see flourish and become great. 'Etain', the Cork Ballet Company, was not enough. 'Etain' was a symbol of something formed at the beginning—the fruit of their initial fusion.

He drove it forwards partly because it could not satisfy him. He needed a pinnacle to strive for, and tangible goals to reach, both in general and in their relationship. He needed evidence that their collaboration had led to something more significant. He also wanted the adrenalin-charged excitement of acting out the bringing-of-gifts. Since she got her self-esteem purely from her work, she went with the momentum to expand.

Joan was an ideal candidate for the 'goddess'. Their shared aims and strategies, their regular adventures together—the 'battles'— strengthened the bond. Whilst their joint mythological game was conscious, their own motivations were not consciously apparent to them. They were both deeply 'in love' with each other in a way which made both feel safe: she had a narcissictic tendency to prefer being loved than to love. This meant she did not have to venture out of herself and become emotionally vulnerable, and also that she could be sure of being needed. This is the love of the power person, the love of the control freak. As long as the ballet went on, she could feel secure, and sure of him. He was the secret hero—she owed it all to him, and was certainly not going to allow the ballet to end. In a curious sense, it was for his sake that she had to keep going. She wanted to keep his love.

Aloys perceived himself to be in love, but the hero that he was really serving was himself. Even in his own everyday life, Aloys was constantly pondering and invoking classic ideas and themes, but with Joan he was Jason questing the golden fleece over and over again. He got huge excitements and satisfactions from his love relationship, but what he was really in love with was with his own ability to achieve his own objectives. That was the narcissism in his approach. As one of his own main objectives in life, he had chosen the ballet. In order to achieve in that world, he needed Joan. The essential role of Joan Moriarty in his driven life, was that of the muse, the vehicle.

Their relationship had other dimensions, but essentially he was the powerful one, and she was the instrument. She provided front-of-house glamour and mystery, and he pulled the strings. It all became bigger than both of them, and over time, the sexuality of both partners was sublimated into energies which fuelled the enterprise and perpetuated it. This gave them a united 'spiritual' status which could be strongly sensed by others. As far as the public was concerned, their union, seen in full flower, was 'ideal'.

Both were skilled at PR, but where he was romantic, she was always prosaic. Joan would affect a romantic attitude at times, but she had a very dogged sense of her own advantage. Whenever she talked to the press down the years, Joan repeated the same things over and over; statements that smacked of mundanity. Her calculated talk about money, about hard work, and about dedication was thick with coded messages and rebuffs.

At least she said things about wanting a professional company that made some sense in terms of the dancers, and dancing training. She said that dancers need not leave this country if they were properly trained here, and in turn, this country would then not need so many guest dancers.

In the conscious mind of Aloys, however, getting her a national company was not all that much to do with dance. He simply enjoyed heaping ever more praise and glitter onto his darling. His PR work became a great edifice. Over many years, he created 'truths' about her which concealed lies. In heroic style, these were the gifts he brought back to her over and over again.

At that time, Joan was living in a flat in Lover's Walk in Montenotte, within a few minutes drive from his family home. She later bought a large house in the same fashionable district, which was even nearer to Aloys' own house, and which therefore made her more accessible to him. It was called 'Dreenagh'.

'To my darling on her birthday', Aloys wrote encouragement in July, 1971, 'A small prop for her letters and lectures—my indomitable one, overcoming all handicaps, reigning over students and academics, serenely, with the poise of a queen—from her Colm.'

The other sheet got down to the business of the moment—raising money:

'All the details would need to be verified (from the letter to the Gulbenkian people) shall ring tonight, love Colm.'

But it was proving difficult to stage a showcase ballet in Dublin, and her response was typically withdrawn. In March, 1972, in connection with his work, he was away on a trip to London, staying at the Royal Hotel. He followed up a telephone call to her, with a letter:

'My darling,

What a terrible blow! Behind your quiet, seemingly unconcerned voice I noticed a trace of despair. And no wonder. All your hopes and plans dashed to the ground. On top of your present over-work, it is too cruel.

Am phoning (illegible) this morning to see if he can find out if the political situation was responsible. If so, if and when a settlement is reached we shall have to try again, and use every possible pressure.

Shall ring and come to you to-morrow night.

All my sympathy and love—

Colm'

They were to try again, and it was to be *Swan Lake*. She needed to invite someone more experienced to reproduce this ballet. Choreographing was a great struggle to her. She knew that her approach was simplistic, and that she had problems translating ideas into dance form and in communicating. Her notes accompanying her diagrams, were inarticulate, halting and mis-spelled. She constantly dreaded disaster, but he understood very little about her insecurities, and unthinkingly elevated her methods to the ranks of art. The great scapegoat he used was the public. If Joan's work was not popular, he reasoned, it was because the public—which included the government and the Arts Council—were philistine. He was going to educate them all to appreciate a noble art.

He constantly dramatised their own efforts. He sent her a stark, black and white picture of Pont-na-Spania at Giant's Causeway, with great white foaming waves dashing against dark rocks.

'This shows the present climate,' he wrote. '—The battle against apathy and lack of support.' He gave her a postcard showing Oskar Schlemmer's regimental robot figurines. 'This shows the grim, machine-like work process,' he wrote. His correspondence to her is full of worry about her illnesses. Much of the time, he was preoccupied with giving her encouragement, both in illness, and in professional setbacks.

His notes down the years often made vague mention of her recurrent maladies:

'On our.... birthday, with love and admiration, and in high hopes of a proper recovery from present physical troubles.'

He always wanted more rest for her. Sending her a card of Alfred Sisley's *The Seine at Marly*, he wrote:

'This is where we should be—having a holiday, a few weeks of ease in a warm climate.'

He invested her with all sorts of virtues, but it was himself who showed true heroic qualities like a willingness to take risks and an unflagging determination to take on the opposition, not Joan.

He was an honourable man, but blinkered by his own obsessions. He slanted truths in his own favour, ignoring inconvenient facts. He made sure the right lobbying letters, favourable presentations and positive articles on Joan's behalf were placed in the right quarters, and this usually meant the top brass. Aloys had no time at all for little people. He only ever dealt with bosses, and those with pull. Where he had no influence himself, he was adept at using others who had influence of any sort whatever in high places, to further the cause of his ballet.

In 1972, influenced by the opinions of others who knew more than he did that the quality did warrant the upgrading, Jack Lynch decided to give the company a grant to allow for the creation of a professional company. It would have been more appropriate to seek funding through the usual channels, like the Arts Council, but in this case, it was Jack himself who made the decision.

The Minister for Finance was George Colley, who was considered by the leader to be a man of good judgement. Jack had a word with George, with whom he had a good rapport, and a good working relationship. 'It is about time,' he said, 'we made a move on this.'

And so the Cork Ballet Company secured the Gaiety Theatre in Dublin for a week in 1972, for their showcase presentation of *Swan Lake*. It was a very big occasion. Publicly, it was the silver jubilee year of the company, and a great splash could thus be justified. Privately, the symbolic child of Joan and Aloys' union 'Etain' was twenty-five years old, and the lovers were utterly confident that on this special occasion a new, greater offspring 'Dreenagh' was about to come into being. It was the highest peak of their secret love affair.

17

Swan Lake

'And it is going to lose hundreds and hundreds of pounds,' said Joan to *The Irish Times* writer, Elgy Gillespie, who was interviewing her for a women's page profile (4/11/72) in advance of *Swan Lake*. 'I mean, think of all the dancers and orchestra members, all staying in hotels, think of the special train and the costumes.... everything. But it's worth it.'

As always, she was ready to present her best face and muster the right kind of support, but this was the unguarded moment. Elgy wrote that with her 'no nonsense clothes and severe pony tail', there was 'something oddly childlike mixed in with this governess aspect'. Elgy also wrote that Joan had studied in Paris for three years, and become a graduate of the RAD. Like every other writer, this one wasn't heartless enough to check Joan's credentials.

'Ballet is always financially difficult,' Joan went on pointedly, 'but don't forget, it's a challenge. Sometimes when I see some of the things which get grants I only wish we could have the money they've wasted. We have jumble sales and whist drives and what have you to raise money for the ballet. But it's taught us versatility, anyway.'

Joan knew she was getting a grant. It was the company's silver jubilee and everything had been done to make sure that the answer from the government would be yes. The martyred observation that other people waste state grants was one she was fond of making. She also knew that whist drives and jumble sales raised almost nothing. This kind of comment was purely about PR. She seemed more than just impressed that for this great event, huge amounts of money were available, and were being spent. She was bragging.

As usual, the Cork Orchestral Society was sponsoring the Cork Ballet Company, with the help of the Arts Council. And for this big production—the first time in a decade that the four-act *Swan Lake* would be seen in Dublin—enormous sponsorship had been raised from businesses and individuals all over Ireland. As usual, dancing fees, air fares and hotel expenses were to be paid to professional dancers and also to a choregrapher, and for this production, Dublin hotel bills were to be met for the entire *corps de ballet* and attendant experts, as well as the whole orchestra.

It was not Joan Moriarty who was to choreograph the showcase performance but Helen Starr, from the Royal Ballet and the Royal Festival Ballet, who had danced the lead role of *Giselle* with the Cork Ballet Company the previous year. Most of the main players had worked with each other before. Sandra Conley, who was to dance *Odette*, was a soloist with the Royal Ballet, and guest dancers, Mary Hanf, Alain Dubreuil and Dubliner Gerald Byrne were with the London Festival Ballet. Alain had also danced in Cork the previous year. As usual, Pat Murray designed the set, and Maeve Coakley the costumes. Opening at the Opera House on 6th of November for Ballet Week in Cork, *Swan Lake* was then to travel immediately to Dublin, opening on Monday 13th for a week at the Gaiety Theatre.

Press coverage down the years had fed the image, and by summer 1972 had built up to laudatory pitch. On Monday 17th July 1972, the *Irish Press* had published a profile of Joan, written by Susan Nicassio, and headed, 'Bringing beauty to people'. Alongside a portrait picture of Joan, the sub-heading read:

'Joan Denise Moriarty is a remarkable woman—a professional ballet dancer from Cork who for a quarter of a century has been working towards her ambition, to give Ireland a professional ballet company...'

Extracts from this article illustrate the way in which the fiction of Joan's past had become fact, and illustrate the kind of treatment Joan and the ballet received from the press.

'Joan Denise Moriarty was a professional ballerina in Britain', Susan Nicassio wrote, 'when a tragic accident ended her career and brought her back to her native county of Cork twenty-seven years ago'.

Without specifying where Joan was dancing professionally, or what the accident was, Susan went on to quote Joan, as she gently confided the story of her efforts:

'"When I came back to Ireland I made a vow to myself—I would give my country a professional ballet company. I hoped to see it in my lifetime but now I just don't know...

'"There is simply no opportunity for professional dancers: all of them must eventually emigrate. This is just L S D, you know. We have the talent but we don't have the money...

> "'When we first began I would ask for subscriptions and people responded. They might only send 5 shillings, but they responded. Now there is almost nothing. People seem to be only interested in themselves. It's the same all over the world, of course, this materialism…'"

What Joan did not tell Susan, was that from the start, Cork people and businesses had been, and had gone on being generous to her annual requests, and that for the special ballet currently in production, which would involve huge expenses, she was well underwritten. Thousands of pounds had already been raised from individuals and from businesses, and thousands more had been guaranteed. Joan was used to pleading poverty, but she had Jack Lynch all ready to act, so she did know that she would see it in her lifetime. It was important to her that the Arts Council, as well as possible sponsors, should take notice. Knowing nothing of all this, the interviewer continued:

> 'Why does it seem so important? What drives these remarkable people to spend their lives in hardship and physical labour that would make a navvy collapse: When the tea-sipping ladies speak of bringing art and culture to the masses, it reeks of condescension. When Joan Denise Moriarty talks about ballet, the effect is quite different.

> "'It isn't condescending to want to bring beauty to people. It is a matter of loving your own art, and wanting to share it. I don't want to make dancers out of everybody—good heavens, that would be terrible! I only want them to enjoy the beauty of it. So many people have been enraptured with just one ballet, it has touched their lives…materialism…but the mind is more important. And I don't say that from an ivory tower—when I first began I went a year without having a full meal. There just wasn't enough money. I had two complete breakdowns, just from lack of food. Why did I do it? I suppose because I was stimulated by beautiful things. The cynics will say that beauty is not as important as having a full stomach. Well, I've been through it, and I say that it is."

> "'The important thing is not to waste time. I realised that when I was 15 years old. I remember thinking, here I am, 15—there isn't much time left! Foolish but it taught me something. We are here for such a short time, we must do the best we can, and no one can ask more."

> 'Joan Denise Moriarty does the best she can. And Ireland is the richer for it.'

In the last interview she ever gave, almost twenty years later, Joan was saying exactly the same things. A woman whose whole life was an act, she had a honeyed knack of seducing interviewers, and it worked every time. Since she had never told the truth, and had only ever invented chunks of history, and manufactured nuggets of quotable, if boring philosophy, which she repeated over and over again, it was conscious manipulation of the press right into their faces. Irish journalists may have erred by writing too positively and too unquestioningly. It is likely, therefore, that she despised the press. Presenting herself as a saintly, vulnerable ballerina starving for her art drew sympathy and admiration, and she had seen such manipulation lead people to put their hands in their pockets.

'What does she do with the bit of her life that isn't ballet?,' Elgy Gillespie asked, in the women's page of *The Irish Times*, two days before *Swan Lake* opened. "I'm afraid my life is seven days a week ballet," Joan answered sweetly. "You see you must give everything. You must know your work and you've got to have the idealism and the practicability. I'm not a very practical person, but I've had to learn how to be.'"

Mostly, she was successful in stage-managing her interviews. Aloys could make the odd gaffe. Part of the reason his letters so often appeared in the newspapers, was that he could be amusingly immoderate. (Towards the end of his life, he attracted a lot of hate mail for suggesting that the national anthem should be changed.) In the Silver Jubilee Souvenir Programme, the language describing Joan—'idealist'; 'grinding hard work and almost fanatical zeal'; 'unbelievable courage'—suggest that he wrote it. It also contains this, which only himself would have dared write:

> 'Miss Moriarty protests strongly against any suggestion that she has a good business instinct, but despite all her idealism and enthusiasm she is endowed with a large measure of sound common sense. It was this attribute which drove her to maintain the non- professional ballet company between the years 1959 and 1964, while the professional company was endeavouring to bring to the remoter parts of Ireland a knowlege and appreciation of ballet. She knew only too well the number of small professional companies which, over the years, have had to fold up for lack of funds, and when Irish Theatre Ballet met with the same fate, Cork was lucky to find the non-professional company still going strong.'

Joan did not like the idea of being known for her business acumen. She would not have liked the 'business instinct' comment, but the rest of the paragaraph is larded with flattery of the sort she approved. The fact that she had paid so much attention to her amateur company, would later become an issue that would cause her deep embarrassment. For now though, in 1972, things were going according to their plans.

On 3rd November *The Cork Examiner* ran a picture of the ballet stars arriving, and being met with bouquets at Cork Airport by Joan, Aloys, Maeve Coakley and manager, Pat Leonard.

The 'lavish production', wrote Deirdre McCarry in the *Irish Independent* on Monday, November 6th, as she profiled the 'Man hehind the ballet girls', would cost at least £10,000. And a documentary film, she reported, was to be made of the jubilee celebrations, by Norris Davidson for RTE.

The Irish Times ballet critic, Seamus Kelly, came down to Cork for the opening night. He reported on November 8th, that audience reception on the Silver Jubilee first night in Cork was 'rapturous—and deservedly so'. Aloys Fleischmann and his orchestra, he went on, played superbly.

In his regular *Irishman's Diary* column, Quidnunc, in *The Irish Times* of November 9th 1972, Seamus Kelly continued to gush admiration: 'a quarter century of dedicated and indomitable work reached its triumphant pinnacle in the Cork Opera House last Monday night when Joan Denise Moriarty and her Cork Ballet Company, with Aloys Fleischmann and the Cork Symphony Orchestra, achieved their ambition of mounting the full four acts of *Swan Lake* with guest principals... supported by Cork's own talented company. Critical appraisal of this production has been high, and deservedly so...' He went on, 'formidable undertaking.... full value for money... amateurs with professional standards and professional competence'. He attended the post-performance reception in the Imperial Hotel in Cork.

The next morning, inundated with well-wishing bouquets, and with news of full advance booking, Joan and Aloys set off for Dublin, where they held a press conference to announce their coming season at the Gaiety Theatre. Advance articles in the *Cork Echo* the previous Saturday, and reviews after the first night, hadn't mentioned the staggering cost of this production at all, but now, full of success, Joan herself was there, and in a mood to talk.

Even if they managed full houses in Dublin, *The Cork Examiner* noted (8/11/72), the company would make a loss. The press conference was told that without travelling expenses, hotel and living expenses for 145 people, including air fares and hotel fees for so many guest artists, the full-length production would cost more than £10,000. An Arts Council grant of £2,000 had been given. 'It has taken us 25 years to build... audiences in Cork', said Joan, 'but this week we are booked out at the Opera House'.

JJ Finegan in the *Evening Herald* (11/11/72) in Dublin, was impressed by the scale of it:

'For more than ten years Joan Denise Moriarty's Cork Ballet has been making firm forays into Dublin's theatreland. On Monday next comes the greatest ever invasion of the metropolitan theatre scene from Cork—a special train, no less... bringing 60 dancers and 70 members of the orchestra... It is Miss Moriarty's finest hour. For the entire project, which she directs, is the realisation of her dream for this, the Silver Jubilee of the Cork Ballet Company.

'... at Cork Opera House, every seat of the seven performances was sold before the curtain went up last Monday.

'Yet, even if every seat in the Gaiety next week is taken, the company will not make a penny on the huge £10,000 undertaking—indeed, they stand to lose, even with capacity audiences.'

David Nowlan was reporting for *The Irish Times* (9/11/72) at the Dublin press conference, in which Joan had talked about the huge cost of the production. He had been struck by her saying, 'calmly', that unless they got full houses in Dublin, they'd be sunk, and that poor houses could wipe the whole company out. He discussed the matter in print.

'Now, in a production which is costing £10,000 (and that's before a truck or a train or a hotel room has been engaged to convey and house the 145 people involved...). Joan Denise Moriarty is bringing *Swan Lake*...

'So why choose...a ballet that is both technically and artistically demanding in addition to involving a company of 145...? Certainly it was a huge risk and certainly poor houses in Dublin could wipe out the whole Cork Ballet Company: "Unless we get full houses in Dublin we'll be fairly sunk," said Miss Moriarty calmly.

'Is she crazy, then, this quiet and elegant lady from Cork: Is she blinded by her own enthusiasm for ballet and by an unjustifiably rosy optimism? Having met her for the first time, I would say, definitely not. Enthusiastic she certainly is, and optimistic up to a point; but she is undeniably realistic.'

She had gone round 'school after school', she told him. David Nowlan ended up full of praise, but the immense calm that she showed in the face of all risks and possible disasters was unfathomable to those writing about her and the ballet. Aloys was always on hand to murmur reassurances with gravitas, that she was a wonder to behold, and so, without having to say anything, was the influential figure of Jack Lynch. The fact that Seamus Kelly was an acolyte helped her PR too, because he was working for the serious, prestigious daily, *The Irish Times*. The other Dublin papers, as well as the provincials, were likely to follow his lead.

Seamus Kelly was rooting for them in their hopes. In the *Quidnunc* column of 15th November 1972, he made much of the 'Silver Jubilee achievement" and reported on Aloys' onstage political banter.

The Taoiseach's speech at the Gresham Hotel reception that evening, Kelly reported, included a hint from the Corkman that 'I hope it won't be another twenty-five years before Miss Moriarty realises her life's ambition to found a professional ballet company in Ireland'. Jack Lynch had gone on to mention innocently, wrote Kelly, 'that he had seen to it that the Professor had been seated at supper beside Mr George Colley!'.

'*Swan Lake* triumph at Gaiety,' wrote Noeleen Dowling in another opening-night newspaper review.

'The decision by Director Joan Denise Moriarty to spare no expense on the production has paid off in a presentation of richness, density and artistry.'

There was almost no adverse criticism.

Thanks to Jennie Dowdall, there were even greater glories for the company. On 15th Novemebr 1972, in the *Irish Independent*, members of the Company were pictured at Áras an Uachtaráin, the Presidential mansion, surrounding a bewildered-looking President de Valera. A happily smiling Joan flanked him on one side, wearing a hat with a brim and long suede boots, and Jennie Dowdall, who had obviously pulled the stroke off, sat proprietorially on the other. Looking on, in the company of the guest artists, were Aloys; James O'Donovan; Pat Murray, set designer; Pat Leonard, administrator; Ray Casey, lighting director; and Maeve Coakley, wardrobe director.

The Press coverage went on, with the terminology at times, veering towards the mythological. Seamus Kelly called Joan, 'indomitable' (*IT Annual Review*). The Aquarius column in *The Longford Leader* named Miss Joan Denise Moriarty as its 'Irish Showbusiness Personality of 1972', whose production 'enthralled packed houses for a week.'

Joan gave many clues and hints about herself at the Tuesday press conference in Dublin. She was a mass of contradictions. Instead of exhilaration at the Cork sellout success, here was the strange, unfathomable calm that struck writer David Nowlan. Here at the same time was her inappropriate equanimity at the prospect of loss. Here was Joan apparently flying in the face of reality at immense risk, with an attitude that baffled and stupefied people. Here were extravagance and big spending. Here also was the grind of the core schools that she valued. Here were the bought-in big stars

Fostered at about four years. Courtesy of Aloys Fleischmann.

Earliest picture of Joan Denise Moriarty aged around two years. JDM Collection.

Dreaming in Costume. JDM Collection.

Blossoming and competing. JDM Collection.

Glenapp Castle, Ayrshire, Scotland.
Courtesy of Lord and Lady Inchcape.

Marion's home (extreme right) in Broom Lane,
Mallow, where Joan lived and held class.
Courtesy of Kieron Bolster.

Joan and her 'brother', Sid.
JDM Collection.

Joan in Cork, 1936. Picture has been
doctored to make waist and arms appear
thinner. JDM Collection.

Aloys' mother, Tilly Fleischmann, in Munich, 1910.
Courtesy of Aloys Fleischmann.

Aloys Fleischmann. Author Collection.

Dancing on the gatepost of Aloys' home in Cork, 1947.
JDM Collection.

Ecstatic as the slave girl in La Calinda. *First collaboration, 1947. JDM Collection.*

Joan and Aloys. Taken by each other in Germany, 1958.
JDM Collection.

The piper, 1940.
Courtesy of The Cork Examiner.

Aloys and Joan in Germany 1958 with company members.
JDM Collection.

Joan with Pat Murray in the 1960s.
JDM Collection.

Happiness for Aloys and Joan at the Limerick Tóstal.
JDM Collection.

With Swan Lake *cast and President de Valera at the Áras, 1972. Jamie*
Donovan is on the right of picture and Senator Jennie Dowdall is seated
beside the President. JDM Collection.

Devastated after the Brinson Report, with the cast of Playboy.
Courtesy of The Cork Examiner.

Presentation by Jack and Mairin Lynch, at the fortieth birthday of the Cork Ballet Company. Aloys' wife, Ann, stands to the extreme left of the picture. JDM Collection.

Terminally ill, Aloys buries Joan. Jamie stands immediately behind Aloys,
Pat Murray to the right of picture and Pat Fleming to the extreme right.
Picture by Billy MacGill. Author Collection.

Joan.

that made it all work—a troupe of strangers from abroad. Here was the political pull going full steam ahead. And here was Joan actually spelling it all out.

The truth about Joan's superhuman calm was that, apart from the possible effect of antidepressant drugs, she simply did not care about the risk. In the Cork Ballet Company, when productions were being put together, it was not herself that was taking the risk, and it never would be. Her mind was compartmentalised. Joan Moriarty the person was the woman who had started the ballet schools and personally trained young girls to teach in them, and from these she had managed to make a living. She was safe. Privately, she placed a very high value on this security.

Also, although she craved the security of money, her greatest personal attribute and skill in the running of the Cork Ballet Company was nothing to do with money, and certainly not with risk. It was that she had built up an intimate hard core of volunteers who could be totally depended on for continuation of the performing aspect of her business, fed by her own schools. This was another constant in her life, and she relied far more on these people that had cost her nothing than she did on any hired professional. She valued and trusted these people, and they also gave her personal security.

Hilda Buckley, for example, an unmarried Cork secretary who danced the Queen Mother in *Swan Lake* on this twenty-fifth anniversary, had been a pupil of Joan's at the very start, and loved her. Hilda went on dancing, and giving her evenings to ballet concerns, to board meetings, and to her dear friend until the very end, when she was made one of Joan's executors.

Joan had a lot of problems in ballet, and facilitated by her powerful volunteers, she was enabled to throw other people's money at them. Since the very start, she had been completely underwritten by Aloys and the various organisations he was plugged into from his UCC vantage point.

Joan found that money meant power. A gravy train started rolling, and she was in control. There were many good professional people whom she trusted—designer Pat Murray, for example, and these were given the jobs. Money could buy people who could do things, and the plans became more and more ambitious.

When ideas were dreamed up for the following year's Ballet Week, money was needed. It didn't much matter what everything cost; whatever the bottom line turned out to be, that was the target.

The machine went into action. Joan did not so much stop and count the cost, as ask about more and more ways of getting more and more money. Then she spent it quickly. The thousands of pounds that were raised and swallowed up by the ballet company were put up for 'Miss Moriarty' by someone else, and whatever the profits and losses, it all took place at no risk to herself.

Not only that, but where she managed her own money shrewdly, driving a modest old car and fixing up pensions for herself, she was increasingly extravagant and lavish where production funds were involved. Joan hardly had to do a thing. She just glanced around her, and was blessed. When she agreed that she needed big names from abroad, money had to be found for it, and her perpetual suitor went on bearing gifts. She found that the more spectacular the result, the better it was liked, and the rave press proved to her that she was doing the right thing.

There is no doubt that the *Swan Lake* fortnight was a glittering success, and that by the end of it all everyone was delighted. In their subordinate function to the guest dancers, the *corps de ballet*, and supporting dancers had proved commendably competent. What had been completely overlooked, was that Joan had no real function in a production of this sort, except almost as a sort of impresario. Choreographer Helen Starr, though given hardly a mention, had obviously done her job well. Joan's sitting back artistically, largely went unnoticed. She was the figurehead of it all, the 'Artistic Director', and the press duly reported that *Swan Lake* was under her 'brilliant direction'. She got top billing, as well as all the laurels, but what she actually did, apart from overseeing the schooling of her *corps de ballet*, nobody actually knew.

In addition, this special expensive production had very little, if anything, to do with the Cork Ballet Company, and was hardly a reflection on it. On the face of it this *Swan Lake* provided no justification in itself for the forming of a professional company, but its excellence and success was used, it seems by everyone, as a yardstick of how good the company, and Joan herself were. In reality, all the production showed was that if you care nothing at all for the box office factor, and can afford to pay star dancers, as well as afford to deliberately make enormous losses, big money can buy a really good show.

18
Irish Ballet Company

I n January 1974, Aloys wrote a letter to Joan from Dublin, where he was spending a few days working. After some discussion of work, he finished:

'Do hope things are working out for you. Before the season is out let us plot one trip to Dublin, in better weather scalp (sic) again, galleries—and a box at the Olympia! Thoughts darting back to an eyrie perched high in Montenotte, where poetry and visions and sometimes ardour meet, to fuse and lead to fine achievement. Shall ring you Friday night.

Love Colm.

P.S. Frieda had only this paper—in case you think I'm carrying on like Charles Lynch!'

The script was cramped, and he had written on both sides of octavo-sized paper. Perhaps the pianist, Charles, had written cramped letters on both sides of small bits of paper, hence the joke.

The reason Aloys took a box when they went to the theatre in Dublin was so that they would not be seen. Wherever he went alone, he tended to think of her, and of how much better they would enjoy everything together. In this letter, he was explicitly acknowledging the power of their private and personal bond, in perpetuating the ballet. His part in it was clear in his mind. For Aloys, it was the fusing of their joint experience of poetry, their joint experience of visions, and their joint experience, sometimes, of intense passion, which were the ingredients that formed the 'fine achievement' of the ballet, and the vital chemistry all took place in Joan's house up on the steep Montenotte hill. The tone of this letter is that of justification: the creation of the IBC had justifed and validated the liaison.

The forming of the new professional Irish Ballet Company, and the state grant in 1974, of £45,000 was for Aloys the tangible, mature fruit of their long love affair, and an opportunity to reach the peak of their experience together. For Joan it was the beginning of the end.

'Miss Moriarty' was Artistic Director of this new enterprise, which was called the Irish Ballet Company, and because Aloys did not want too high a public profile, he installed James O'Donovan as chairman, and gave himself the position of vice-chairman. There were wages and salaries to be paid, and Joan took on a personal secretarial assistant, a 'Girl Friday'. Amongst the new professionals, Muriel Large, an Englishwoman who had managed the Scottish Ballet, took up the post of Administrator. She was directly answerable to the Artistic Director, required to seek Joan's agreement on all decisions, and keep her briefed at all times.

There was an interesting twist. A special clause, a proviso, was inserted into the new arrangements. The new company was one thing, but the original company, it was stipulated in the terms of the grant, was to remain, and should not be allowed 'to die', as Aloys put it. 'Miss Moriarty' was also to continue on as Artistic Director with the original company. The only reason they gave for having it set in stone that they didn't want it tampered with in any way, was the obvious one that it was 'established' and could act as a 'breeding ground' for young dancers.

This was perfectly true, and personally for level-headed Joan, who was now middle-aged, it was reasonable to continue earning her living from the amateur schools connected with the Cork Ballet Company. But she had other reasons. After twenty-five years she was afraid to move on. Her fears were partly her own rigidity, and partly her deep fear of success. Just as her ambition welcomed the new professional Irish Ballet Company and its huge income, she was also instinctively full of mistrust. This discomfort was justified. The whole new thing been engineered by other people, however well-meaning, and although she had partly manipulated them into it, she was far from on top of things with IBC. One crucial difference was that she and her champion were no longer completely in charge. She was as exposed as a young doe in the middle of an open snowfield.

Aloys had the rather more personal idea that 'Etain', the symbol and fruit of their union, should not be 'killed off', as he put it. He was confident and aggressive, and would never understand how she could feel depressed and apprehensive in the midst of all the success they had achieved, and neither, unfortunately, in her closed world, could she fully comprehend it. With 'Dreenagh' now in the arena, the love letters flowed, the music continued, and the dance went on.

The Irish Ballet Company gave its first performance in the Cork Opera House in January 1974, and the programme included *Billy The Music*, a short ballet choreographed by Joan, with music by the gifted Irish composer, Sean O'Riada, an ex-pupil of Aloys at Cork and also a lecturer in his music department. There were twelve dancers at first, soon to increase, and Domy Reiter-Soffer was principal choreographer.

The founding of the Irish Ballet Company roughly coincided, for Joan Moriarty, with the beginning of the menopause. When her menses countinued at the wrong times, she went into hospital for a D&C, a minor operation. Her stress levels also immediately increased, and she had recurrent attacks of diverticulitis, her irritable bowel syndrome. When she got these attacks, she would go on the drug Buscapen for a few days. With the exception of Billie Hunt, who usually nursed Joan when she went into Shanakiel Hospital, people around her didn't dare intrude into the mysterious world of her illnesses. Aloys who visited her on the numerous occasions when she went into hospital was always full of sympathy.

She was ill at Christmas 1974, and Aloys sending her a Virgin and Child card, wrote:

'To My Love
With longing for her recovery
and with bright hopes for 1975
From
Colm.'

The IBC statement of accounts for the nine months, ending 31st December 1974, showed an income of £53,793, which included a grant of nearly £3,000 from the tourist board, Bord Failte, and performance receipts of nearly £6,000. The total deficit was £1,518. Not enough of a deficit to really worry anyone, but now there were two companies and several schools for Joan to worry about. At IBC board meetings, which took place firstly in the Imperial Hotel, and soon afterwards at the Music Department at the University, a lot of her thinking, right from the start, was about money.

Amongst the notes she habitually made, as meetings progressed, were jottings of amounts of money allocated and estimated. Little sums fringed the notes she made on her printed agendas, endless addings-up amongst the doodles, which ranged from notes that her PA was to receive £15 wages, through items like £80 for a new sewing machine and £150 for a new washing machine, to the tottingup of tens of thousands of pounds in total grants. She also took separate lists of petty expenditures, and tea, coffee, meal and taxi expenses to these meetings.

By August 1975, Aloys was getting a little uneasy, too. He was beginning to want to get away from it all with Joan. In his letter from Germany, he is also clearly worried about the business, as well as being anxious about her health:

'My darling!

How I wish you were here! Apart from many fascinating papers, and interesting people to meet, there are so many museums, galleries, churches to visit. Next year we must really plan well in advance.

You would have been intrigued by the paper on dance research, by a professor of dance from Columbia University who looked the characteristic ballerina, and brought a film on the Shakers—really a ballet based on the folk dancing of a sect who dance to free themselves from sin!

Most anxious to know how you have been, and how things have gone since. Home Saturday night, and shall ring at once. In haste—love Colm.'

Things were not going well. So soon after its formation, the IBC was far from safe. Joan felt that it already appeared to be suddenly on the brink of disaster. The 1975 accounts showed an income of nearly £63,000, comprising £52,500 from the government, £4,993 theatre returns, £4,000 from Bord Failte, £1,000 Erasmus prize for choreography, and £350 from the Gulbenkian Foundation. With an expenditure of nearly £72,000, the deficit was around £10,000. Added to the deficit for the previous year, and to the first year's deficit of £405, the total deficit was more than £11,000.

The breakdown of salaries for 1975/76 in IBC, included £2,500 annual Artistic Director's fee for Joan rising to £3,000. There was a fee of £1,460, for an Artistic Adviser, for which ongoing service she chose Domy Reiter-Soffer, and additional choreography fees were budgeted at £500 each, for six ballets. The dancer's salaries varied from around the twenties per week, to the thirties and forties. The Girl Friday was down for £35 pounds a week, and the Company Manager was down for £40. US fares were authorised for Miss Moriarty and Mr Reiter-Soffer, the studio was to be redecorated, and additional barres were to be put in. A studio cleaner was also engaged.

Whatever the fortunes of the new professional company, Joan appeared to keep on with her amateur company in exactly the same way as she had before. In November 1973, Ballet Week took place as usual at The Opera House in Cork. *Nutcracker* was combined with a ressurrection of Fleischmann's *The Golden Bell of Ko*. The following year, in the usual early November slot at the Opera House, the Cork Ballet Company went ahead with Ballet Week, and staging *Giselle*, with another short ballet called *Full Moon for the Bride*. Apart from the questions of whether there was enough public interest in ballet to support performances by both companies; and whether the public thought they were seeing the new professional company, or thought that her amateur company had been grant-aided, it is clear that Joan kept her amateur company a high-profile distance away from the professional company from the start, and that Aloys was of similar mind. The prime slot of the year, Ballet Week, was retained exclusively for the amateur Cork Ballet Company, and the professional Irish Ballet Company had to find other performing outlets.

Joan's amateur dancers took part in IBC productions, providing a *corps de ballet*, and professional members of IBC now starred as guest artists with amateur CBC, for Ballet Week. In 1975, for example, Richard Collins, a professional dancer who for four years was a member of the Bolshoi Company in Moscow, was borrowed from IBC for Ballet Week, to dance the lead in Polovtsian Dances from Prince Igor. A stylish, vigorous dancer, he was popular with the public.

On opening night that year, Aloys sent her the usual ritual bouquet: 'To my Queen,' he wrote on a plain card, 'on our 28th battle together—in love and devotion—Colm'. She later added the date, '3rd Nov 1975.'

1975 was exactly twenty-eight years since the amateur Cork Ballet Company had started with a single performance. At this time, the professional company, IBC, was supposed to be in full swing, and had toured the country the previous month but Aloys had not counted any IBC performances in his card to Joan. These did not qualify, it appears, to be counted as 'battles'. So far, the annual notching up of the 'battles' was reserved for the Cork Ballet Company.

A few days after amateur Ballet Week in 1975, there was an IBC board meeting of 13th November, in which *Romeo and Juliet*, a ballet for touring on big stages, was ruled out as being too expensive, partly because the new company found it was unable to afford a sixth male dancer. On 23rd November Joan wrote to Domy Reiter-Soffer at his home in Tel Aviv, with the financial news. Addressing him as, 'Domy Dear', her typed confidences to him were panicky and intimate.

'....And now to the bad news—We had a board meeting a week ago, and much to the horror of all it has been discovered that we are very deeply in the red! (nearly £12,000) with no hope of getting any more money! It seems the rising costs, the drop in numbers attending over the last year is the cause, now the Bank has said it will not give any more overdraft!!!! so it has meant that we have to cut right and left. I have given up my "girl Friday" and we have cut out all spending apart from the wages, and even this we will have to cut where ever we can... I am very upset, but the main thing at this time is to see that the Company can keep going, the last thing we want is to have to fold up—We have managed to make an appointment with the Goverment (sic) representative for next Wednesday in Dublin to discuss the matter—but they have already said there is no more money available—in fact said there was no point in going to Dublin— but we pushed and we are at least going to discuss the position, but we have not much hope. We tryed(sic) to see the Minster (sic), but no, we have to go through his office—one cannot get pass(sic) the red tape of Goverment (sic)!!!!!!

'...Please Domy We are all very sorry that R & J cannot go on at the moment, but I am still hoping it may be possible in time'...

'One of the things that I am sad about is that at the moment we have not got a work by you...I would like one of your works. can you think of something dramatic? I know you have made the suggestion of Yerma, but one thing worries me is the music, it has been used recently by Rambert, and on top of that it would be very, very costly to get permission to use it, is there any other composer that you could turn to?'

Typing at nine in the morning, the only time, she pointed out, available for writing, she finished this letter, 'From us all love Joan,' and filed away a copy. Here her warm regard for, and dependance on the young choreographer is apparent. She also is clearly out of her depth. Without waiting for a reply, she wrote again on 2nd December 1975. Her tone was more alarmed.

'My Dear Domy

'I hope by now you have received my letter of a short time ago? To follow up on what I said, we went to Dublin for a meeting with the Goverment (sic) man Mr Scully, well, alas we got no "Joy" as the modern expression goes. he informed us that there was no money for to pay off our over draft, AND, NO EXTRA FOR THE COMING YEAR OVER WHAT WE RECEIVED IN 1975—This will mean cuts, cuts every where from now on!!!!!! it is most depressing, But we were told in no mean words that we have to run within our present buget (sic), or close?!!!! as things are at the moment the country cannot even afford what we already get. All the other companys (sic) will get the same treatment. I asked this point!

'I am so sorry to have to paint such a black picture, but there it is. it seems one no sooner get (sic) something, and almost at once it is about to be taken away again! the struggle never ends......

'We are putting on Studio Ballets in Dec and Jan to an invited audience for four performences (sic). this will include class work, Pas-de-deux, Contrasts, Pas de Q, and I have asked the dancers to arrange four short mimes, comedy, one for each of the performences (sic). they seem to like the idea. These will be held in the Studio, with coffey (sic) and biscuits(sic) and a chat after. I am going after people who do not on the hole (sic) go to the Ballet—no charge will be expected. It will I feel give the dancers something to do—now that R&J has been posponed (sic) for the moment.

'I will let you know the out come. I go into hospital next week for long over due treatment, which I have put off for the last two months, but cannot be put off longer!!!! how ever I managed to get all my work finished, that is something!

'Must close, let me know about a new work. I mentoned (sic) this in my last letter. hoping you are well.

'Love from us as always.

Joan.'

Domy wrote from London in the new year with his own news, and expressed his belief that the grant situation would improve.

Pat Murray was one of the fortunate experts in the company who was completely independent. He dared to call her 'Joan', was disarming and brotherly towards her, and had no sexual interest in her whatever. Since the results of his work usually delighted everyone, he could be depended upon to get on with it. Joan gave him carte blanche regarding the sets and costume designs, and felt comfortable enough with him to go on holiday with him. Domy was more like a favourite nephew. He was full of filial affection, and solicitous of her. She relied on him for artistic input and advice, and had a personal need for his reassurance and support. The ballet which Domy offered, for the following June in Dublin was *Yerma*.

Joan was devising ways of getting more money, and she prepared some notes for an extraordinary meeting of directors on 2nd January, 1976. She wanted to increase the draft budget.

In the event, the government grant for the year to IBC was £93,000. In the same year, CBC received £1,000. The Gulbenkian Foundation later paid for equipment to video ballets.

In the meantime, the IBC prepared to perform the five short pieces in Cork, and Domy came to help. The orchestra was engaged, and the amateur Cork Ballet Company joined in, as supporting dancers and *corps de ballet*. For this production, Joan herself kept handwritten lists of petty costs incurred by the CBC, and payable to them, for bits of lace, elastic, tights, bangles and teacloths.

Joan was capable of paying attention to detail, and, in the early days, her involvement at the most basic level in the outgoing finances of her own business was appropriate. But after twenty-five years, the responsibility for dispensing petty cash to cover running repairs, and for keeping such piffling records, ought to have been delegated to her wardrobe department.

That she was so meticulously preoccupied, at this crucial stage in her career as the head of IBC, with all monies, including the most petty expenditures imaginable, when the organisation was fully staffed with professionals, was inappropriate. She had a new professional company that was £12,000 in the red, and as well as trying to keep tabs on all expenditures incurred, she was also busy making sure that the cost of every nineteen-pence bit of elastic, and thirty-five pence fragment of lace bought by her amateur company was recovered.

She was the chief decision-maker. At board meetings, most items under discussion were respectfully, 'subject to Miss Moriarty's approval'.When Kathleen Smith was to appear with Richard Collins at the Ljubljana Festival in Yugoslavia, for example, Kathleen was very anxious to create a *pas de deux* for the occasion. The idea had to go through the administrator, Muriel Large, who told her that it could not be a definite suggestion until approved by Miss Moriarty, and until Miss Moriarty had seen the final thing.

Yet Joan was not just the utter skinflint and busybody that she would appear, but a woman motivated by terror. Her misplaced preoccupation with money was an attempt to protect her own interests, and thus to protect herself. Deeply afraid that the Irish Ballet Company—over which she had little real control—would be the cause of robbing the Cork Ballet Company, and therefore robbing herself, her real intention was to make sure that did not happen. She chose an ambitious way of clutching at straws.

Money represented control. Fiddling with capital expenditure, as well as the cost of bits of lace, was for Joan a means of control. So far, she had succeeded in her life by using money to buy experts and stage productions. Now, staying abreast of tens of thousands of pounds worth of grants made her feel she had some power even though the matter was largely outside her remit. Watching even the petty cashflow vigilantly gave her a sense of control over transactions with the amateur company.

Yerma, choreographed by Domy Reiter, was approved by the board of IBC, and went ahead in the summer of 1976. It cost a lot of money to produce and was performed for one expensive June week at the Abbey in Dublin, and also for a week in Cork. Then it went touring. *Yerma* was danced by Kathleen Smith, supported by Richard Collins and Anna Donovan, with Patricia Crosbie and Babil Gandara. At considerable cost the production was taken to thirty-eight small towns in Ireland, and also in Northern Ireland.

As well as Domy, other choreographers engaged included Peter Darrell, from the Scottish Ballet, and Royston Muldoon, also from Scotland. Anton Dolin came from the UK, Michel de Lutry from West Germany, and Charles Czarny from the Netherlands. Hans Brenaa was from Denmark. The music of many composers was used by the assorted choreographers, but for the few ballets which Joan herself choreographed, it was O'Riada's music that tended to be used.

In 1976, the Arts Council became responsible for giving grant aid to the professional company, by which time their total allocation had risen to £93,000.

The 22nd July 1976 was Joan's birthday, and she was away on tour with IBC in Killarney. Her birthdays passed unnoticed amongst her colleagues. She was commonly believed to be roughly in her mid-fifties, but she was at least around sixty. The summer had not been going well for her, and Aloys was attempting to console her. Normally he would have gone to her in the morning, on his way to the college, but on this occasion, he let himself into her empty apartment with the key she had given him, and left flowers for her, so that she would find them when she got back. He wrote:

'My darling

'All I can do, in wishing you a happy birthday, is to leave a small bouquet, for remembrance. What a pity we cannot go to our pool tomorrow! This summer has seen a whole shower of disappointments for you. But there have also been major triumphs, and these will continue to bring forth the fruit of the big personal sacrifices you have always made.

'Do hope your trip to Killarney worked well. Shall ring you at lunch-time—in the hope you will allow me come to supper! My love, and best wishes for your coming year! Colm.'

The disappointments were to continue. The Arts Council report looked rosy enough, and £126,000 had been requested by IBC for the following year. The money required to finance a show of this nature was soon swallowed up. In the draft budget for 1977, the payroll was around £82,000 for a permanent staff of approximately twenty-five people. Touring costs amounted to more than £30,000. Apart from annual artistic advisory fees, a planned *Romeo and Juliet* was to cost £600 in choreography fees, and £3,000 in production costs. Four additional ballets were to cost £400 each in choreography fees, and £500 each in production costs. Hire of the orchestra was £800, and the design fee was £1,500, with £1,000 allowance in the event of Mr Murray's unavailability. Fares and living expenses for Domy as artistic adviser, were £750. Joan's annual payment was increased to £3,000. She crossed this out, and altered the figure to £2,500, adding a note: 'no increase please', but this gesture did nothing to prevent the further losses that were looming.

In 1976, a total of less than four thousand people went to see the Irish Ballet Company at the Cork Opera House, an average of less than six hundred people in the house per night. In 1977, the box office was down to nearer five hundred people per night. It was not enough.

Other procedures adopted at this time would eventually become problems that Joan would not be able to handle. Some dancers trained with her original company had become professional and were installed on the IBC payroll. That was fine, but by now, in her furious secret drive to guard against CBC being swallowed up or in some other way harmed by IBC, Joan—assisted gamely by Aloys, as well as by other devoted supporters—was overcompensating. Rather than the little amateur company being properly used to feed the professional one, it increasingly seemed to be the other way round.

19
76&77

The one department in which Joan objected to Aloys' admiration of her smartness, was in the matter of business. To be promoted as someone who was good with money, was too near a truth that she did not want to look at. She didn't want him to go round innocently telling the world that business sense was one of her gifts, so she scotched the idea. With poetic aptitude, he took to weaving this embargo into her mystique, presenting her as someone who had no money, and who took nothing at all for herself. So convincing was she, that he believed it, and his own sense of awe, and her aura of mystery, increased. People who dedicate themselves to work without pay, are saints.

Yet she had more money than he did. She spent her life drawing income from her schools, and sensibly salting it away. Though he insisted that her hard work at the professional company was given freely, she took a decent salary for years as artistic director, as well as generous expenses. She secured a pension, as well as investment dividends. All these practices, given usual procedures, would be a normal part of any business. The fact that money loomed large on Joan's agenda went right over Aloys' head. It was easy for him to invert facts. In some ways, it was as though he spent his time paving the artistic way, and she spent her time quietly reaping the economic benefits.

The significance of her schools was completely lost on him, as was the part her own amateur ballet company occupied in her life. He perceived the schools to be a small matter; she didn't bother to enlighten him. He saw the amateur company as the ongoing product of their love, an artistic oasis which must be cultivated. She perceived it firstly as the source of her own self-worth. She pursued her own secret freedoms, astutely playing both her amateur company and her schools into the IBC equation, in ways which ensured maximum involvement and benefits for both.

It was very easy for the sheltered Aloys to think that other people did not care about wealth, because he himself never thought about money. Born affluent, he had never had to think about it. In everything he had ever done, money was an unseen, natural part of it. His parents both had prestigious jobs, and he had been brought up in an intellectual atmosphere where everybody was preoccupied with ideas, and the only time anyone thought about money, was when they were taking up scholarships. At the university, a salary had cocooned him since the moment he had stepped off the boat from student days in Germany. He was Head of Department, his assured money just flowed into the bank, and he did exactly as he pleased. Composing commission followed commission, and as far as grants and bursaries were concerned, he was in the right place. What hustling he did for money with the Arts Council, and in looking for sponsorship for the ballet in Cork, added fun to his artistic life.

In spite of her conviction that she had a percentage of blue blood, she was fully aware that she did not belong in the charmed circle of privilege. With the realism of one born destitute and raised in poverty, Joan had always rightly seen her survival as a dance teacher in terms of money. She was a teacher by default—if she'd been able to fulfil her real desire, she would not have started teaching at all when she was young. If she could have, she would have been a dancer. By opening up the world of grants and subsidies to her, Aloys propagated the idea of her as an artist, so she became a choreographer, and for that she was grateful.

Most importantly for Aloys as a creative artist was the role Joan occupied as his muse. He sent her bouquets as 'tributes', and habitually paid devoted homage to her in romantic style—like his offering of the first laburnum every year to his goddess—but it would have been unthinkable for him to marry her, and not just because he was already married. He would not have wanted her as a wife and partner. He wanted her as a thing apart, and, no matter what the tensions, blistering rows, denigrations and discomfort in his marriage, he was determined to pursue his relationship with Joan inside that framework. Joan and himself were not to be an 'everyday couple'. He wanted the romance and excitement of having her illicitly.

It was an elaborate, if wonderful game, and they both knew perfectly well that his intellect and education went far beyond her own, and that it was he who had the political clout as well as the bravura. He claimed that she 'ruled over' him, but, far from ruling him, she relied totally on his judgement: She would make a tentative suggestion; he would say yes or no, and she would go along with it. When it mattered to him to take a stand, she did exactly as she was told.

In 1976, amateur Ballet Week went ahead as usual. For this, Joan's 1956 short ballet *The Seal Woman* was revived, and Geoffrey Davidson, ballet master in the State Conservatoire in Istanbul, choreographed *Viennese Caprice* and *Scheherazade*. Joan did not have to look far for the guest artistes. From the professional company Richard Collins was once again a guest soloist partnering Julia Cotter, and other male dancers from IBC also performed as guest dancers, including Eric Gibson, Terence Grizzell, and Radu Ciuca. Patricia Crosbie, who also performed as a soloist, was a graduate of the amateur company, and had just been added to the IBC payroll. The amateur company thrived on the accessible professional input, and the luxury of a resident orchestra gave it an edge over the professional company.

'The principal roles were danced with such skill,' wrote Geraldine Neeson in *The Cork Examiner* on Tuesday, 9th November 1976, the morning after opening night, 'that it is neccessary to raise one's critical sights and bring them well above the amateur level. *Corps de ballet*, too, has arrived at a higher level...'

On the same day in the *Echo*, Noeleen Dowling wrote of gasps of admiration and loud applause for Richard Collins' 'almost barbaric dancing, full of acrobatics, fire and brilliance' and Patricia Crosbie's 'very sensitive performance, full of detail and observation'. Seamus Kelly wrote in *The Irish Times* of the 'tremendous reception from an almost full house'. By the following Saturday, in the *Echo*, Robert O'Donoghue was reporting full houses for the week. Once again, Pat Murray had excelled at design, and Maeve Coakley at costumes, and once again, amateur Ballet Week in Cork was a great success.

Back at IBC, *Romeo and Juliet,* amongst other suggestions, had been under discussion for 1977. The professional company also prepared to appear as guests in festivals at home and abroad. There were at least eight or nine choreographers under discussion, including Joan. A full-length ballet was needed. The idea of doing a ballet based on John Synge's classic work *The Playboy of the Western World* was raised. Joan had misgivings. At a board meeting of IBC in the Music Department of UCC, on 2nd September, 1976, Joan had expressed her private reluctance to proceed with it herself. At the foot of her agenda, she wrote:

'Dublin theatre Festival Play Boy? Don't want to go on working.'

Joan was tired. She was around sixty or so years old, diverting her energies, whenever she could, to her amateur company, and surrounded in the professional one by ambitious, aggressive young choreographers actively submitting ideas. *Playboy* was added to the list of new productions, and lighter works were needed to balance it. She told the October 6th board meeting to leave the arrangements for that to her. It was planned for IBC to appear at Cork Opera House in February 1977, and at the Abbey in Dublin in June. At a director's meeting on 17th February 1977, she pencilled-in 1978 for *Playboy*, and also noted the figure £17,000, which in the interim, the company seemed to be down. With estimated total outgoings of £140,000, which included production costs of £3,000 for, *Romeo and Juliet* alone, the estimated total box office receipts were only £13,650. The following day she wrote to Domy, with the assumed responsibility of it all weighing heavily:

'. . . By now you will have received a telegramme from the Board. we had a meeting last night which really shattered all of us! at this the financial position of the Company up to last week showed a huge loss LOSS—add with this, the loss of 1975 (which we are carrying a bank Overdraft for) the position is VERY SERIOUS, and the Goverment (sic) through the Arts Council has said over the last two years that they will NOT stand over any losses that Company s (sic) accrue over and above their grant! We find that we have to cut down on everything, to keep going. and with costs raising (sic), and raising (sic), I just do not know how we are going to manage!

'At the meeting the planing (sic) of the Companys (sic) next productions were discussed backwards and forwards, and the position is this.

'1. We cannot think of doing R&J as we just have not got the money, or the cast to make a success of it

'2. that from now on Ballets must be able to be put on in all theatres and halls. As you know Yerma is a wonderful Ballet, but it has cost us a huge sum of money to put on, for one week in the Abbey last June...

'Now, inview of all our tale of woe, we came to the dicision (sic) that We would ask you if you would be so kind as to create a new dramatic work of 30 minutes for the company, perhaps not using all the dancers, say half, or three quarters as we always have the trouble of not being able to have a good running programme! and over using some dancers and others not enough. If you feel you can do this, give a think to the music, so we will not have to pay big royaltys (sic), please Domy do not think I am tying you, but we just have to cut down, or the company will not continue! If the latter came to pass I feel it would be the end of every thing that we have all been working for!

'Sorry to be so glumy (sic), but I am once again fighting to keep my lifes work alive!!!!!. I hope to see you in Dublin, that is if I get there . . . perhaps we can then discuss any ideas you may have.'

Joan was known amongst the inner circle, for her, 'poor mouth'—she was good at crying poverty; always going round saying how little money there was for productions. She may, therefore, have been laying it on a bit thick to Domy, but even so, her distress shows through.

Dame Ninette de Valois, the founder of the Royal Ballet in Britain, was the valued patron of IBC. A Wicklow woman who had worked with WB Yeats at the Abbey Theatre in the 1920s, and subsequently left Ireland to pursue ballet in England, she would have been in complete sympathy with Joan, although she only ever knew her remotely. The idea that Joan had worked in pantomime and music hall would have held no terrors for Dame Ninette, even if she knew about it, for that was how she herself started dancing in England. Things which would have made her feel that Joan was competent as well as established, were that Joan had attracted very large private sponsorship, as well as a government grant, and that she had an orchestra at her disposal. Equivalent circumstances would have been much more difficult to achieve in England.

Since there was a budget, Dame Ninette could be persuaded to fly to Ireland at IBC's expense for special occasions, but was not keen on speaking. When RTE made a sugary radio programme about IBC in 1977, at which time the professional company was being criticised because most of the participants were imported, the Wicklow woman came forward. Her objective was not to praise, but to gamely tackle the flak. Her few tart words in defence of dancers, stuck out amidst the other, more glowing contributions, but she made no mention of choreographers:

> 'The progress in the last two years is the most marked thing' . . . 'I was really thrilled last night with the performance they gave. There is a great deal of talent in the company. It is all very well to say, "oh, they are not all Irish"; it's got nothing to do with it. It is orientated in Ireland. It is an Irish ballet company. It has its own principals. I hear that it is going to follow through, and what ever country you come from, to join it, you become a member of the Irish Ballet Company, and that is the end of it.'

The Arts Council did not feel it was being kept sufficiently informed of developments within IBC. Requests for information seemed to be met with obfuscating answers from the IBC board, which left them no wiser. Over time, an uneasy need grew amongst those members of the Arts Council who dealt with the company to find out what was happening, and to find out how IBC actually worked. On the 5th April 1977, Colm O'Briain, a representative of the Arts Council, was installed on the IBC board of directors. He emphasised to those present that his presence was in a liaison capacity which would in no way affect decisions to be taken independently by the Board. Miss Moriarty was in London for auditions.

Richard Collins was on the agenda at the board meeting. He wanted more power, and had requested a discussion with Miss Moriarty before signing his contract. He wanted more time off, and wanted his official position in the company improved. He wanted more consultation with management, equal authority with the ballet master, and a means of having his objections on casting or performance taken seriously. It was decided in Miss Moriarty's absence, that, subject to her approval, a further two weeks leave should be given to him, for teaching at the Royal Ballet, but little else, if anything, was conceded.

The Wexford Festival was also on the agenda, for which Domy was to choreograph something. The producer had written complaining that although eight female dancers were available to him for *Orfeo*, he had been offered only one male dancer. Muriel explained that since the Festival had declined to use the full company, the particular group of dancers had been proposed since October 1976. The offer, she said, was based on that group. At his first board meeting, Colm O'Briain was puzzled. Why not more males if Wexford wanted them? According to the minutes of the meeting, he was not only told that the male dancers were tied up with the amateur company, but was reminded of Joan's entitlement to do this:

'The Chairman explained to Mr O'Briain the conditions under which the Government grant had originally been given to the Company.'

Colm O'Briain did not ask whether this practice could hamper the functioning of the professional company but, on this occasion, it clearly was.

Richard Collins, the son of a Canon at St Paul's Cathedral in London, was a charismatic dancer, and he was extremely attractive to women. He could develop a marvellous rapport with a female partner, and he was equally charming and winning to Joan. He was also a triumphant drinker and a womaniser, and he could afford to drink champagne. Wherever the company went, Richard would always spend a lot of time chasing women and generally living it up. Joan was a woman who unhesitatingly refused a lot of dancers, and refused a lot of teachers, but she had a sense, in a world where male dancers were difficult to get, that not only was Richard a valuable dancer, but that he was compatible with herself. For this, she would put up with anything.

When he got drunk and behaved outrageously, or disappeared *en route* to a venue, in pursuit of a woman, and then turned up hours later, having lost his credit cards and his passport, Joan turned a blind eye. She could turn a blind eye to anything she wanted to.

Mostly, the only thing she would talk about with dancers was the production in hand. Everything else was dismissed abstractedly— she was 'too busy' to bother with mundanities. There was an asexual, spinster-like, drawing-room quality to her own work. It was safe, anodyne; it was tepid. There was no passion in her, and there was no passion in her work. The injection of fire and impact into ballets was left to choreographers like Domy; to dancers like Richard. She understood what homosexuality was, she assented on a rare occasion to a group of dancers who were discussing lesbianism; homosexual females? She shook her head. That couldn't be possible.

To the IBC dancers and choreographers, most of whom had come to Ireland from almost the four corners of the dancing world, Joan appeared deeply old-fashioned. Many of them had greater experience than she had. Out of touch with the profession, she was uneasy, and affected a grim veneer to her aloofness that repelled familiarity and questions—but many knew. A dancer could tell by the way she did not take class that she was not willing to teach trained professional dancers. She made it clear, by the vague way she asked one dancer to teach another, that she was unable to spell out the dance steps. And she made it clear by her dismissive attitude, by her constant turning away, by her brushing-off the details, that she was unsure of her ground.

Observers wondered that one who was reputed to be so gifted, so charismatic, could appear so limited; could be so pitiless in her rejections, so unyielding in her refusals. There were no answers.

'Unfortunately,' said manager Tom Donnelly, speaking about touring on a 1977 RTE radio programme about IBC, 'Miss Moriarty, because of many commitments at her schools, can't always be with us. People want to meet her, because she is the myth, the woman who worked for thirty years to establish Irish Ballet Company.' Tom was one of the people who was proud of Miss Moriarty. He was one of the people who would have seen her commitment to her schools as pure dedication. There were others who saw it as a threat.

Publicly, she got top billing, but there was no discernible stamp of herself on the professional company. She had commissioned too many bits and pieces. She needed to justify the Irish Ballet Company, and justify her position in it. Thanks to Aloys, with his tricks of consulting the top people at all times, she was well used to the idea of consorting with big names. Yet, in choosing really big names on which to hang her own choreography for a full-length ballet, scheduled for the following year, she was to expose herself to far wider scrutiny than ever before.

Before the end of 1977, there were huge tributes waiting just around the corner for Joan and Aloys. In October, to mark the forthcoming 'Ruby Production' of the Cork Ballet Company, a 30th Birthday Celebration was held at the Metropole Hotel in Cork, at which the Lord Mayor and Lady Mayoress, Gerald and Sheila Goldberg, were guests of honour. Old friends both, Sheila was also active in the Cork Orchestral Society. The party was arranged by other long-time friends like Hilda Buckley, Meta O'Mullane and Monica Gavin, all of whom would not have dreamed of calling Joan anything other than 'Miss Moriarty'.

'Taoiseachs are dispensable, Lord Mayors are dispensable,' said Taoiseach, Jack Lynch in his speech, as reported in *The Cork Examiner* on October 21st, 'but two people in the city of Cork are totally indispensable, Joan and Aloys.' He went on to talk about the 'remarkable qualities of this single-minded, determined woman, Miss Joan Denise Moriarty, born in Mallow ...'

The main ballet chosen for this ruby production was *Vltava*, the story of the River Vltava, flowing through the city of Prague, in which Joan had appeared as the river-goddess on the magical first night in 1947.

Julia Cotter, a professional dancer with IBC, danced the river-goddess for the week, as a guest artist. Babil Gandara and Eric Gibson were among the IBC dancers who also appeared as guests.

'The soloists,' wrote Geraldine Neeson, in a glowing, 'best performance ever' piece in *The Cork Examiner* on 8th November, 'can take their place with confidence on a professional level in good company.' Under the circumstances, the general public perhaps couldn't sort the professionals from the amateurs, but this careful reviewer of ballet performances was a mature friend of Joan and Aloys, and was close to the ballet. Whether or not she had any idea that the principal soloists she had seen were professionals, and not part of the amateur company, her statement was confusing.

Because of all the patchwork, the changing around, and similarity of company names, with both based in the same place, it was far from clear in the mind of a public for whom ballet was simply ballet, which company was which. Some people watching the professional, heavily grant-aided national company, thought they were seeing the amateur company they'd seen in the fifties. To some extent, they were.

Seamus Kelly was full of praise and superlatives. 'Regrettably,' he finished, in his *Irish Times* review of 8th November, 'Miss Moriarty, who founded it all, failed to take a curtain call.'

She hated taking curtain calls. Perhaps on this occasion her reticence had something to do with the fact that she'd had another fall on brittle bones, and her arm was in plaster. In general, when people making speeches talked about this wonderful woman, she stood regally aside and let them do the talking. The effect was of humility, of reticence, but she did it without yielding any high ground; she acted out her part. On the one hand, if pushed, she could declare herself to be just like anyone else, and say it was all a team effort. On the other, her posture, demeanour, and soft gaze suggested, that what people were dealing with, in herself, was indeed some dark and mysterious force, almost of nature.

She often stood quietly at the edge of the applause, a faint, enigmatic smile on her face. That night was more special than usual. The strains of Smetana's magnificent music had rung out, as they had on the first night Aloys had conducted the whole orchestra especially for her. And tonight, once again, with the glitter of VIPs, the excitement of the special performance, and the house full, he had been conducting for just one person. A special bouquet stood in dressing room number eight, where he had come in, as usual, to fix his bow tie and smooth his hair down before the performance. In her pocket she had a little card, his accolade:

'To My Dearest One
As we journey on, after
thirty years of happiness together,
Like Vltava, to our
ultimate goal—the sea.
— Colm.'

20
The Playboy

*T*he *Playboy of The Western World* was to succeed beyond Joan Denise Moriarty's wildest dreams, at the same time as being the most bafflingly complete failure of her entire career. To many it was a sign that she must indeed be a great Irish artist; to others it only provided conclusive evidence at last, that her calibre was seriously substandard.

The company was fêted at home and abroad over the *Playboy*, applauded by most critics in Ireland, and savaged by some in England and America. In the event, and long after it, Joan, Aloys and many other people, could never understand why *Playboy* did not elevate her at last to the ranks of the great. To the end of her career, she and her supporters continued to point to it as an example of her work at its best. It also paraded her weaknesses. When in later years, Joan would ask repeatedly, 'Have I succeeded, or haven't I?', her confusion and bewilderment were real. At the end of it all, she—along with Aloys and her close, inner circle—genuinely didn't know where, if at all, she had gone wrong.

During the preparations for *Playboy*, which was to be premiered in the capital city under the sponsorship of the Dublin Theatre Festival later in the year, Joan was tired, she had a broken arm, and she was not contributing to the current IBC season. Other choreographers, mainly Domy Reiter-Soffer, and Toni Beck, had prepared several short pieces for the IBC spring season, and her own *Devil to Pay,* as well as Domy's *Chariots of Fire* had been revived.

Having an employed set of people, from the professional manager downwards, rather than a crew of devoted volunteers, made both Joan and Aloys very uneasy. A professional company was an unwieldy enterprise, and in his opinion, dancers were a demanding breed. Compared to CBC, he felt that the whole of IBC were what he called 'incredibly difficult people'. There was also the matter of Joan's ill-health. But there was another reason why Aloys was despondent in 1978. It was that he was to receive the honour of being made a

Freeman of the City of Cork. The problem for him was that there was to be no mention of Joan. He felt that his acceptance without recognition for her would not be right. He needed to get something for her, and immediately prepared for battle. He did not intend to let her down.

His own career was in a different class from Joan's. He was Head of the Music Department at UCC, and was still the director of the Choral Festival, the chairman of the Cork Orchestral Society, and the conductor of the Cork Symphony Orchestra, which had engagements other than that of Ballet Week. He also remained a member of the Irish National Commission for UNESCO, and a member of the Advisory Committee for Cultural Relations of the Department of Foreign Affairs. He was chairman of the Music Teachers' Association, chairman of the Cork Ballet Company, and vice-chairman of the IBC. In 1961 he had become chairman of the Cork Sculpture Park, and had been a member of the Royal Irish Academy since 1966.

He was involved in many other things—he conducted concerts, composed, lectured extensively, and it is no exaggeration to say that he went straight from one thing to another, all day long, every day. His articles featured in music and academic publications, and his political letters littered the pages of the popular press. Since the 1960s, he had been working on his mammoth work, *Sources of Traditional Music 1583–1855*. He was tirelessly gracious to students, and generous with his time for them. He held the amateur orchestra together, mainly by charm, and choirs responded to his style. He had taken over the music scene started in Cork by his parents, and music had thrived under his influence. Aloys had been awarded the Silver Medallion of the Irish–American Cultural Institute in 1973, and the United Dominions Trust National Endeavour Award in 1976, for his promotion of tourism.

Friend and ballet fan, Gus Healy, a Cork Lord Mayor who was later appointed to the board of the IBC shared Aloys' view and concern about the Freeman question. It was also his wish that Aloys and Joan be conferred together, not that one should be refused. When Gus and Aloys tried to insist on Joan's inclusion, they were advised that a Cork-born person may not be made Freeman, and that whilst Munich-born Aloys qualified on those grounds, Joan, being born in the County of Cork, had been ruled out. Gus complained to Jack Lynch.

They agreed this was nonsense, since Jack himself had been made a Freeman of the city, and he had been born in Cork. Neither was he the first Freeman of Cork who had been born in the county.

In June, Joan travelled to Dublin to welcome Dame Ninette de Valois, who had travelled to Ireland at the IBC's expense, to the opening of two weeks of ballet excerpts at The Abbey.

Joan, far from feeling confident about the work she had in hand, was in no mood to stick her neck out. 'I'm in no hurry to go to London', she told Richard Davies in a summer 1978 issue of *Classical Music Weekly*, in an interview to mark the fifth year of the IBC.

'Everybody wants to run to London, but there, and in New York, one failure and you're finished—it takes five years to recover. I've seen too many companies who have folded up because of that. We're booked up to 1980 ...We were invited to New York, but I have not accepted...In England, they don't know much about us, and I want the company to mature first before they see us. Walk before you run. It's very easy to shoot at the highlights, but it's very hard to stay there.'

Before the year was out *Playboy* was to be staged in New York, and the following spring, to appear in Sadler's Wells, London.

It was reported that Joan Denise Moriarty had been intending to do the *Playboy* for twenty years. At the same time, it was reported that she had never once seen a stage production of Synge's internationally known play. She didn't want to.

'She has done this deliberately,' wrote Seamus Kelly in *The Irish Times*, on 4th July 1978, 'on the premise that knowledge of a stage presentation might affect her choreography, which she hopes will come off with more originality if she bases her dance treatment of the theme purely on the text.'

The beauty and richness of the language contained in *Playboy*, was one reason why people were dubious about Synge's work being successfully translated into any dance form. Admiration for Irish playwright John Synge, particularly abroad, was all about the language he used and his reputation naturally would have been based on what was considered to be his extraordinary gift for inspired, authentic dialogue, as well as the presentation of strange, quirky philosophies full of fascination. Amongst admirers *Playboy* ranged from being considered his masterpiece, to being taken with a grain of approving salt.

His detractors tended to be Irish cultural nationalists, often living in Ireland, and included those who would have strong feelings against his work. Synge was accused bitterly and repeatedly down the years, of conspiring in the worst sort of stage-Irishness.

Aloys would have had enough confidence in Joan, and would have known little enough about ballet, not to worry about the question of translating Synge's extraordinarily moving dialogue into dance. Whether he thought to alert Joan to the possible stage-Irish pitfall of tackling Synge's Irish characters and their sentiments, or whether, if he even considered it, he felt that pondering such niceties of offence would be unneccessarily splitting artistic hairs, is not known.

But although the project was given advance publicity, there was never at any point, any discussion or evaluation of the theme in public, either by Joan, or by any feature writer. It was merely stated that she was doing *Playboy*; that she had first thought of it during a holiday in the Aran Islands, where Synge had collected much material, and that she had never seen the play.

The Chieftains' music had, in 1977, been used for the short *Lugh of the Golden Arm*, and had given the dance performance a vital ethnic dimension. The Chieftains had become hugely popular by 1978, with box office appeal on an international scale, and it was an obvious move for Joan to try to hitch her own heavily-subsidised wagon to their star. They were an approachable, obliging crowd, they were the biggest and best she could have wished for, and they had Cork connections. The late Sean O'Riada, whose music Joan had used for previous ballets, had been a founder member, and had performed with the Chieftains, until his appointment to UCC in the sixties. Another reason they would have been enthusiastic to join in, was that she would have appealed, with such an Irish project, to their sense of Irishness. In addition to this, Joan would have deserved their respect as a most unusual musician, a female piper. When Joan asked Paddy Moloney and the rest of the band whether she might employ them for *Playboy*, they gave permission for her to use any of their music that was already recorded, and offered to provide links, and write whatever additional music might be needed.

The work was not actually a ballet; there was no dancing *en pointe*. It was an anecdotal mime of the text, and manual gesture was the main vehicle of expression. The dance repertoire consisted of slight variations on three basic steps. These were Irish steps, but without the complexity and diversity of the true traditional form.

This robbed the steps of the sense of virtuosity that is possible in the Irish dance framework. An absence of creativity is another striking feature of the restricted traditional Irish form, which might in this case, have been transformed by explorations of the theatrical and creative strengths of classical dance. That would have been the challenge—to draw on the great strengths of both and transcend limitations.

In the choreography of *Playboy,* there was to be no intensity of fusion, no exciting breaking free of forms, no harnessing of primitive undercurrents, no flowering alliance of the raw with the refined, no symbolism, no exaltations and erotic tensions implicit in the bodily arts. It was as if, with her vapid, non-sensual, drawing-room approach, Joan had simply watered everything down.

Of all the music Joan might have chosen from the Chieftain's magnificent repertoire, and of the additional special-effects and embellishments she might have commissioned from them, she chose a series of very similar tunes almost all of which seemed to be the same frenetic, wearing, too long jig. In doing so, she robbed the Chieftain's music of its impact, and made them sound eventually, not only samey and boring, but irritating. Her reasoning might have been that she wanted to base it on a 1-2-3 step, and although this factor ended up working with her, the whole thing ended up seeming like a massed, tiresome, and interminable jig.

It was a great big theme though, and the great big names were there. It was Synge's famous play, taking a new form, and it included the wonderful Chieftains, whom everyone wanted to see. It was the Irish Ballet Company, whose patron was the Irishwoman, Dame Ninette de Valois. Pat Murray's Irish costume designs, made up from traditional fabrics added hugely to this celebration of Irishness— Irish audiences loved it.

Taoiseach Jack Lynch opened the Dublin Theatre Festival. The dressed-up opening night of the Irish Ballet Company's contribution to it, took place at the Olympia Theatre, and the premiere ended with stamping and cheering approval (*Cork Echo* 10/2/79). 'They were dancing in the aisles,' said Aloys Fleischmann, with satisfaction.

In *The International Herald–Tribune* (Paris 10/10/78), Noel Goodwin, who knew the stage play, reported that Chieftains' fans, and IBC fans, had made *Playboy* the 'hottest ticket' of the festival, and was repeatedly quoted in the Cork papers. 'Despite a certain amount of repetitive dancing,' he went on, 'there was hardly a dull moment.'

John Finegan of the *Evening Herald* (3/10/78) wrote that the audience was on its feet at the end, applauding frantically, the stage littered with flowers thrown from the boxes and stalls. Members of the Chieftains, he added, were dancing with the ballet stars.

Ireland Today, the bulletin of the Department of Foreign Affairs, (15/11/78), reported that *Playboy* was a 'splendid native production which could not have happened without Festival encouragement and backing ... it delighted overflow audiences ... something new and of exceptional quality has been created'.

The odd dissenting voice was an echo of old Irish–English antipathies. John Percival, of *The Times* in London, was irritated by this 'strong appeal to patriotic emotions', where the 'national flavour is just a little too determined'. He blamed Synge '. . . the prototype stage Irishman was invented by the country's own authors, not imposed as a caricature by foreigners, and they do not come any more Irish, or any more stagy, than in the *Playboy*'. Even with the Chieftains' skill, he felt, 'one jig or reel sounds rather like another when you have two solid hours of them . . . The only trouble is that, once on stage, there seems little response to any situation but another jig.'

Impresario, Noel Pearson, who would later be associated with the Irish movies *My Left Foot* and *The Field*, immediately signed up the *Playboy* for New York. He knew nothing about dance, but had seen the festival audience's reaction to it, and was told the production was respectable, which it was. Not everyone went along with the instinctive flow.

Colm O'Briain, who represented the Arts Council on the board of IBC, was a man who had a passion for ballet, about which he had some knowledge. He felt disloyal to the company; more than willing to be fair and supportive, his truth was that he didn't like *Playboy*. He was not the only one. There were cynics about, and Joan was a stranger in Dublin. In Cork you would hear her friends as well as her enemies talking, but in the arts world of the capital city, Joan had cultivated no friends. The Irish Ballet Company was a big show to be putting on the road, and it was trundling up to the metropolis from a couple of hundred miles away in Cork. 'Joan who?,' asked some.

The success of the *Playboy* satisfied Aloys. Using its acclaim as a lever, he had been busy behind the scenes arranging things for her, and he too had succeeded.

Seamus Kelly, *Irish Times* writer and longtime supporter of Joan and the ballet, had been recruited. He also approached Jack Lynch. What could be done about the Freedom of Cork and Joan? Jack had no influence over it. Then if Joan was not going to be made a Freeman, Seamus argued, couldn't she be given an honorary doctorate to compensate for this failure to recognise her work in the city? Jack Lynch felt that Joan richly deserved this, and duly had a word with a member of the Senate of the National University of Ireland, with whom he was friendly, and argued for Joan's investiture. Before any CV or any credentials or any scrap of a newspaper clipping about Joan's work reached the desk of the President's office, the answer came back to Aloys from the NUI in the affirmative: Joan was to be given an honorary doctorate. It was in the bag. As the amateur company prepared for curtain-up on Ballet Week 1978 in Cork, Aloys' annual present to Joan was accompanied by the following happy note, anticipating his crowning gift to her:

'To My darling,

'In the most fantastic of seasons—of Playboy, Princess and another honour to come—in love and admiration.

From Colm.'

By the time the IBC opened their spring season in 1979, with an extended two week season, during which they would perform *Playboy* before taking it to New York, Aloys was provoked to greater flatteries of Joan, in a mood to affirm his allegiance to her, and to acknowledge the professional company. He wrote:

'Opera House Feb 1979. Miss Joan Moriarty
'To my darling
On our 6th IBC season together.
I had planned the Margot
Fonteyn latest autobiography—
As of one Queen to another—
But the wretched post wrecked that.
So some red flowers
Instead—Red for love
and devotion.
Colm.'

The Cork run was heralded by an enthusiastic Seamus Kelly in *The Irish Times* (10/2/79), who considered the 'sparkling combination' by 'Moriarty–Moloney', an 'outstanding triumph'. It arrived at the Opera House to a standing ovation.

At the Civic Center in chilly New York, the atmosphere was different. Advance notice had attracted a dance audience, and it was not well received by ballet lovers. Clive Barnes, of the *New York Post*, did not like it at all, and another particularly scathing review by an American dance writer analysed the production classically piece by piece to terrible effect.

Aloys later told the story that on arrival in America, Joan had been forced to take out her personal cheque book and write a cheque for two thousand pounds to pay the dancers because they were ungratefully refusing to go on stage and threatening to go on strike for more pay. This story was intended to illustrate that the IBC dancers were incredibly difficult to manage, and had a tyrannical relationship with the besieged and generous Joan. The truth was that, according to union rules in America, a certain basic rate had to be paid to performing dancers, and IBC dancers were paid below this rate.

Arts Council money could not be used outside the country, and the trip had been paid for by sponsorship, which included a grant of £2,000 for air fares which Aloys had extracted from the Department of Cultural Relations. The ballet company had managed to get Equity in Ireland, to agree to the dancers travelling on Irish wages, but American rules would have none of it. Joan merely paid up on behalf of the company, but Aloys claimed that she had paid the money out of her own pocket. It was Noel Pearson who lost money.

In Ireland the response to *Playboy* was instinctive. Whether the production worked or not, the hugely important thing that this Irish event did for the Irish consciousness, was that it cut an old enemy down to size and in doing so, it thumbed its nose at the ancient matter of foreign oppression, in all its forms. Here was this alien, bare-all, sensual form of dance expression, for centuries dreaded and preached against as a primary immoral influence on the population, suddenly being transformed by a well-known tale of Irish guile, and being not only safely earthed by the most elementary of Irish dance steps, but being itself bewitched, by the most quintessential Irish element of them all—music.

When the incessant music became hypnotic, folk-memory clicked in. Where had all this whirling madness happened before? It had happened countless times in the realm of myth—in stories of infancy. In the books of schooldays, never-ending dancing is an element of stories of the fairies. The sheer interminableness of the music; the monotonousness of it, provided a never-ending, inside-the-mountain atmosphere, reminiscent of the stories all Irish people grow up with, of little people capturing mortals, and playing music to them all night long, and letting them out in the morning, years later.

The *Playboy* was the trickster. This was the victory, and this was the subconscious Irish secret of it. This was the reason why some could love it passionately and others view it with deep disdain. It was a fleeting, elusive, sub-gut response, and it was never articulated. No analysis was ever made of the significance of Joan's *Playboy*, but it was the nearest she ever came to producing art.

Joan was not in America to see how badly it was received by a classical audience. As the show opened, she was flying back to Ireland on a first-class ticket to meet Aloys in Dublin, and to join Jack and Mairin Lynch for the conferring of her honorary Doctor of Laws degree at Iveagh House.

She stayed on in Dublin for a few days, because inevitably, with *Playboy* going on in New York and her LLD being conferred in the same week, she had come to the notice of the *Late Late Show*, and was due on Friday night to be interviewed by host Gay Byrne, on the most watched chat show on Irish television.

21
Cresting the Myth

'We have been receiving many and variable garbled accounts of the reception for *Playboy* in New York,' said *Late Late Show* host Gay Byrne to Joan, on live television. 'What is the latest word as far as you are concerned?'

'Well,' said Joan brightly, 'at half past seven this morning I got a telephone call from New York, from our General Manager, to say that last night the house was full, and we received a standing ovation at the end. So that is the absolute latest news that I have.'

So far, so good. Gay's introduction of Joan had pointed out that it had been 'a traumatic and interesting week', but Joan's publicity machine had been at work, and Gay had also been handed the myth on a plate. His introduction of her to the show had contained the lies that were by now a regular feature of media coverage of Joan's life. He said that she had started ballet dancing at the age of six, whilst on a visit from Cork to London with her mother, and had decided on the spot that dancing was to be her life.

'Since then,' Gay went on, 'she has ploughed a very lone furrow, with very little backing or encouragement from anybody in Ireland. She has ploughed a lone furrow in the cause of dance and ballet dancing in Ireland. Now she is receiving recognition, but there were many sparse and lean years when she did not receive any recognition at all.'

Since Joan was responsible for allowing this story to be put out, and for allowing it to spread unchecked so widely, it is a wonder that none of her devoted supporters, who had given her so much, and shored her up so well, ever accused her of disloyalty, and failure to acknowledge the enormous support she had enjoyed from so many individuals over the previous thirty years work that had led to this.

It is also a wonder that this 'lone furrow' story was never challenged by her very many generous sponsors in Cork and elsewhere, on the grounds that it was deeply insulting to the people who had provided her with the thousands upon thousands of pounds that she had used to put on lavish ballet productions over many, many years. Joan's fleeting lean years had been before anyone knew her; they were nothing to do with the ballet, and there had never been any lone furrow. The list of supporters was endless, from the O'Connor family's early generosity, to the work of skilled people like Aloys, Jennie, Jamie, Mrs Hunt, and the rest of the volunteers, and thirty years of free service from the whole Cork orchestra. Mairin and Jack Lynch had been ardent and unstintingly influential supporters since Joan's first ballet performance in 1947, and had that very week sent a telegram of good wishes to Joan in America, through the Consulate General of Ireland in New York.

She had mentioned her general manager. Tom Donnelly was the sort of highly articulate, charming talker that radio journalists would immediately latch on to. He was extremely good at the blarney. The tone of his languid anecdotes happened to deify Joan, but his talk was also frank and off-the-cuff. He seemed to believe that the world owed Joan a living. Tom had said, during a radio interview in Cork, that the government subsidy in 1973, was:

'a tribute to her life's work—twenty-six years of uphill struggle, and the tragedy that she lost all her dancers in 1964. It was a tragedy, they all emigrated. They've done very well, but as a result of this, the government gave her a grant.'

This reference to Irish Theatre Ballet shows clearly the compensation theory of recognition. Tom spoke of the tremendous sense of occasion on opening nights, the dress suits, the coiffeurs, the 'enthralled, proud' audience, that had 'rarely experienced such pleasure'. Joan Denise Moriarty, he would say, inspires awe and admiration, and so does the Irish Ballet Company. This talented man could go on endlessly. In a sense, there was a great ring of truth to what he said. Audiences were enthralled; Joan did inspire awe. With the chemistry of the colours, the lights, the fabrics, the sets, and the music, ballet is transforming. Whilst he was with IBC, Tom was the charming, fairy-tale, PR face of it all, and he put this aspect across wonderfully. Joan wasn't in it for the same reason as the audience.

Gay Byrne next made an opening reference to the unfavourable reviews *Playboy* was getting in New York, but Joan was ready to savage the savager:

'Clive Barnes was not all that kind to you, this dreadful man.'

'Well, you know,' began Joan, 'he used to be the drama critic for *The New York Times*, but to use the American expression, he 'gutted' so many companies there, that in the end the companies all said, "please don't come and review our performances at all; we don't want you". Because he really literally broke up companies, who went financially—crashed, and everything, and he is no longer with *The New York Times*. I don't know whether he was exactly sacked or anything like that.' She continued, her voice mellow, 'but he is not there. But he is now drama critic of *The New York Post* which has a fairly small sale.

'Well, we were a little bit unfortunate that he was sent to us for our critic from that particular paper, and the reason being that of course the ballet is based on a play, so that is how we got him.'

'On a technicality, yes,' agreed Gay, chivalrously.

The interview went on.

'Do you feel bitter that you got very little backing,' asked Gay, in innocence.

'Not at all,' she answered promptly, with the assurance of someone accustomed to her views being sought. 'I think it is all a process of growing. I was very young at that time. I have no bitterness. I was sensible enough to realise, first and foremost I realised, the health wasn't good. The boys selling papers were barefooted. I thought, I will continue, I will try, but first things first—you must get better education; you must get a better standard of living and health, and I think that has come. It is one of the great pleasures that I have, when I go round to our schools, to see the wonderful healthy children bubbling over with vitality and looking marvellous. That I find wonderful.'

This was disingenuous. The children in all Joan's classes had always been healthy. Right from the start, with term fees and mandatory uniforms, Joan had seen that only middle-class kids applied. The boys selling newspapers on the street may well once have been barefoot, but the paper-boy sector was never one she cultivated. She had never given any thought to ways of including working-class children. It would have been a less outrageous suggestion if she had said that numbers in her schools had increased because more ordinary people had now become affluent, but that would have been admitting to a middle-class orientation.

'There is a lot of foreign blood in the IBC, said Gay. Is that deliberate?'

'Yes,' she replied. 'I would never like it to be 100% Irish. I think mixed blood, like we have in our Radio Éireann Orchestra, which is so marvellous; mixed blood can give you a new style, a new vision, a new emotion, particularly in dance. It is very good that way. That is why I would like to keep it. I would like a few more Irish dancers, but it is only now we are really starting to get fully trained. It is no good me taking a dancer just because they happen to be Irish. That's no good; they've got to have a standard. That is what we are fighting for now...'

It was a way of hitting back at the critics who were complaining that the Irish national company, with only 25% of Irish dancers, was far from Irish. A female dancer's career, she stated, was over at age thirty-five. But what about Dame Ninette? asked Gay. Joan interrupted him.

'—not Dame Ninette, Dame Margot Fonteyn. She is a legend. After all, it is her artistry now that carries her, rather than technical dancing. That is the difference. She is a great artist'.

This was followed by a snippet from the myth machine. 'You strike me as a woman who just doesn't have 'can't' in her vocabulary,' said Gay.

'I think all my friends here will say that. That is the one word that I don't have in my dictionary. There is no such thing as 'can't'. You can do anything you want to do, provided you have the determination. Maybe you have to compromise a little bit on where you wanted to get to. The only thing I won't compromise on is the standard of the work artistically. That is the point. But you can— Ireland is a wonderful country for opportunity, provided you are going to work, and work means work. There is no five day week.'

After this dig at the dancers, Joan introduced the word 'dance'. 'I don't use the word ballet any more. Ballet conjures up a nineteenth century classical ballet, like *Swan Lake* or *Giselle*, which I can understand a lot of men hate. But you have all the contemporary work, as we do in our own company. We have jazz ballets, rock, discotheque. It is dance more than ballet. Ballet is the wrong word.'

Ballet for Joan had been very much the right word, when she had been nailing her colours to the mast. It was true that choreographers like Domy Reiter-Soffer and the others were a modern influence, but now that she was exposed to criticism from classicists she was disowning ballet and calling it 'dance', as a way of trying to deflect purist evaluation. From now on she kept at this, urging people to use the word 'dance' instead of ballet. It was at this point—and even well before it—that if she'd had enough independent creativity and courage of her own, she could have opted for the truly *avant garde*.

She had an ideal framework to encourage dance forms from other sources.

Her sweeping views on the Irish as dancers, as she gave them on the *Late Late Show,* appeared nonsensical, as well as racist.

'Irish people have a great advantage in that they are very musical, and emotionally, they are great actors and actresses. We have difficulties physically. We have rather weak backs, slightly curved, which is the first thing we have to try and straighten. The feet are not altogether pliable, which means a lot of hard work on the feet again, but then we make up for it in musicality and emotion.'

'You mean,' wondered Gay in disbelief, 'we have less straight backs than English people?'

'Yes, that is quite true. The English have marvellous flexible feet; very straight backs on the whole, but are far less emotional. They are very straight —'

Gay interrupted, heading her off. 'You mentioned this emotional tie up. I think you need this fire in the gut to drive you on.'

'You must, you must, you must have it for dance. Dance is a silent thing...'

'Alas methinks we lack the work ethic,' Gay prodded.

'—well, this is another little thing, you see. I think it is changing now, a lot. In the beginning it was, [breaking into a false Irish country accent] "sure it'll be alright tomorrow; it'll be alright tomorrow". We are very ambitious and want to get there, but—in my world, anyway, it is changing now. I think the young people are realising you don't get there quickly.'

Quite what this means isn't clear, but it was at least another racist allusion. In New York, the *Playboy* was falling down around their ears, but on *The Late Late Show,* Joan had bluffed it all through. From the lies about her childhood, through the myth of her mission, to the nonsense of her views on dancers, it was all over in a few minutes, and she was finally and fully on the national media map. From now on the whole of Ireland would know who Joan Denise Moriarty was. The following morning, Joan flew on a first-class ticket back to New York, to see at first hand how *Playboy* was faring.

In New York, the Chieftains, who by now could command huge Irish-American support in their favourite touring city, where they had lots of friends, and were always well received, were seeing at first hand, as whistle player Sean Potts put it, 'the power of the critics'. The verdict of Clive Barnes of the *New York Post*, meant, people felt, that New Yorkers stayed away in crowds. Noel Pearson was losing money. Friends in the city later told Sean Potts (*Sunday Press* [10/6/79]) that they would have gone to see it if it hadn't been described as ballet.

For the second week, the promotion tack was changed, to appeal to the ethnic sector. It was to be an Irish event, rather than a dance event, and with a strong Irish slant on publicity, the Irish-American population was tapped, and audiences for the second week improved to the point where they became reasonably good, but not on anything like the scale that the Chieftains normally enjoyed.

After not succeeding in America, Joan's feelings when she returned to Cork must have been fragile, as well as confused by the simultaneous high praise in Ireland. Aloys, the primary exponent of the compensation theory of recognition, the man who had orchestrated the honorary doctorate she had in her pocket as a compensation to her, was ready as usual to sweep reality away. Determined now, to call the bruising excursion to New York a victory, he was looking forward to spending time alone with her on the evening of her arrival:

'Miss Joan Denise Moriarty, LLD.
My Darling!
A 100 thousand welcomes
to our victorious Queen—
battle-weary surely, and
what a battle!
Shall ring, and then call
to-night
love
Colm.'

Having already been carried by sponsorship to New York against her own instincts, Joan was minded to think twice before venturing out again, but a prestigious sponsored international gig came up. The biggest Irish festival ever staged anywhere was in the offing, to take place in London, and the Irish Ballet Company was invited to appear for the first time in London, at Sadler's Wells Theatre, as part of the Sense of Ireland Festival, sponsored by Waterford Crystal.

The festival was to cover north and south, involving over 90 separate events in music, literature, theatre, visual arts, cinema, dance, crafts, design, photography, architecture and archaeology. It was to take place from 1st February to 15th March, at 42 different venues, including the Royal Albert Hall, The British Museum, and the Royal Festival Hall. Participants ranged from the RTE and the Ulster Orchestras to rock bands, Thin Lizzy and the Boomtown Rats; literary figures included Seamus Heaney, Edna O'Brien and Brian Friel. The Chieftains were also included in their own right, in the traditional music section, and were confidently expected to fill the prestigious Royal Albert Hall on the 5th February. There was a rush for tickets for the Chieftains and for Irish mod-trad group, Planxty.

Joan wanted to appear at the Irish Festival, because she could not pass up the opportunity to appear at Sadler's Wells, a most prestigious ballet venue with the capacity to hold 1450 people, but she was undecided about which ballet to take. It would be the first time an Irish professional company had danced at Sadler's.

If she had put on something contemporary of Domy's, she could have hidden behind it, but Domy's work was already showcasing in Chicago, and as far as any other ballet egos were concerned, the dynamic Richard Collins had already decided to get out and had left the company. In London there was the Irish exile factor to be taken into account and Joan, assisted by the adoration surrounding her, could not resist it. It was decided that for their first London season, 4–8th March, *Playboy* would be ideal for a captive Irish audience at this Irish event.

The Who's Who of celebrities at the opening night was headed by Sadler's Wells incumbent, Dame Ninette de Valois. Eamonn Andrews and Cyril Cusack were there, and Irish Minister for Foreign Affairs, Brian Lenihan. The Irish Ambassador, Dr Eamonn Kennedy, actor TP McKenna, and Mr and Mrs George Crosbie of *The Cork Examiner* attended. Brendan Smith, director of the Dublin Theatre Festival also attended the ballet. Aloys travelled to London for the occasion. This was Joan's opportunity to invite her old friends, and Ethel Beare, friend from the very early days in Cork, was delighted to come down from Manchester to see, and to be part of, Joan's success. George and Maureen Collins were also invited. Joan's godson and Aloys' son, Alan and his wife, Vanessa, who lived in England, were also invited by Joan.

In London, *Playboy*, as part of a mammoth Irish event, did 100% business, with the Chieftains playing a big part in its success.

Audiences were enthusiastic. But this time there was not just cosy Irish reporting. *Playboy* was at the mercy of the English critics.

'The company has, in a way, cheated,' wrote Ian Woodward, in an overall favourable review. 'There is no real ballet dancing as such... no point work, and no way of judging, therefore, the dancers' technical strength... If you do not know the plot... then you must read the programme... The music was charming at first but eventually wore me down.'

Irish exile, Maeve Binchy, reported for *The Irish Times* (6/3/80). Maeve quoted mainly approving reviews, mentioning the capacity houses. '*The Times* was not so enthusiastic,' she wrote, quoting: "even the tender passages revert to jig time ... and the choreography as a whole lacks mood and inflection... It was cheerful and apt, but I am afraid most jigs sound alike to me".'

In the *Sunday Telegraph*, (9/3/80), Nicholas Dromgoole hated it. He wrote:

'Synge's play about credulity and ignorance in Ireland's primitive country areas.. caused riots in Dublin in 1907, and again among Irish Patriots in America in 1911. It would be difficult to guess why from the Irish Ballet's frenetically cheerful dance version. Nobody seems to stop, and like those relentlessly cheerful folk dance groups, a grimly determined smile forever plastered on their faces, everybody just goes on and on. The Chieftains' score does its best to provide variety, but there is finally a depressing sameness and a pneumatic drill quality about the music that makes it all sound like a never-ending Irish jig. Every movement acquires the same exaggerated pantomime quality. Anybody pointing at anything, points not once but three times. Anybody nodding, gives at least four nods. Every domestic article becomes the excuse for a frantic dance, a broom, a bottle, a plucked hen, a coat, etc. Yet in all this galvanic activity...the Irish Ballet never seemed to create a step; and ultimately its attempt to hide this by dancing every routine step three times over, seemingly at three times the speed, fails to convince.... a pity the London showing is restricted to... this limited work... sets and costumes imaginative...company looked technically accomplished, and worked with a praiseworthy vigour at their sadly intractable material.'

A favourable review appeared in *The Stage and Television Today*, two weeks later, on 20th March 1980, written by 'A.N.':

'Many people were disappointed by the IBC's debut at Sadler's ... but I found myself rather impressed by the honest craftsmanship.'

The Dancing Times in England was the one to watch, for this organ of the ballet world has authority and prestige. In the April issue, writer 'MC' noted that the theatre was sold out, the audiences were full of enthusiasm, and the press were somewhat guarded.

> '. . . and the notices which found least to enjoy in the *Playboy* urged the company to return with a sampling of their full repertory. About such a return visit I would be cautious. Without the Chieftains and without the lure of such a popular title I think the little company might find London a rather tougher nut.'

Whilst the company were away in London, the Evening Press in Ireland (6/3/80), reported that a person called Janet Lewis had announced the start of Dublin City Ballet.

As soon as Joan returned to Cork, she began writing letters of thanks. There appeared to be no confusion in her mind. She wrote to supporters dismissing the antics and stressing that '1,500 people at each performance can't be wrong.'

Joan's hope of returning to London in the near future was a vain one. Perhaps the folk-dance experience in Europe had given her a misplaced assurance, as well as an equally misplaced tendency to believe that the same song and the same step would suffice every time. Festivals in Europe were still the safe avenue to complacent performing that they had always been, where there was a budget, a happy climate in celebration of European unity, and a complete absence of critical scrutiny. *Playboy* would go to Rennes, but after the London debut, there was to be no return to Sadler's Wells, ever.

22

Crisis

Joan's relationship with the professional dancers was not good. She was gracious and she was regal, and she inspired love as well as awe in many of the amateur dancers, but she was aloof, and she distanced herself greatly from the professionals in many ways.

She never gave class, she did not mix, she kept the dancers ill-informed of company developments and morale was low. Busy with her own company and her schools, Joan did not go touring with the company unless it was near Cork. She was not entirely responsible for wages being so small, or for touring conditions being below reasonable standards, but for many years dancers were not allowed representation at board level and had no voice at all.

Joan, who would even ask a journalist to use the title Miss Moriarty, was referred to facetiously behind her back by some company members as 'Madame'. This satire was because Marie Rambert, who was French, was naturally known by her pupils as 'Madame', and Dame Ninette de Valois was entitled, by virtue of her DBE, to be addressed as 'Madam'.

The male dancers were paid more than the female dancers, and the more important dancers of both sexes were paid accordingly. There was some playing-off on Joan's part, of the professionals against the amateurs. 'These are trained, professional dancers', she would say to the novices, whenever a visit from some of the professional company was in the offing. The young ones were intimidated. To salaried dancers she would say, 'my own company dance because they love it, and not for money'. It was true that a lot of pupils and ex-pupils in her own company had stars in their eyes, but Joan thought paid dancers were spoilt. She took refuge in feigning disdain for the capabilities of dancers, and coolly fostered unease between the two companies.

Whenever the professionals made demands for better conditions, Joan sweetly told them that, not only was it different in her day, but her own dancers would still put up with any amount of privation. It was as though she did not properly respect the working dancers. Her ideas did not always translate easily into movement, but she could belittle a dancer who had difficulties. It was her technique to single out one dancer to demonstrate steps to another, in a way which could make both dancers feel uncomfortable.

The amateur company, which had an orchestra every time they went to perform in the Opera House, did have a certain edge over the professional one though, which was dependant on recorded music played over a sound system that was prioritised neither for quality nor for servicing.

When light and sound were under review, company engineers were asked to investigate, and submitted meticulous reports on the defective state of equipment. Since the board consisted of loyal supporters of Joan and top management employees who were expressly contracted to carry out her wishes, final decisions were often down to Joan, and the whole board waited for her ruling. She agreed to the replacement of some sound equipment, but ruled against the lighting, on the grounds that both at once would be too expensive. It was a matter of rule-by-whim. The lighting badly needed upgrading, but whilst the subject of lights was under discussion, she had her own delaying solution. Pointing out that the ESB electricity bill was too high, she suggested that a great deal of money could be saved if lights were put off when studio or other rooms were not being used. The message was, that if only dancers would penny-pinch, money might be found for new lighting equipment. In terms of a professional touring company with a sizeable budget it was madness.

For the professionals, the studio floor was uncomfortably cold for dancing, and the heating was an ongoing problem. Out around the country it was worse. The company would sometimes arrive at a venue to find inadequate changing facilities, poor heating, and sometimes, as in venues at Ballina, Galway and Nenagh on the autumn tour in 1981, just one toilet to share between all the dancers. They got ready in cold dressing rooms with concrete floors, and danced on unsprung stages.

The dancers and stage manager wrote independent painstaking reports on the 1981 tour in an attempt to have their grievances heard. The stage manager, Mark Galbraith, wrote of electric shocks to himself from the faulty wiring he had to deal with, and the real danger to dancers from the electrics, and from the seriously defective state of some of the vans the company hired. Mark argued for the provision of a company vehicle as well as a tour manager to look after the dancers. He also wanted consultation on tour schedules, because some venues were impossibly far apart. Instead of performing at a different venue each day, he said, the company needed two days to fit up, and performances should start on the second day.

The dancers' report contained verdicts on conditions in halls as ranging from 'dirty' through 'very dirty' to 'filthy'. Almost everywhere was too cold for dancing, and resulted in injuries, and recurrences of old injuries, to dancers' feet, legs, hips and backs. The lead dancer, Wayne Aspinall, once had to wash his hair in cold water after dancing, and another time had to boil a kettle to wash away his make-up. Six months later Mark Galbraith left. Wayne Aspinall soon followed.

On one icy winter occasion, the dancers finally went on strike because it was far too cold to perform their warm-up exercises. Management could have alleviated many of the problems the company found around the country, but dancers were expected to simply put up with miserable performing conditions. In Aloys' mind, the strike was remembered as unreasonable.

Where something could be done, dancers had to fight hard. Joan, backed by Aloys, responded to requests as though there was a war of attrition on. When the dancers' electric kettle broke there was no procedure for dealing with the situation other than bringing it before the board. The answer came back that dancers were responsible for their own repairs. At the same time, Joan's expenses on behalf of visiting guest dancers could run into hundreds of pounds for restaurant meals.

On contract matters, Joan could be unyielding. There was a clause in the dancers' contracts that serious misconduct, or not carrying out duties, could result in one week's notice of termination. The dancers requested a concession of one warning before a contract was terminated, which would be a normal procedure. Joan simply wrote, 'no' on the agenda. Another clause was that all classes were compulsory unless permission had been given by the ballet master. The dancers requested one optional class per week during rehearsal periods. Again Joan's recommendation was a terse 'no'.

At a time when the touring meal allowance was £3.00, the dancers asked for more, pointing out that on long journeys, only set meals were on offer at pull-in hotels, which cost more than this. 'No,' she wrote, adding that £3.00 was the public sector rate. In view of the strenuous and gruelling nature of the dancers' work when on tour, this refusal seems mean-spirited. Expenses that she herself incurred with the company were unquestioningly taken care of, whether it was for cups of coffee and cakes in the company of guests, or taxis to the airport, or restaurant meals. Anything else she wanted she simply asked for, and was given.

The dancers also asked for a salary increase, or else a reduction in the number of hours worked per week, plus an increase in overtime payment beyond 10 p.m. at night. Joan ignored the salary and worktime questions, and agreed to an increase in after-ten overtime, which gave the dancers very little indeed—a matter of just a few pence. Joan was financially comforable herself with an annual salary of around £3,000, and an income from her own company and schools, to be in a position to regally claim 'no fee' for additional specific choreography. She had also invested in pension funds. This occasional 'no fee' syndrome, gave rise to the propagation of a myth, via Aloys Fleischmann, that Joan never took a penny from the company for herself.

With the help of their union, Equity, the dancers managed to get a representative in attendance at board meetings in the role, at first, of an 'observer' for a 'trial period', subject to being asked to leave the meeting if and when matters not deemed relevant to dancers' concerns were discussed. When the newly-appointed Roger Wade was to speak at the following meeting, Joan was taken aback. 'Roger to speak on behalf of the dancers?,' she wrote on her agenda, 'thought he was an observer? observer does not speak?' If she could have, she would have silenced him at the start, but he was allowed to go ahead.

When dancers held their own Equity meetings in company time, Miss Moriarty complained to the board that it was discourteous of them to keep guest teachers and choreographers waiting whilst they had meetings. When the 'discourtesy' happened again, a directive was issued to the company that meetings must be held in dancers' own time. In time, the dancers were also looking for the financial statements.

Muriel Large, whose previous experience was with the Scottish Ballet, appeared sympathetic to the demands made by the dancers to bring their working and touring conditions into line with union agreements. Joan, who was accustomed to being sovereign, and disliked the idea of union activity, was not. Neither was Aloys, who was too cloistered and well-paid to grasp workplace issues.

When Kathleen Smith, a valuable dancer, took two weeks leave of absence to go home to America, the board deducted two weeks salary from her pay packet. When she applied for a reinstatement, they were unanimous in their verdict that there was no justification for it because she herself had requested the leave. It was a matter of a few hundred pounds for the company, but for a hand-to-mouth dancer, which is what the dancers were, a deduction meant difficulty.

By contrast, Domy Reiter-Soffer's fee of £3,238 for *Medea* the year previously, inclusive of fares and expenses, had willingly been met, and salary increases totalling £6,000 to non-dancing members of the company had been budgeted.

When dancer Leith Ridley, returning from home in London after injury, missed the ferry through no fault of her own, a day's pay was deducted. A deputation of dancers appealed to Aloys to have this decision reversed and it duly was. It was not the only case where dancers resorted to the compassion of Aloys, but Leith soon left the company. Beverly Knight had permission to be absent for a week from the tour, but had omitted to inform the company of her whereabouts. Only a deputation to Aloys restored her pay packet. She did not renew her contract.

A young male dancer, Donnachadh McCarthy, was lost to the company because Joan had offered him only a three month scholarship with no guarantee at the end of training. He accepted a contract with Dublin City Ballet. Joan was later asked to explain what had happened.

'I decided to offer three months,' she wrote, 'with another three months to follow, as I felt this arrangement would make this young man work harder'. She added that it would appear he'd been told that he would never be accepted as a member of the company, but that she herself had hoped 'if and when' to add him to the number. It was the usual alienating iffy imperiousness with dancers, but like Richard Collins, he was gone.

Joan's lack of vision was duly endorsed by the board, and unless Aloys knew better, she had the last word. She had a reputation for being kind, but could be most unkind too. When her influential patron Dame Ninette de Valois asked a special family favour—an Irish family favour—it was refused. According to Joan, the Dame wrote asking for help in getting a trainee stage management position for her grand-nephew. It would have benefitted everyone to have accommodated this young man, but it was merely agreed at the meeting, to write and explain the 'practical difficulties' this would entail. The older woman must have keenly felt this rebuff from her own country. Joan gushed to Dame Ninette when she herself was hosted, as she was by the Dame at Sadler's Wells, but when it came to her own power, Joan was no respecter of persons.

The Táin, a new ballet based on the epic bloody Irish legend, choreographed bloodlessly by Joan, had been premiered in Dublin in 1981, to mixed reviews, and small box-office. Aloys had composed the music, receiving £4,000 from the Performing Rights Society.

Although, in featuring Queen Maeve and her epic battles, it referred directly to their personal joint mythology, Aloys knew that this ballet was a difficult one. In the summer, whilst they both had been working on *The Táin*, he had sent Joan a birthday card.

'Birthday greetings to my love, ahead of the toughest campaign she had ever faced. May she again emerge victorious, As ever before! Colm.'

The picture showed two little children drawing, with the caption, 'Aren't you glad we have each other'.

When the ballet opened, his card to her, bearing a picture of Van Gogh's *House at Auvers,* was tinged with sadness:

'To my darling on the eve of the toughest battle of her career against ill health and every kind of disillusionment. But some peace must come, typified by this Van Gogh Cottage—and we shall work together for a freer easier and still creative existence. All my love—Colm.'

The Arts Council Report for that year did not contain a reference to the Cork national company, reporting instead on newcomers, Dublin City Ballet. Aloys queried this, in the light of *The Táin* having been premiered at the Dublin Theatre Festival. Whether there was any import in the omission, his response, as always, was dogged bewilderment that the success of the new production had been overlooked.

High touring costs for the IBC had meant cancelling tours, which affected the dancers. With its low overheads, the strategically-placed Dublin City Ballet, run by Louis O'Sullivan, was inadvertantly further contributing to low morale at the IBC, by undercutting costs. The small metropolitan company got £40,000 in grants that year, and was expanding the repertoire into modern work. Dublin Contemporary Dance Theatre also received a grant of £6,000, but since funds were so tight, this enterprise was not helped in 1982, and was assisted again in 1983.

In 1981, more little companies were springing up, and a new scheme of dance scholarships was underway in Ireland. Peter Brinson, a British dance critic, ex-dancer and a member of the Gulbenkian Fund board, was one of the adjudicators. During discussions, he suggested holding two seminars on the future for dance in Ireland. These were duly held in June and October.

In June, *Phoenix* magazine, the Irish investigative and satirical equivalent of the British *Private Eye*, had requested information on attendance figures from the IBC office. By September, Professor Fleischmann was voicing extreme worry to the board, that the query 'was part of a wider scheme to blacken the company'.

It was all getting too much for Joan. If the IBC meetings clashed with rehearsals of the amateur company, she skipped the board meetings. She had asked earlier in the year, that some of the 'burden' for the professional company be taken off her shoulders. Whatever she meant by this, it was agreed that Aloys take a supportive role. It wasn't enough; she was exhausted.

She roughly prepared a presentation for the September meeting:

'…work increased so much … mornings with dancers, and about two hours each day in the office, that I found I just could not continue to take classes each day, and asked the board if the board could agree to employing a teacher to help me to be free for IBC. 6 years ago this was granted.

'Again as time went on I found IBC was becoming full time, and employed myself a part time sec 2 afternoons a week to do accounts and interview parents etc.

'But this was not enough & I asked the board if it would pay to employ 1 sec each after noon. I would share the experience which I have — this was granted.

'The position at the moment is, and for the past 3 to 4 years 2 teachers employed

1 sec

I pay for 1 teacher

IBC pays for 1 teacher

IBC & myself share sec expenses

I employ (illegible) and all other expenses.

188

'Last year I was not able to take and classes & only travelled once to the classes outside.

'Now that I am not taking classes teachers must be qualified to be able to take all ages! Exams

'My work for IBC has become more than full time—choreography—more and more time spent in office

'I also have C B Co at night.

'The only 1 in IBC no holiday

'If I was not with IBC I would only employ 1 teacher.

'As Artistic Director I have 50% extra work which is really no part of being Artistic Director

'such as

'1. Every idea for IBC comes out of my head

2. Publicity

3. New ideas for promoting IBC

4. Watching stock…'

Her bottom line was simple: 'give up schools which means C B Co. or resign IBC'.

She continued not taking classes, and the board duly took notice that for medical reasons, she would not be able to do any choreography for a year. She suggested that Domy Reiter-Soffer should be invited to produce in her place. The professional company also agreed to pay two teachers for Joan's own company, but this created problems with the Arts Council.

Following discussions with Colm O'Briain and with Mr Joe Grey, the auditor, it was agreed that the IBC could give a grant of £7,500 to the Cork Ballet Company based on salary scales, for training pupils so as to find suitable recruits for the IBC. Joan was pleased, and she had the wording changed to 'a bursary to the Joan Denise Moriarty School of Dance'.

'I am very worried,' she noted in December, regarding the future of the company, 'that there is very little coming up. We have rather priced ourselves out.' There were certain Equity restrictions regarding performing and touring, but Cork seemed an expensive distance from metropolis gigs. With no invitations coming in, Joan wrote, 'I can see we will be losing our position!!'

Arthur Lappin had taken over as Arts Council representative on the board of the IBC. Arthur was appointed in 1979 to the newly-created post of Drama and Dance Officer on the Arts Council. The previous representative on the IBC board, Colm O'Briain, remained as Arts Council Director, and continued to take a close interest in the ballet company.

On 4th December 1981, Colm O'Briain wrote to the company, seeking to broaden the board, by suggesting that it should be enlarged to twelve members—three from the Taoiseach's department, six to be appointed by founder members or their successors, and three to be appointed by the Arts Council. It was a stiff enough letter, but considerate of the present board, and it stated plainly at the outset that 'the Council has been examining the structures of the major national companies with a view to determining whether or not it would be appropriate to introduce some amendments'. The letter concluded with mention of the difficult years ahead.

The minutes of the IBC board meeting record their decision: 'After discussion, it was agreed that the Chairman should reply to Mr O'Briain, offering him various counter-proposals for consideration'.

Jamie did not send any letter. On 25th March, Arthur Lappin asked when it would be possible for the Chairman to reply, and the Chairman agreed to do this, following further discussion with the present directors. Arts Council members felt they were getting the runaround.

The coming year was a difficult one for the Arts Council since the government had reduced their own budget in real terms by about a fifth. At the end of January the Arts Council suddenly completely withdrew all state funding from the Irish Theatre Company in Dublin. At the time of axing, that company had been in receipt of £278,000 per year. A touring company like the IBC, it was set up in the same year as IBC, 1974, and its objective was to bring professional theatre to centres outside Dublin. It also had a similar board structure to IBC. The decision to axe the subsidy was a controversial and unpopular decision, yet attempts to reverse it failed.

In Colm O'Briain's opinion as Director of the Arts Council, the Irish Ballet Company had clearly been underfunded the previous year, with £244,000. For the coming year, the intention of the Council was to find a significant increase for the Cork company, to bring the grant up to about £300,000. But review and possible cuts would be needed across the 26 major organisations being funded. The regions and education were to be prioritised, and after that, he said, the plan was to look at cost effectiveness, value for money, and to ensure that the money would be carefully and usefully spent.

The Irish Ballet Company gathered momentum in cutting costs, from reducing touring, dancers and new productions, to eliminating small expenses, however vital. The professional company sometimes had the use of the orchestra during the Cork season, but when attendances were not good, this expense was slashed. Early in 1982, based purely on box-office losses for a week (£858) at the Opera House, weighed against orchestra costs (£1,730), it was agreed that for the following year, exclusively taped music would be used in Cork. When Aloys pointed out that orchestra fees were £600 less than the previous year, it was agreed to review the position after the 1983 season. Audiences preferred the amateur orchestra to taped music.

Salaries were an issue. Application was made through the Arts Council to the Department of Finance for a supplementary grant to allow public service increases to the dancers, and around £30,000 was secured. James O'Donovan also met Colm O'Briain to discuss the composition of the board.

In May, Tom Donnelly resigned, and took up a post managing the Opera House. Mr Graham replaced him, and a development officer, Eric Peard was engaged.

The May 1983 board meeting minutes reported that, 'Professor Fleischmann produced a press cutting entitled, "Battle of the Ballets", alleging that the Dublin City Ballet was becoming more important than the Irish Ballet Company'. This emphasized, they agreed, the need for a swift change of title to include the word, "national". It was passed that the name of the company be changed to 'Irish National Ballet' (INB).

But Joan was marvellous at best-face public presentation of the name change:

'Before admitting the word 'national' into the title of her company Miss Moriarty felt that it had to prove itself,' wrote Tom O'Dea, in *Image Magazine*, in June 1984. 'They have worked from time to time for RTE,' Tom went on, ' but the concrete floors of the studios are less than ideal for dancers.'

RTE, which had paid for ballet pieces in the past, had stopped hiring the company explicitly on the grounds of expense. Muriel Large had been a tough negotiator, but Joan herself knew that as far as outside agencies were concerned, the company had priced themselves out of the market by demanding big fees. Here, in the middle of a crisis, she was airily telling the press that her company had proved itself enough to warrant being called national, and that RTE's floors were at fault. The view she voiced most often, was that things weren't good enough. It worked.

By 1983, Dublin Theatre Festival was no longer willing to take on the INB, without substantial guarantees. The festival director declined eleven of Joan's suggestions to perform certain works, and there was some perceived delay in getting commitment from Dublin. Also the Festival wanted to protect itself financially, by taking a specified first slice of the box office. With a possible £10,000 bill to face, the INB withdrew from negotiations, and company morale sank lower.

Also in May 1983, when the approved Arts Council grant for the coming year was £352,100, dancers contracts came up for renewal. Weary of the consistent intransigence and refusals from the board, they had reached the serious stage of resigning *en masse*. Muriel Large asked permission to raise their salaries by two and a half percent, explaining that this gesture might persuade the majority of the company to remain. Arthur Lappin agreed that the salary range was modest, and the board relented.

A good deal of cut-and-thrust is normal and desirable in arts organisations, as well as egotism and power-play. The problem here was that at the top, there was little energy being directed into the company as a national resource. They were isolated, they were insulated, they were very far, idealogically and geographically, from where artistic exchange could flourish, and they were sinking. Money was their sole currency, and they gobbled it up. Creating opportunities and generating developments were unknown concepts. Outreach into schools had always been a priority, but there was a divine-right approach to the subsidy, and attempts by the Arts Council to interface and to modernise policy were fly-swatted away.

Joan was tired, sick much of the time, on medication, and pouring her waning energies into the ongoing camouflage. Long-term use of drugs had led to osteoporosis, and she was still breaking bones. Aloys was misdirecting his considerable energies and talents into shoring up Joan's position, and vigorously defending her against everything that appeared in her path.

Jamie O'Donovan was tired too, and he was still working at supporting the now clearly ailing Joan, and protecting her position. They were getting old. Helped by other board members whose overwhelming dedication to Joan had no place in a normal working relationship, they had been so busy copperfastening Joan's position at the apex, that the rest of the board were as good as hog-tied in some respects.

Nothing of all the backroom ferment was apparent in the public realm. Press coverage was more supportive than ever, with publications littered now with endless interview profiles of Joan and her life and work. She loved taking the laurels. In 1982, she accepted the Harvey's Award for her outstanding contribution to Irish Theatre.

'Recessions are nothing new to me,' she said in Dublin. 'I've been through recessions that the economists have never heard of ... People simply must get up and fight this thing.' Referring to her as the 'first lady of Irish ballet', the *Irish Press* said it was a speech that 'drew thunderous applause'.

That was followed in 1983 by a 'People of The Year' award from the Rehabilitation Institute ('Ireland's undisputed Grande Dame of Dance'), and The Variety Artistes Trust Society Award for 1983, in recognition of her contribution to the Irish entertainment world. The VATS organisation baked a birthday cake for her, having heard, said the Chairman, that she'd never had time for a birthday. Joan looked ill, and very, very tired.

The whole atmosphere in Ireland suddenly changed in the early 1980s. Subsidies were going backwards, but new developments in the arts suddenly began burgeoning unassisted in Dublin and everywhere else. Dynamic new efforts began to be noticed as deserving of a little help to develop further. Both the Dublin Theatre Festival and Wexford Festival were hit by the Arts Council because they were healthy and attracted commercial sponsorship.

The response of the national dance company in Cork to the upheaval that was going on, was to continue trying to think up ways of getting ever larger slices of gratis revenue, and Aloys was as inventive as ever. He had impressively secured Gulbenkian Fund money and Cultural Affairs money for the company in the past, but much of it was petty, as well as arcane. When *La Dame Aux Camellias* was proposed by Domy, Aloys pointed out that, since the ballet was based on a French classic with music by Saint Saens, 'an approach for sponsorship should be made through the French Embassy to the Dublin branch of the Banque de Paris and it was agreed that this should be followed up'.

Agreed at the June meeting in 1983, was a suggestion that the Chairman write to Ted Nealon, Minister of State for the Arts, with a request that, as a tenth birthday present to the company, the accumulated deficit of around thirty thousand pounds be cancelled.

On a more realistic level, the stage manager again suggested that some kind of permanent transport be acquired, to avoid the annual thousands of pounds spent in continually hiring cars, taxis, vans and trucks for touring and general use.

A meeting with Mr Nealon revealed that for the following year, the government was planning to cut the grant to the Arts Council, which implied a cut from the Arts Council to the company. The dancers themselves submitted an idea to the board, that they take a cut in subsistence allowance for the autumn tour. However minimal the saving was, and however expensive personally to each barely adequately paid dancer, it was passed unanimously at board level that a vote of thanks be conveyed to the company. Unknown to them, the dancers were rewarded by a proposal in the revised budget for the coming year to cut costs by reducing the number of dancers.

In October 1983 *Phoenix* published a small piece on Arts Minister Ted Nealon's resolve to slash the Arts Council budget, and his apparent intention to force companies to raise their own money.

'If that is Nealon's strategy,' said *Phoenix*, 'then he will be anxious to replace the cultural élite who make up the Council's board with a broader-based selection of people. For when money is tight in the Council, the first to feel the pinch are the new, innovative enterprises — not the Council's expensive, prestigious pets like the National Ballet.'

An article about a small new company, the Ranelagh Ballet School, appeared in which the principal, Jill Wigham, was pointing out that the Arts Council was funding the INB to pay for English dancers to come over to Ireland. A bell was tolling, but nobody in power at the INB was listening. They thought they were surrounded by begrudgery.

Joan spent time looking at minutiae. When she was told that it was difficult to switch studio lights off because they were linked to one circuit, a request was sent out to investigate whether the electrical circuits could be separated. Whilst Joan went on scribbling endless sums of money in her margins thinking of ways to save pennies, other solutions gathered momentum.

The Dance Council of Ireland was set up, an umbrella organisation in the contexts of dance performance and education, and the Arts Council announced its intention of commissioning a report of dance organisations in receipt of grant-aid, with the objective of informing future Arts Council policy.

As it was, the Arts Council seemed to have been screaming at an obsolete board for years, and not being able to make itself heard. More than £300,000 was going out to the INB annually, and the isolationist company seemed to be showing a centre-of-universe attitude, at the same time as getting deeper into the red, showing a dwindling box-office, and failing to develop dance.

The Arts Council was aware that there was a lack of dynamism about the organisation. They knew that, at least as far as money was concerned, to increase revenue, rather than to cut costs, might have made sense. They were aware that dancers had problems which were not being addressed. They were also dimly aware that, contrary to public perception that Joan was a fighter, there seemed to be no aggression and drive at the top. They knew that the figurehead was being chivalrously supported by a charming champion, and by other faithful supporters who were now getting old.

The INB was swallowing up a huge subsidy that might better be distributed some other way, but nobody at Arts Council level knew just exactly how it had all happened, and how it was all being perpetuated. They were in the dark about the dynamics of this secretive, sleight-of-hand decision-making few. Although nobody at Arts Council level was qualified to evaluate dance, they perceived that the whole organisation was in some way strangely wrong, out of date, and that they couldn't get through to it.

Their solution was to pick an outside expert to find out what needed finding out. Peter Brinson, along with his young assistant, Andy Ormston, was commissioned by the Arts Council to prepare a report on dance in Ireland. For Joan, the Englishman's conclusions would be devastating.

23
The Firkin Crane

'I don't know if you have heard our awful news?,' wrote Joan to Domy in August, 1980. 'On Sunday July 6th The Butter Market was burnt down—no one knows how it happened—the doors were locked and all light (sic) off. we are still waiting to hear from the experts if it was malicious or accidental. This has been a big sad shock to all of us. as you know we were looking for £400,000 now it will be nearer £600,000—were (sic) this kind of money can be found at the moment, in view of the World situation and the shortage of money! How ever we can only look forward—and keep hoping!'

The butter market which Joan referred to was the Firkin Crane, an historic, circular building in the Shandon district, near the cathedral where Aloys' father used to play the organ. It was built on the site of a castle, which had earlier been an earthern fort, and which gave the district its name. At Joan's request in 1979, the Arts Council had bought the building as a permanent home for the professional ballet company, as soon as it came on the market, at a cost of £60,000.

Dame Ninette's blueprint for success was that having a company is not enough; you must have a school, and you must have a building. As it was, professional rehearsals, administration, scenery and wardrobe all took place at different venues in the town.

Aloys and Joan, together with solicitor Jamie, had spent a lot of time and energy in trying to get a building for the ballet company. The Arts Council had agreed to the purchase of the Firkin Crane and supplied the money.

'She gave me one instruction—get it,' Tom Donnelly had said to *The Irish Times*. 'Money never enters into her calculations. That comes afterwards.' This airy public praising of Joan, for taking money and the future for granted, fostered the myth, and encouraged her. They'd gone ahead right away and started hiring experts for proposed massive renovations. Exhibiting an architect's model of the building in the foyer of the Abbey Theatre in Dublin,

Joan, Tom and Muriel Large, had announced a campaign to raise reconstruction costs of £400,000.

When the building was completely gutted by fire just two weeks later, it was revealed to have been insured for only £19,000. 'Ballet Stars Lose New Home in Fire,' said the *Irish Independent*. 'Ballet Group Determined to Rebuild,' reported the *Cork Evening Echo*. Tom Donnelly lamented that the locals from the little houses in the Cork back streets around the building, would have been the first honoured guests to view the ballet.

Sympathy poured in. Five children turned up with five pounds— the proceeds of their jumble sale to help rebuild. A nun came up and gave Joan two pounds, and a man stopped her in the street and handed her a hundred pounds. Other local people who had very little money of their own sent Joan small amounts they could afford, and the donations totalled two hundred pounds.

Through an Order of Court, the company secured £41,000 from the Cork Corporation, in payment of a malicious damage claim, and an undertaking of a further £40,000 grant. Church and General insurance company paid out nearly £9,000. Pfizer Chemical Corporation guaranteed £10,000. Once again, private businesses and individuals were approached for money. Working on how to get nearly half a million took time and energy, and as well as having special fundraising meetings, Firkin Crane matters were featured in the monthly INB board meetings.

Joan's head was full of plans. She took lists to meetings of all the different requirements for the company, from a boardroom and offices for everyone, to barres, mirrors, and even a cupboard for the cleaning materials. Discussions were endless, but since it was an opportunity for Joan to leave something solid and enduring behind her, she diverted much of her waning energy into it.

Tom Donnelly said that he expected Mr Donal Crosbie of *The Cork Examiner* to donate £1,000, and it was agreed that this might encourage other people to donate the same amount. Joan wanted to start an appeal immediately, before public sympathy died down after the fire, but company fundraiser, Maurice O'Brien, of European Corporate Services Ltd, and other board members advised caution. For such big money, a more organised approach was advised, and with a fundraising committee formed, various methods were tried. Maurice's initial plan was to raise around £310,000, but it was soon realised that if money had to be borrowed from banks, the sum needed would double.

An *ad hoc* study group, consisting of all the main players plus a few more noted:

> 'consideration should be given to the future viability of an organisation which is almost totally dependent upon government funding to meet the operating costs.'

Colm O'Briain, then at the Arts Council, agreed that more than £300,000 should be raised, and advised forming a trust fund to administer the money. He also asked for copies of all correspondence, especially to the Departments of Finance or Education, or to the EEC. It would be helpful to the Arts Council, he said, if the company would keep him advised of developments. He was particularly anxious that they should consult with him before borrowing money from banks.

Joan was not just unafraid to ask for money; she also appeared to believe that it was very easy for others to find it, and to give it to her. Her letters to sponsors were syrupy and pushy. When Pfizer Chemical Corporation offered to donate £10,000 to the restoration fund, Arthur Baker, chairman, who was also on the Fundraising Planning Committee for the ballet company, wrote to Joan early in 1981, to confirm this, and to say that the contribution would be paid over three years. Joan wrote back:

> '... I am thrilled with the wonderful news that your firm have agreed to contribute £10,000 per year over three years. This is very heartening...'

He wrote back telling her that she'd misunderstood.

> 'How very stupid of me', she responded. 'I fully appreciate that at the moment a larger sum could not be made available... I am indeed very grateful for the kind offer...(of course £20,000 would have been very acceptable!!)'

Maurice O'Brien had drafted the initial letter, asking for £20,000. Joan and Aloys were to be the signatories of it, but before she signed, she wrote to Maurice thus:

> '... do you think it would be unwise to ask for the £25,000 rather than the £20,000 but surely these firms a matter of £5,000 wouldn't make that much difference ... I feel it is better to ask for the big amount first.'

By the end of the year, they were looking for a bank loan of £26,000 to pay the first instalment of a fee to engage the Wells Organisation, a professional fundraising company from England, who were to administer the trust fund.

A sighting of Rudolf Nureyev's picture in a Cork newspaper, in connection with work the renowned Russian dancer was doing in Norway, gave Aloys and Joan the idea to get Nureyev to appear at a Cork fundraiser.

At the end of the meeting a few days later, Joan mentioned that the Dublin Grand Opera Society had brought Luciano Pavarotti for an evening to Dublin, and it had been a great success. She very much wanted to run a gala evening in Cork, she said, featuring Nureyev or Markova.

Aloys composed the letter to ex-dancer, Anton Dolin, who was on familiar terms with 'Rudi', couching it in language which was in keeping with Joan's informal style:

'Dear Sir Anton,

I do hope you are in the best of health, and as active as ever!

When you were in Ireland perhaps you heard that the Rotunda Building which the Arts Council bought for our company went up in flames, and we are at present trying to raise over half a million to rebuild and adapt it for our purposes.

Among the enterprises we are planning, we thought of arranging a really big Gala Night at the Cork Opera House. For this some major attraction would be essential, and I was wondering whether you would ever be so kind as to approach Nureyev on our behalf, and to ask whether he and a partner would be willing to honour the occasion, and on what terms.

We would appreciate it enormously if you could do this for us. It would of course have to be a Sunday night, but any Sunday within the coming year could be arranged. We would love to have you as our guest if you happened to be free.

I shall look forward greatly to hearing from you.

With Very Best Wishes From Us All in 1982.'

With one or two minor alterations, like, 'I know only too well how busy you are', Joan duly copied this out, and signed it, and Anton Dolin co-operatively passed it on to Nureyev's management, Sandor Gorlinsky Ltd. It was impossible to arrange, Joan was informed with regret, since Mr Nureyev was completely booked out for the coming year, with no free dates at all. They might have known. The approach to such a big star, complete with restrictions, seems breathtakingly crass. Rudolf Nureyev was blatantly not of value in this case for his dancing; he was merely one of the people whom, because he was influential and important, might be of help in getting money for Joan.

The Wells Organisation was recruited, but an economic recession and a bad budget were affecting the corporate sector, from where the company expected to get funds. The outlook was bleak. The Arts Council grant was up by only two percent. The number of dancers was to be reduced.

Jamie wrote an understated letter to Joan, telling her that the bottom line from the costings, on what money would be needed for the Firkin Crane, was now the 'shattering sum' of £1.1 million. The idea of launching an appeal in the depressed financial climate, looked doomed. The question was, he said, whether to go ahead, and spend another £10,000 in having detailed plans drawn up for the Planning Authority, on top of the fifteen thousand already spent on plans, or wait until two meetings could be held in Dublin and Cork, which Jack Lynch had agreed to host, in order to gauge potential support amongst influential, wealthy people. Jamie included the rebuilding costings from Quantity Surveyors, Patrick Coveney Associates, which were in the region of £592,000. Other costs, including bank interest, salaries, and fees to the Wells Organisation of £50,000 sterling, brought the total up to more than a million pounds.

It was a sober letter, full of reserve, but Joan was extremely elated by it. She wrote thanking James for the 'impressive document' of the new costing lists, congratulating him on 'making it all so clear to an unbusiness head!'

'...while one half of me asks will we get such an amount these days, the other half says go ahead we may as well try as we have gone so far!!! I would dearly love for the Irish Ballet Company to have such a beautiful home—SO I AM SAYING GO AHEAD! and the good Lord look after us all!.'

She concluded this almost manic letter:

'James may I say how very grateful I am to you for all your loyalty, thought, and devotion to the "Goodess(sic) of Dance" I feel I can never show my deep appreciation enough...thank you for everything.'

For all the years of work that Jamie did freely for Joan, this is the only surviving reference to the nature of his personal involvement and to their relationship. The goddess referred to here, was obviously an ideal outside herself, of which she was a representative or an emissary. She herself in later years, began to talk of a 'goddess of dance', which she said took no form, but which existed 'up there'.

In one of the last interviews she ever gave, she said that the goddess had goaded her on all her life, to do more and more, until she was weary, and pleading, 'goodness, how much more are you going to ask of me?' Few people, however, remember Joan mentioning this goddess, and she did not talk to dancers about it until near the end of her life. She eventually incorporated it into her own story as a motivating influence.

Whether she took the notion of the abstract 'Goddess of Dance' from Jamie himself, or whether it was an adaptation of Aloys' goddess, what is certain, is that Jamie was serving this abstract 'goddess' when he was serving Joan so dedicatedly. The 'goddess' which was ardently worshipped by Aloys, differed from Jamie's vision, in that for Aloys it was personified by Joan, and in that Aloys was pursuing a 'love' relationship as a suitor and a lover, as well as a servant. In any case, Joan had two men serving a 'goddess', and she was the focus and recipient of their lifelong energetic service. If Aloys knew of Jamie's devotion to the rather more acceptable abstract goddess, it is likely that Jamie never knew the details of Aloys' intimate adoration of her.

Jack Lynch agreed to be president of the Irish Ballet Company Trust Fund, and agreed to host a reception at the Abbey Theatre in Dublin, to which he would invite influential people and heads of the main potential corporate donors. In the event, Jack had another engagement and Mairin presided, along with Gordon Lambert, chairman of WR Jacob, and trustee of the ballet company. By this time, the loss of the talented Tom Donnelly, particularly in his public role, was being felt. He had left to manage the Opera House, and Desmond Graham had taken his place as manager of the company. Joan, Aloys and James all missed the special charm of this imposing figure at functions, and his ability always to remember names, as well as faces.

John Green, of the architects acting for the project, reduced their fees by £20,000. Outgoing chairman of the trust, Arthur Baker, also waived fees. In December 1982, Joan was presented with a grant in excess of £7,000 from the Ireland Fund by its chairman Dr Tony O'Reilly. The restoration fund already had £50,000 in compensation payments in the bank, and had raised more than £30,000 in the Cork area. Yet all this money was swallowed up in expenses. If it hadn't been for the Ireland Fund contribution, and the waiving of fees by

201

John Green, and Arthur Baker, there would have been no money at all in the kitty.

The income and expenditure account for the period ended 30 April 1983, shows that the Irish Ballet Company Limited had income of £54,926 in compensation for malicious damage, and had accrued £3,051 interest. Funds raised in the Cork area amounted to £31,670; funds raised in the Dublin area amounted to £250; and the Ireland Fund had contributed £7,184. The grand total of income was £97,081. Expenditure amounted to two thirds of this: There were fundraising consultancy fees of £36,674; salary and travel expenses for the trust executive, Eric Peard of £7,279;, and his training fee at Wells, £666. Secretarial salaries came to £4854; bank interest and charges were £5549; audit fees were £250; the model of the Firkin Crane building was £3740; the Trust Brochure cost £3680; printing and stationery cost £1081; furniture, advertising and petty expenses came to £1431, and fundraising receptions cost £1742. Total expenditure, therefore, was £66,946.

The total in hand that was left, in the middle of 1983, amounted to £30,135.

The fact that the building had a preservation order on it was a big plus for Joan. It meant borrowed perpetuity for her own legend, as well as funding for rebuilding. When the Cork Corporation, which was to some extent holding the purse-strings of redevelopment in the rundown area, and was planning a craft centre nearby, had things to say about whether the Firkin Crane should be for the exclusive use of the ballet company, trade-off negotiations took place. The Ireland Fund also welcomed the idea of community use for the building. The ballet company acknowledged that the Firkin Crane was to be designated partly for community use.

It duly appeared in *The Cork Examiner* that, 'Dr Joan Denise Moriarty would like to see the premises used for the needs of the company and for the local community. She thought it would be an ideal centre for small exhibitions by young Irish artists, and hoped that it would also serve as a community centre.' No provision whatsoever was made in the plans to this effect.

The Arts Council was supportive of the venue as a ballet school and as a rehearsal venue, but not as a performing venue. It eventually reconsidered over a few years that the appeal would be greater, the huge cost could be justified, and funds found from various sources, if the use of the Firkin Crane was extended to include that of an arts venue.

Accordingly, it eventually appeared in newsprint that Joan Denise Moriarty was a champion of culture as well as of ballet. When a nationwide appeal was launched in early 1984, it was backed by such people as trust president Jack Lynch, and trustees, Dr Tony O'Reilly, Michael Smurfit and the Earl of Rosse. All the ambitious details were in place; the historic nature of the building was emphasised, and attention drawn to its potential versatility.

'This building is the chosen location for a proposed national centre for arts, drama, opera, and a home for the Irish National Ballet Company,' reported *The Irish Times*. The venue for arts, crafts and drama was to be 'in full use at all times, providing a venue for workshops, lectures, exhibitions and educational programmes for children and adults alike'.

Whether people believed all they read in the papers or not, there was no memorandum or query or statement at board level as to whether the plans allowed for versatility of use, or whether consultations with other groups, or adaptations, major or minor, needed to be made. It was merely noted internally that other artistic groups were to use the building when the ballet company was on tour. Fundraising was the main thrust. Progress was slow, but the target was achievable, wrote trust executive Eric Peard in his 1983 report, partly because of 'the tremendous admiration and esteem for Dr Joan Denise Moriarty felt by everyone in Ireland'. The other two bases on which the target would be achieved, he wrote, were that the building was historic, and that other artistic endeavours would take place there.

All three of these bases for optimism were flawed. The historical nature of the building was real enough, but it had nothing to do with the ballet. The idea of the building being used for other artistic pursuits was dubious, and the respect and esteem that Joan was held in throughout the country, was largely due to her publicity machine, and the susceptibility of the press.

All contributors to the Sean Dun Appeal, as it was now called, in a reversion to the original name of the site, were promised to become honorary 'Friends of the Irish Ballet Company', for the first year of its formation. Because of the name change of the company, the name of this organisation later became, 'Friends of the Irish National Ballet'. On the ground, this organisation was competently planned as a most user-friendly outfit, with invitations to rehearsals, lectures and workshops being part of the benefits of membership, plus luncheons and an annual Friends Evening. The idea of invitations to rehearsals was dropped.

'The Friends of the Irish Ballet Company is an association of ballet-lovers all over Ireland who aid and support the Company in many ways,' said the circular, outlining the benefits of newsletters, social activities and priority bookings. Women around the country expressed interest, including the wife of the Labour Party leader, Mrs Spring.

Internally, the line from the top was a little harder. Included in the objectives of those engaged in company publicity to this end were:

'... to seek out in all centres where the Company performs people of wealth and influence and in particular those who are interested in Ballet and from amongst these persons to form a group who will consent to act as 'Friends of the Irish Ballet Company' for the purpose of (1) ensuring that all publicity sent to such groups prior to performances in their particular area shall be distributed by them to as many of their friends and acquaintances as possible (2) ensuring that the halls and theatres in these particular areas where the Company is due to perform are well-filled on the evening or evenings of the Company's performances and (3) encouraging the 'Friends of the Irish Ballet Company' to make an annual subscription to the company.'

At the same time, it was necessary, 'to prepare at suitable intervals but not less than times each year a résumé of the Company's work during the preceding period giving details of the places visited, the result of the performances given in other areas, the progress of fund-raising and such other details that will stimulate the minds of the 'Friends of the Irish Ballet Company' and encourage them to seek further friends and funds for the Company.

'... on each occasion that the Company performs in any area where a group of 'Friends of the Irish Ballet Company' has been established to call on the Chairman or President of that group and report later to the Board of the Company as to the result of that visit.'

In a country where much is achieved by word of mouth, it had been possible for both Aloys and Jack Lynch, both of whom were held in high national regard, to have influence amongst big names in Ireland. Top business people might naturally have been expected to have some interest in ballet, and also some interest in patronising worthy causes. All they had seen were glittering first nights, with elegant receptions laid on, ballet stars and choreographers from all over the world at the tops of bills, and a string of awards for the taciturn, mysterious Dr Moriarty. They had also seen Arts Council support, a hugely supportive press, and a very high-powered, state-of-the-art fundraising drive. They had no idea what it was all about, and less idea that the board of the ballet company had been cautioned by their Arts Council member, Arthur Lappin, that even though they might get the building, there might not, in days to come, be any ballet company to go into it.

Not everyone was happy to hear the new description of the Firkin Crane as a national centre for the arts. Since 1977, a hard nexus of Cork talent had been extremely busy persevering to establish the Triskel Arts Centre, and only that year had received a capital grant from the Arts Council to buy a city centre warehouse for use as a major new arts and recreation complex in the second city. The total cost of the project was to be a low £175,000, and the range of activities was far-ranging and flexible. Young, vibrant and educated people were involved from all disciplines of the arts, and together they combined to form an exciting, thrusting and energetic arts facility, with links extending from the university to the back streets. The board of directors at Triskel reacted with consternation at this apparently competitive move from the ballet company, saying that public confusion could divert public goodwill from themselves.

In *The Sunday Press* Aidan Dunne reported that:

'Ambiguity allied with the prestigious names associated with the Firkin Crane project could, they feel, actually injure Triskel's chances for success.

'The Irish National Ballet Company does not seem to have any definite ideas for arts involvement beyond the obvious and immediate one of establishing a permanent and much-needed home for itself. The manager of the Ballet Company, Desmond Graham, is actually quite unaware of any wider ambitions whatsoever. The executive of the Trust, Eric Peard, does however talk in terms of an arts centre, but not in any structured or specific way.

'The idea would seem to be that the Firkin Crane premises could serve as a performance venue for other individuals and groups when, for example, the Ballet Company is on tour. Other ancillary activities are also possible, but there are no definite plans that the premises would function as an arts centre in the same sense as Triskel. Mr Peard does not see the project as being in competition with Triskel, and it seems fair to say that the term "arts centre", as it is generally understood, is inappropriate for the project.'

It was Mairtin McCullough, Chairman of the Arts Council, who travelled from Dublin to Cork, to hand over the £60,000 cheque to Triskel Arts Centre, as an instalment for their capital programme.

As a member of the Arts Council, he was in the habit of getting out to see the work of the artistic organisations which were being funded around the country by the Irish government. He would have seen the Irish National Ballet in Dublin and when he had occasion to be in Cork, if it was on, he would have gone to the Opera House to see the ballet. Money to the Arts Council had been cut by the government, and adaptations were being made by the Council to their new lower budget. Whether money was being well spent was a reasonable question to ask, particularly of the heavily-subsidised. Standards were being looked at, and this became a particular emphasis. Mairtin McCullough, chairman of the Arts Council, was looking for excellence. He was not seeing it in the Irish National Ballet.

24

The Brinson Report

When Peter Brinson started interviewing individual dancers in Cork, Joan was completely spooked. For her it was a time of heavy silence and deep suspicion. It wasn't just that she didn't like him poking around—she had a ghastly, crippling feeling that the game was up. She had nobody to confide in. She could not talk frankly, even to Aloys. There was a lot that she had not told him, much that he had not realised, and more that he did not want to know. Never could she have imagined, at this stage of her life, at the top of her profession, and with so many awards, so much support and love, and so much public acceptance, that she would be facing the inquisition.

Peter Brinson had written several reports on dance and the arts, and was head of research and community development at the Laban Centre for Movement and Dance in London. He had been Director for many years of the UK branch of the Gulbenkian Foundation, and during that time had come to know people involved in the arts in Ireland. He had been the founder/director of the Ballet for All Company, of the Royal Ballet, and had written and produced for this company for a decade.

'He writes articles and things,' Joan would say defiantly, 'but he is not a dancer'. To the end of her life she went on asking another indignant question: 'What does the Arts Council know about dance?'

One thing that soon became clear to everyone, was that whatever Peter Brinson's mysterious brief, he was doing a thorough job. For the first time in her professional life, the thought that her champions and acolytes might not be able for this entered Joan's head.

There had been plenty of time. It should have been clear throughout the early eighties, from Arts Council interactions, that the Cork company was facing a radically altered situation. The Cork company's needs were threatening to outstrip the total dance budget. Other new dance companies which were generating box office income and sponsorship, were also considered to be deserving of grants for their development, and the intention of the Arts Council to re-appraise allocation of funds was serious. The establishment of the Dance Council of Ireland was felt to be an important development, and the declaration of the Arts Council intent to become reliably informed, was included in its 1983 Annual Report:

> 'The absence of a broad professional base for the practice of dance in Ireland makes it difficult to establish assessment criteria for artistic policies and standards. In 1984 the Council intends to commission a report on those dance organisations in receipt of grant-aid so as to inform future policy in this discipline.'

It could not have been clearer. In the autocratic world that Aloys inhabited though, where he had power—power over the orchestra, power over his students—it was a matter of demolishing the opposition with argument, and bashing on regardless. He was convinced of his own correctness. What Aloys perceived himself to be doing with the Arts Council, backed by the legal brain of the charming James O'Donovan, was quelling all objections that arose from them about whatever the company happened to be doing, and pacifying any tiresome unease. Frustrations expressed by the Arts Council representatives with whom he had to deal from time to time, would merely have been taken by him with a pinch of salt. Whilst he would have been accommodating, polite, and considerate, he would also have seen them basically as objects getting in his way, which needed to be thrown aside. Whilst operating in a pseudo-democratic style, his own confidence was so great, that he felt anyone who didn't agree with him, to be simply wrong. His other conviction was even more misplaced: he had an unshakeable belief in Joan's supremacy in the dance field in Ireland. In his mind, she deserved all the money the company was getting, and more.

Peter Brinson's terms of reference were firstly, 'to identify the nature, provision, standards and administration of professional classical and modern dance forms currently available in the Republic, with particular reference to The Irish National Ballet, Dublin City Ballet, and Dublin Contemporary Dance Theatre.'

He was then expected to suggest ways to improve skills in every department of dance and to refer to vocational training at all levels. It was within his brief to consider fringe companies, as well as to refer to the relationship between amateur and professional dance. Finally, he was to 'make recommendations with particular reference to audience access and funding from all sources'.

He wrote to Irish newspapers, outlining his inquiry, and requesting them to publicise his availability to personal approach, in confidence, by members of the public. In the half dozen national dance studies he had undertaken around the world, he wrote, he had always found such individual contributions invaluable. Letters to him at the Arts Council, Merrion Square, were to be marked, 'personal'. The cost of the report to the Arts Council was £8,100.

Peter Brinson's investigations and deliberations went on for weeks and into months. Where previously Joan had been facilitated in imperiously batting away criticism, now she smelled a newly-changed atmosphere, an awful lull. She suspected sabotage, and so did Aloys. She was uneasy, but he felt that any potential saboteur had no grounds beyond the pure malice of betrayal, and was in battling form.

Joan was not well. Since her deprived childhood, she'd had osteoporosis, and her hallmark faintness and falling—the effects of prescribed drugs—had led to many broken bones. Long-term use of corticosteroids for asthma had increased her tendency to break brittle bones. The fractures allowed her to retreat periodically to the safety of hospital, but she could never bear to be in a room where people were smoking. She had also developed a peptic ulcer, another possible side-effect of extremely powerful asthma treatment. She suffered with bad headaches. Side effects of both the medicine for her ulcer, and her emphysema drug, were both likely causes of these. More seriously, she was developing a slight, constant shaking of the limbs—unmistakable signs of Parkinsonism, a likely side-effect of the prolonged use of antipsychotic drugs for depression. She had diverticulitis, caused by the high stress of her lifestyle, and recurring diarrhoea was the debilitating sign of this. An injury to her foot, a legacy from her dancing days, was giving her a lot of pain.

When people asked her how she was, she would always say that she was fine. When she fell ill, and retreated to her bed, or to hospital, nobody save the very closest friends had any idea what was wrong with her, and even they were given only the scantest of information. She took her drugs and her painkillers, but her illnesses were a mystery.

Though friends, as ever, fed her whenever possible, and she still had never cooked Sunday lunch, her determined lack of interest in food meant that she had become run down. Joan appeared to bother so little with feeding herself that Aloys, who normally had no appreciation of the psychological aspect of illness, had by now become convinced that she was suffering from anorexia nervosa.

The Brinson problem occupied her, but she had to keep it all bottled up. In the daytime, she kept her back straight, as ever, and her head high, but with her usual keen intuition, Joan had a dark terror, that in some way, someone, somewhere, might have seen through her. Joan tended to reject anyone who wasn't altogether supportive of her, or in awe of her, whenever it was possible. She could take instant dislikes to people, and those she didn't like, she absolutely refused admittance into her life, but increasingly, there were people whose presence in her professional life was beyond her control.

She did not like outsiders on the board, she was not comfortable with her administrator, Muriel Large, and she disliked Arts Council officer, Arthur Lappin. The professional dancers were always a breed apart, kept by her at as far a distance as possible, but if she occasionally mistrusted one of them, and got an opportunity for arguing against renewing a contract, she would take it. Mostly, she weeded out possible troublemakers at the audition stage.

Depressed as she was, and with the spectre of her unhappy and suicidal Aunt Joan haunting her, she had never really trusted her own thought processes. Now a fresh period of insomnia was making her thoughts in the small hours ever more fragile. Filled with a sense of doom that no amount of reassurance could remove, Joan spent anxious nights. She felt she needed to do something to deflect Brinson's attention, and defuse any criticisms he might have. The answer she came up with was a pitiable gesture: she decided to advertise for an assistant.

Such a delaying sop might have worked in the past with the Arts Council, but in Brinson's hands, it would soon serve to help dislodge her.

Also trying to resolve her own inner tension, she quietly but deliberately suggested one spring day, that it might be a good idea at this point, if she were to resign. Joan was past the normal retirement age, even in terms of her fictitious younger age. Led by Aloys, her supporters would not hear of it. If she had called a small special meeting of intimates, possibly including Jamie, Maeve Coakley, and Billie Hunt, as well as Aloys, and put it to them that she was old enough to retire, and that she really was tired enough now, or sick enough, to announce her retirement from the professional company, they might have held a party for her, and a special farewell performance might have been organised. This was her eleventh-hour moment to get out and depart gracefully, but she let the moment pass.

Bona fide, old-age retirement never entered her head. She only offered to resign, and with nobody but herself aware of what was at stake, the offer was not taken seriously. The ageing and devoted Jamie, who had always done as she pleased, saw no danger whatsoever. Aloys stood firmly against Joan's retirement, and she did not have the drive, the confidence or the autonomy to make the ultimate decision for herself. At this point, as at all others, she needed direction, but the mentor she had chosen to trust, had no awareness of the issues.

In her half-world, where a lifetime's libido had been subsumed in an obsessive, joint love affair with an icon, what she had been looking for was an affirmation. The ascent-to-stardom techniques were long-established; she was reaching out for some do-or-die declaration of allegiance for the ultimate battle ahead. When she looked to Aloys—to Colm—for direction in this new situation, offering the ultimate sacrifice—abdication—she saw no writing on the wall. What she saw reflected still, was the marvellous, legendary figure of herself, and as a counterweight to her nervousness and her weariness, she perceived in him a bristling, aggressive intent.

If he had shown any prudence at this stage, or any real concern for Joan as a human person, the outcome might have been quite different, but he didn't. He was determined to press ever onwards. His romantic secret vision of Queen Maeve the invincible warrior-muse was too closely entwined with his thrilling vision of himself as the battling, achieving devotee of the goddess, for him to think of letting go of his private creation.

In Joan's mind, Aloys had always been incredibly useful to her, and she trusted him. Yet despite this trust, long ago she had realised that a large part of his 'love' for her, had nothing to do with her as a person and had, accordingly, withdrawn some innermost part of her being into a sad and lonely place which was inaccessible to him.

Nor was he capable even of perceiving it. He had never understood how she could look blankly at him when he lavished praise on her, or how she could remain unmoved by rose-tinted admiration. In a crucial sense which she herself did not fully understand, Joan could not afford to take him seriously. This fundamental wrongness at the heart of their relationship, contributed to Joan's depressions. Her own willingness to take part in it all had led, not just to the laurels and acclaim, but to deep self-hatred, and an unease of the soul.

She would never realise that amongst the powerful, tangled interplay of obsessions and motivations that drove Aloys, there were two clear fantasy allegiances which were potentially destructive to herself. One was that he identified very closely with the successful aspect of herself, to the extent that he gained strength from it, saw his own success and even worth in terms of it, and had laid his life's goals along the path of it. The great danger of this, was that his magnificently grinding obsession was in too-stark contrast to the fragilities and inadequacies of her reality.

The other harmful factor for her, was that in his classic love-obsession, he was intent on cherishing and promoting the idealised image of 'Miss Moriarty' which he had created, even to the extent of fiercely protecting it against Joan the human, fallible, frightened, hurting woman. She was in no position at this stage, to call things off; she was as pinned to her fate as a butterfly to a board. What she had become, although neither of them realised it, was his victim.

In Aloys' sparklingly inventive mind, whatever the next battle was all about 'Miss Moriarty', and 'Dreenagh', were at its core and they were going to take it on. He was as sure of that as he had ever been of anything, and judging by what they had so far achieved, he reasoned, they would win.

Thus, insulated as she had been for the past forty years, as queen in a highly-public, yet intensely private, world of increasingly difficult battles, followed by huge booty in big finance, prestigious followers, and handsome awards, she, as ever, went along with it, believing there was every chance that she—that they—could win. Encouraged by this most devoted and committed consort, that she was not alone and that he was in for the ultimate fight, as well as for the long haul, the figurehead of Irish ballet stayed put.

Morale in the INB was not good, but from the outside, things appeared fine. The company was awarded £100,000 in the summer of 1984, by Ted Nealon, Minister of State for Arts and Culture, from the 'inactive' section of the 'Funds of Suitors', a well of cash and security deposits in the High Court. The money was for the restoration of the Sean Dun. Also in the pipeline was a possible grant from European funds, but Joan had begun to waver and to capitulate.

'I can see why only a certain amount of money is allocated,' she had said in a 1982–3 interview for *Theatre Ireland* magazine. She called it making compromises, but her company was swallowing 87% of the total Irish dance budget and 1982 had been one of her most difficult years. Unrest amongst the dancers had reached formal complaint level and, as well as a spell in hospital following an accident, the close of the year had brought bitter reports from the dancers and from technician John McCarthy, following the autumn tour, on not just the poor state of the equipment, venues, and inefficient touring schedule, but on the deterioration in morale amongst the technical workteam.

In June 1984, as the tenth anniversary was celebrated at the Abbey with Kathleen Smith dancing Domy's *Lady of the Camellias*, and a grant cut loomed David Nowlan wrote that it was 'nonsense' to link state subsidy with box-office, and that the company could not 'afford any cuts in its grant'. Aloys himself could not have put it any better, but the time for listening to him, and for taking notice of the press, was gone. In 1985 the Arts Council published 'The Dancer and the Dance; Developing Theatre Dance in Ireland', which came to be known as 'The Brinson Report'. It was sixty-seven pages long, and contained a further ten or so pages of appendices.

All eyes were on the INB, into whose maw nearly all the money was going.

As the first of his fifty-three recommendations, Peter Brinson happened to find firstly, that inadequate government funding was a primary cause of difficulties in dance, but that point was found by companies to be of little comfort or relevance. They were interested in the fortunes of the dance allocations.

Many people Brinson consulted about the INB around the country, he wrote, had questioned the 13% residual subsidy available for dance in the rest of Ireland. He was surprised at the number of people who did not recognise the company's national status, and who reported that they considered it 'regional'. A constraint on touring, he noted, was the subsistence allowance that was needed whenever the company travelled more than sixty miles from Cork, and a constraint on standards was the inadequate facilities. The grant, he said was too small for the company's present structure and 'drastic measures' were needed.

The section on reorganising finance said that the company appeared to be faced with closure or financial and artistic reorganisation. Vigorous fundraising and aggressive marketing to raise box-office revenue were recommended, plus 'a new artistic policy in line with current artistic development in theatre dance to produce new product for marketing which emphasises its national status'. He suggested restructuring the company.

'Our study of the company and consultations with a range of people, from company members to members of their audience', he heralded the section on artistic leadership, 'suggest that policy, especially artistic policy, is a prime cause of current difficulties.'

In public, one of the longstanding 'prejudices' against the company had involved the old rivalry between Cork and Dublin. It was 'Cork as provincial' versus 'Cork as the real capital'. In many minds, Dublin was the only logical place where anything 'national' could be based. Corkonians would have instinctively resented this, and some would have resisted it actively. Aloys had a bee in his bonnet about it, and was out to prove the likes of exiled writer and Corkman, Sean O'Faolain wrong. Joan had jumped on the high moral bandwagon, and for thirty-eight years they had both been fierce and outspoken champions of 'regionalisation'. The rest of the country also had a longstanding notion that Cork was notoriously clannish; those in the second city would support their own, to the detriment of outsiders, no matter what.

However, Englishman Peter Brinson was no hostage to prejudice, and was free to say openly what others dared not:

'Central to artistic policy is artistic leadership. Such leadership … is the same as guided the Cork Ballet Company before 1973 and seems not to reflect now the changed nature and status of the company…The board, for example, is Cork-based rather than national in composition, and is inclined, therefore, to see things from an established Cork perspective.'

He had also sought some sort of agreement, acknowledgement, or admission wherever possible, and however flimsy the material obtained, he had managed, with diplomacy, to use it to full effect in dispensing the *coup de grâce*:

'The Chairman and members of the Board told us they recognised this limitation and agreed the Board needed reconstruction. Similarly, Miss Moriarty drew our attention to an advertisement for an assistant to herself who might one day become her successor. She pointed out that she has responsibilities also to Cork Ballet Company and to her teaching studios around Cork. On these grounds alone an assistant is important. While we might disagree that the qualities of a good assistant are not necessarily the qualities of a good artistic director, we welcome the knowledge that when Miss Moriarty retires from the Irish National

Ballet she will be able to continue with the Cork Ballet Company and ... continue her teaching. Especially we welcome such open and understanding attitudes by those who have led the INB for its first twelve years. Although we have shown that the company's critical situation makes change urgent, inevitable and immediate, this understanding should make change easier. A full-time artistic director is needed, able to give all his or her attention to artistic reorganisation and a new repertory appropriate to a smaller company...'

Previously, board members had been able to give the Arts Council the runaround on what needed to be done, and in the same pseudo-promissory vein, Miss Moriarty had talked only vaguely about a successor. This time, making the right noises had worked to their detriment; their own words were being used to support a case which clearly was against them.

Peter Brinson then recommended that the search for a successor to Miss Moriarty start immediately, in the hope that a revitalised company with a different style and tone might help reverse the fall in box-office receipts. Appoint a full-time artistic director, was his bottom line, and reconsitute the board to reflect national status.

'There is no question that an Irish National Ballet should exist. A standard has been achieved. There is a repertory on which to build... Whatever criticisms are made of the INB, Ireland has nothing else in theatrical dance remotely comparable in quality. To lose the INB would be to lose a creation of great value to Ireland...'

A copy of the Brinson Report was sent to Joan at her studio in Emmet Place. She took it home to the safety of 'Dreenagh', her house in fashionable Montenotte, a secure place where access to her duplex apartment was gained by unlocking a solid metal door with a small grille in it. The big house was perfect for her. The tenant, a classical musician to whom she had let the flat above, gave a sense that someone was near if ever she should need it, as well as giving her the additional financial security of regular rent. The metal door led down steep and narrow concrete steps towards her front door. In the hall were large black and white pictures from the early days—herself dancing *La Calinda* from the very first night; herself dancing *Pierrot*.

Joan read the report at her chipboard desk in the green-carpeted little dining room she used as a study, where a picture of herself together with Aloys and Dame Ninette flanked one of Rudolf Nureyev above her desk. The company had been expecting something like £100,000 to be cut from the grant, and had been ready for a big fight and all sorts of attempted changes, but she read in the most savage of all Peter Brinson's recommendations, that Joan Denise Moriarty should be sacked.

Above her desk were telephone numbers of taxis and other numbers which made her feel safe: numbers of the Gardai at McCurtain Street, of the Gardai headquarters at Union Quay. Her studio had been broken into once. Around the room hung testimonies to her achievements: posters of *The Playboy* and *The Táin*; a picture of herself, exhuberant in the 1940s, dancing on Aloys' lawn.

On her shelves stood a few dusty dolls in national costume, brought back from excursions abroad. The books in the low, makeshift bookshelves had been mainly given as presents to her by Aloys down the years, as he had gently and lovingly educated her, and she had diligently and sometimes laboriously read every one: J.B. Yeats and his World; J.M. Synge and his world; Anglo-Irish Music; books on Nijinsky, Nureyev, Baryshnikov, Diaghilev, Oscar Wilde; books of poetry; books on theatre; Andersen's fairy tales; modern Chinese stories; books on Picasso and Rodin.

When Joan sat at her desk, she was flanked by thick folders of newspaper clippings, full of pictures of herself at triumphant first-nights. Also on the desk was her little red address book, plumply crammed with numbers going back nearly forty years, the old, well-thumbed pages falling out, held in place with an elastic band. On the desk there were some recent, glowing newspaper reports that she hadn't yet had time to paste in with her usual meticulousness.

This naming of only herself, and this utter dismissal of her, the founder, was completely unexpected. Joan was deeply shocked. Years later, in an interview with this author, she described her feelings at the time, saying she'd been unable to believe it. 'My God,' were the words she whispered to herself.

In her bedroom were the things Joan cherished most, the few objects she had accumulated in her lifetime which meant anything to her. The bedroom was a private place of retreat, institutional in its impersonal, monastic simplicity. Her bedroom might almost have been a spare room, so uncluttered was it. Few people had ever been inside her home, and almost nobody ever went up to her bedroom. It was furnished only with things that Aloys had given her. The plain wooden single bed was the one that Joan had slept in when Frau Fleischmann first took her in, and which Aloys had later given her when his mother died in 1967. Joan's three wool blankets were neatly tucked in all around, with a floral bedspread smoothed flat on the top, with an electric blanket underneath.

Her bedside table was the piano stool that Tilly Fleischmann had brought from Germany, and had used all her teaching life. Aloys had given it to Joan. On the little piano stool Joan kept a lamp, a couple of little St Christopher medals and a box of tissues, together with whatever capsule she might need in the night. Across the room was a large, heavy chest of drawers which also had once belonged to Aloys' parents. On top of the chest, Joan kept two pictures; one was of Aloys as an infant, and the other was of his parents, Georg 'Faw Faw' and Tilly Fleischmann, the couple who had parented Joan in Cork, and given her a family life.

The last thing Joan saw every night, and the first thing she saw each morning, as she looked out towards the city sky, was a large framed print of the red-haired goddess Aphrodite. 'You are my Aphrodite,' Aloys had whispered as he had presented the picture to her, and many times since. Joan's hair had remained bright. She regularly and thriftily dyed it herself in the bathroom, even into her seventies. Over past years, the picture had always been a comfort to her, just as all the pictures of herself dancing, that she'd had enlarged and put up on her walls, had reassured her that she was somebody. The huge mountain of greetings cards, heaped in boxes next door on the bare floor of the spare room, had given her a sense of being admired; and the folders full of glowing newspaper clippings had helped to convince her that she had achieved something. The Brinson Report changed Joan's perception of everything, and brought doubts crowding to the surface of her mind.

Aloys lived just a couple of minutes away, and often came over. She kept apple juice in the fridge for him. Sometimes, he gave her his handkerchief to dry her tears. She had many of his handkerchiefs.

Where had she gone wrong? How had she failed? Aloys didn't have any answers either, but the deed was done. The spectacular report on dance in Ireland had given her no options. She would have to resign, she eventually admitted. She would have to resign from the INB. He would resign in support of her, he replied.

Joan remained awake all that first night. Closeted alone in her familiar surroundings, she tried to take in that she had been forced to resign, and that she was publicly discredited. It never occurred to her, during the sleepless nights that accompanied her trauma, nor during any of the days and nights of the rest of her life, that it was partly these very newspaper clippings; these posters of big balletic events in her life; these blown-up pictures of herself dancing; the picture of Aphrodite as herself; that had hurt her.

It was the very things that she was clinging to, together with decades of myth-building from Aloys, that had given her an artificial sense of importance and a false sense of security. Now, in the shocking rawness of dismissal, her sense of her own existence was gone; her sense of self was in fragments. The feted 'Miss Moriarty' which had replaced the rejected and unwanted woman, Joan, was now itself rejected. There was no tearing-down of the pictures from her walls. It was not Joan's form to get angry; she had turned her anger inwards from the start. For the next three nights she did not sleep at all. It was the beginning of another episode of depression.

25

Aftermath

J oan Moriarty became an old woman overnight. People seeing her in the street had always been impressed by the straight back, the regal poise, the sense of calm purpose in the brisk gait. What they saw now was a stricken, and very fragile geriatric. Joan, who said absolutely nothing whatsoever about the matter in public, was very cautiously and quietly engaged in the intensely private and precarious business of trying to put herself back together again.

The public knew nothing more than that Miss Moriarty, the First Lady of Dance, had felt bound to resign. It was enough. Only the most hard-hearted of Cork people would not have been filled with sympathy for her. Dancers at the Irish National Ballet, as well as the whole of the Cork Ballet Company, were shocked. The issues were not immediately graspable by the public, but there was a wave of dismay, not just at what had been done to Miss Moriarty, but at the way it had been done. As one of the professional dancers, Katherine Lewis, later said, 'It tore the soul out of her.'

Still, her phone did not ring. Nobody was on close enough terms with the forbidding Joan, to ring her and commiserate, or even to ask how it had happened. As fragile as she was, she would not have encouraged such overtures, and they were accustomed to exclusion.

She was not a fool. She had read the small print. She knew she had little support at the Arts Council, and Aloys agreed that it was obviously happy with the report. It had been adopted and published with a preface by its chairman, Mairtin McCullough, saying that it was 'a report of great significance which will provide reliable guidelines for the development of theatre dance in the coming decade'.

In private, she had enough of a struggle trying to believe that it was actually happening; that it had happened. Aloys had no answers, except to fulminate, like other board colleagues, that somebody, somewhere, had conspired to dig Joan's grave in this way.

It could be argued that Joan had no need to depart at once, and that she could have announced her decision to retire, remaining for some agreed decent interval. That she did not negotiate an amicable, workable departure, argues that she may unconsciously have wanted to leave the company in some disarray, in order to prove her own value. She may also have resisted a smooth, amicable changeover, because she wanted it to be quite clear in the public mind that she was being forced out. It could have been that she wanted Brinson pecked to death by her compatriots; that she hoped for a huge wave of public opinion as well as influential support, to overturn the devastating conclusion of the Englishman outsider. Her martyred immediate resignation, making a virtue of necessity as it did, was a last-ditch political attempt at manipulation.

Hers were forlorn hopes, but this was precisely Joan's way of playing the game. Whatever her motives, Joan's form was to manipulate, and her immediate departure from the company was as calculated an action as her refusal to cook Sunday lunch. She was genuinely depressive, and took defeat as a dagger to the heart, but as hurt as she was, she lashed out with her usual queenly reserve and gentleness, and did as much damage as she could. Half the board said they would be resigning with her, sending morale within the company into an immediate further spin.

Needing heavyweight public support, she turned with superficial lightness of tone to Dame Ninette de Valois, and asked for the dame's help:

'It is a long time since I wrote to you! and I know you are interested in the Company's progress and what we are doing at this time! Well, like everyone these days we are having our Ups and downs, more downs I am afraid over the past two years!'

The next two paragraphs discussed finances and company numbers, and then the real news:

'Our Arts Council had a report on dance in Ireland compiled by Peter Brinson—this came out a few weeks ago! alas owing to this report and what was said about I.N.B. I find I have no Alternative but to resign as Artistic Director—this decision was not taken lightly, but as the Arts Council passed and accepted Mr Brinsons report there is no other course for me to take. We are now looking for a new Artistic Director from the 1st September, if you would know of any one we would be most grateful for any help. Also we require two soloist boys and one girl, the contract runs for a full year.

'At the moment I have made no statement or comment to the press or such, (of course the phones have been "Hopping") while I am still Artistic Director, but when I finish on August 31st I will then feel free to give my side of the story if I so want to...'

She had no intention of giving her story to the press.

Dame Ninette wrote saying that she was not getting herself in any way involved with Mr Brinson's report, and that her idea was to pay a tribute to Joan, on her retirement, in the Irish press. Adding that in her opinion, Joan coped brilliantly in the beginning, she sent Joan a draft of a letter she planned to send to *The Irish Times*, in which she praised Joan's 'intelligent approach' in the early days. She requested Joan to fill in the name of the brilliant young choreographer (Domy), and also the name of a dancer whom she admired (Babil Gandara).

'I speak only of the past and its beginning,' the Dame concluded her draft to the newspaper. 'Changes must come and, needless to say, are in the end all for the best; but this makes it all the more important that one woman's intelligent effort should not be forgotten or underwritten.'

In paying tribute to Joan, the dame had spoken in general terms, mainly about the early days. She had not mentioned anything in the draft to *The Irish Times* about Joan's actual ballets, and she had not mentioned *The Playboy*, which had been taken to her own theatre in London.

'One small point,' Joan wrote back. '—could you mention in your draft along with the smaller Irish works I have created such as *The Devil to Pay* and *West Cork Ballad* which you saw during your visits here—also that you remember *The Playboy of the Western World* at the Sadlers Wells'.

The omission on the Dame's part, of any mention of *Playboy* must have cut Joan to the quick, but she was humble enough, and politically aware enough, to ask for ammunition against detractors.

James O'Donovan went up to see the Arts Council in Dublin, and came back assuring board members that despite the unfortunate wording of the Brinson Report and the unpleasant publicity relating to Miss Moriarty which followed, the organisation was genuinely interested in the welfare of the company.

Joan was devastated by the report, but her depression was brought under control quickly, for she was functioning quite well again within a few weeks. In July, she attended a press conference to announce that her own company would contribute to Cork's 'Night of Stars' celebration, and she also went to Rennes with *The Playboy*. She attended a Cork street festival in September with a troupe of her dancers. Her misfortunes seemed to be washing over her, and she appeared to be coping, but the medication she took to blank it all out, showed in her ravaged face.

When The Lough Flower & Garden Club asked Joan to open their flower festival, which was to occur in Saint Peter and Paul's church in October, she set to work preparing for it. Yet even this late in life, she needed Aloys to keep her under as close supervision as ever. He was watching out for the pitfalls from a discreet distance.

Joan wrote a tentative letter of acceptance. 'Kindly let me know details of theams (sic),' she wrote, 'or is there one theam (sic)?' They wrote back that the main theme was, 'Let Every Creature Praise the Lord', and that subsidiary ones were fire and heat, ice and snow, darkness and light, etc. She busied herself composing an opening speech:

'My Lord Mayor, My Lord Bishop…

'It is indeed a privilege to be asked to open such a magnificent 'Festival of Flowers.

'Flowers are among the many delights which nature freely offers for our enjoyment. One can never forget the colour, perfume and designs of the different types of flowers which grow wild in the fields and hedges—as cultivated with such loving care by many thousands of gardeners —

'As Francis Bacon says, "God Almighty first planted a garden".

'If we look into the soul of flowers, with their calm—peaceful beauty surely it would help in these days of noise violence and depression.

'In the exhibition there are no less than 10 theams—all beautifully designed and produced—theams which take in so many of the elements of life on this planet

'It would take too long to talk about each theam

'I would like to congratulate the organisers for their vision in mounting such imaginative use of floral design.

'Again the Festival is for such a worthy cause—in aid of the most beautiful church in our city, It is a special place for me, as it was the first church I worshiped when as a very young girl I returned to Ireland.

'May many generations to come experience the same peace, hope and tranquility which I found here over many years —

'and now it gives me great pleasure in declaring the Festival of Flowers open'.

This draft was then submitted to Aloys, for tidying up. On his typewriter, he ordered Joan's thoughts into a dignified and understandable format. He restrained her winsomeness, gently tamed the overblown parts, and guarded against indiscretion. He also excised the glaring lies, namely that Joan had first attended the church as a very young girl, and that she had come directly to Cork city from England.

His faithfulness to the essence of her own thoughts in these transformations proved his worth, and their rapport, over and over again. But his ability to breach such wide gaps, also meant that she was extremely dependant on him. When she went out, what the public were often getting, was Aloys in the guise of Joan. She did not trust herself to function without him.

These drafts don't just reveal that the uneducated Joan remained inarticulate all her life. In an important sense, they are a glimpse into an element of their relationship, which had enormous value for Joan. What Aloys was doing for her went far beyond the writing of speeches; he was interpreting her to herself. He didn't just reveal Joan in the best possible light to the public; he took hold of her simplistic yet strangled ideas, and through them, showed her something of her best self.

Joan officially had left the professional company at the end of August, but the quiet, definite flourish was not intended to be altogether final. Most of her days and nights of worry were spent in wondering whether she was right to resign. Weeding subversives out of her companies was one skill she had unashamedly honed, but responsibility for making her own decisions was one of the most frightening aspects, if not the most frightening aspect, of Joan's trying life.

If a decision was down to her, she would agonise. She preferred things to be written in stone. The decision of whether she was to leave INB was hardly a matter for just herself to decide, but in her muddled mind, it was. Once she had said she was resigning, there was no longer room to negotiate. Domy was installed temporarily in her place, and applicants were interviewed for Joan's post.

If her idea had been to bring the whole thing crashing down it had failed. Similarly, there was no public outcry to reinstall her. Her insecurity left her vulnerable to disastrous advice, and by early September, she was imprudently offering to stay on. If Aloys, or indeed any of her supporters, had been reading the Arts Council mood correctly, they would not have allowed her to be subjected to this possible further rejection. The crushing rebuff that this offer was met with, was as unneccessary as it was humiliating.

It was at board level that the messy decision was made, the night before the INB board was due to meet with the Arts Council, that Joan would be prepared, if invited, to carry out her former duties until a new Artistic Director was appointed. On past form such a tactic might have been the thin end of a wedge, with the possible intention in this case, that future applicants could be rejected indefinitely.

Even though Domy, with other commitments, was leaving the following day, and was to return for a total of only ten days before leaving altogether, Mairtin McCullough, Arts Council chairman, backed by Adrian Munnelly, Arts Council director, firmly refused the offer. The reinstatement of Miss Moriarty, they agreed at the meeting, would be a retrograde step.

At the same meeting, which took place at the Silversprings Hotel, James O'Donovan was given no quarter when he reminded the Arts Council that several directors would be withdrawing from the INB board following the appointment of a new Artistic Director. Mustering all the arguments, Adrian Munnelly made it quite clear that the new board was to be appointed first.

James then said, naively, that the recent performances of the company in Cork showed a splendid mix of styles, as recommended in the Brinson Report. There was more to the job of Artistic Director, he was told by Martin Drury, education and dance officer, than the selection of four or five new ballets each year.

James' floundering intransigence may have seemed like so many red herrings to the Arts Council, but it was a clear sign that, even at that perilous juncture, Jamie hadn't a clue. He went on to ask whether the Arts Council was prepared to submit to the board, names of suitable board candidates. He was allowed this. Finally, he said he was still anxious about the company's immediate future, and was told that Miss Large was competent to run the company until an appointment was made. Aloys was there, but made no contribution to the meeting.

The other board members who planned to resign with Joan stayed on until November. They were Aloys, James, Maeve Coakley and Pat Leonard. Pat Murray did not resign. Factors preventing ambitious international talent from taking over as Artistic Director in the small company, were that the Brinson Report was hanging over the company's future, and that the grant was in jeopardy. Company morale was also low. The Scandinavian Anneli Robinson was eventually appointed, but she did not stay long. The company was falling apart.

The Arts Council set about trying to implement the recommendations of the Brinson Report. Though it hardly registered at all in Cork, Peter Brinson had also advised the axing of one of the two small Dublin companies. Arguing that it did not make sense for the Arts Council's limited funds to support three dance companies, he recommended complete withdrawal of support for Louis O'Sullivan's Dublin City Ballet, and increased support for Dublin Contemporary Dance Theatre. In the same year, the grant to Aloys Fleischmann's Choral Festival was dropped. The INB still had a whopping grant—too big for Arts Council coffers to sustain; too small to run the company.

November was looming and, as usual, without missing a beat, Joan and Aloys went on with their life at the Opera House, with the amateur Cork Ballet Company and the Cork Symphony Orchestra. This time it was to be a collaboration with Graffiti Theatre Company, and there were no imported big stars. Press coverage was favourable.

The following year, during Ballet Week in Cork, Jack and Mairin Lynch made a presentation to Joan of a Galway Crystal bowl, in recognition of her lifelong dedication to ballet. It made front page colour news in the *Cork Evening Echo*. So did a picture of Joan at the airport, welcoming the international ballet stars for her amateur production of *Giselle*. It was glittering business as usual. For all the many times Joan had asked what the Arts Council knew about ballet, she never once had asked publicly what the press knew about ballet.

The following year was the fortieth anniversary of the Cork Ballet Company, and a huge celebration was planned, and efficiently billed in advance, as always. Sponsors rallied, and tributes flowed in. The guest artists were Zoltan Solymosi and Colleen Davis from the Dutch National Ballet dancing *Swan Lake*, and Richard Collins reproduced the choreography. The other distinguished patron adopted by the Cork Ballet Company, Alicia Markova, was invited for the fortieth birthday opening night, and the news made the *Cork Examiner*, but in the event, she sent a telegram to say that she could not attend. Joan understood that the dame had 'flu.

The public may or may not have known or cared which company was which, or whether Miss Moriarty had been reinstated, or even whether the national company, from which she had resigned, mattered all that much. What they saw, was the ballet apparently going on full swing, just as it had for the past forty years, with Joan and Aloys at the helm, and plenty of favourable press coverage with pictures of lovely ballerinas, and princely leading men.

Swan Lake had run for a week in Cork as recently as 1983, but it had been their 'lucky' ballet in the seventies, when they had put it on in Dublin and got the government grant. Now that the national company was gone from Joan and from Aloys, it was as though they were 'reclaiming' this work back into their own company, using their fortieth birthday as a suitably magnificent vehicle for the ceremony.

The national company was floundering. A three-year plan was devised, but the Arts Council was worried because the amount of grant had inevitably risen to £373,000. The development plan was cut to two years, and dancer's contracts were reduced to eight months, but the Arts Council felt that the problems at INB still remained unresolved. The grant for 1987/88 was drastically cut to £285,000, as desperate attempts were made by the company, with its reconstituted board, to survive.

Colm O'Briain was an Arts Council appointee to the new ballet board. It was his conviction that the company could be saved if certain procedures were adopted. He argued strategically, but became aware that the Arts Council seemed suddenly to be interested in the idea of 'standards'. He was baffled.

With no other Artistic Director available, Pat Murray and Domy Reiter-Soffer collaborated on *Oscar*, a ballet on the life of Oscar Wilde. Featuring what was possibly the first ever *pas-de-deux* between two men, it was handled sensitively. The theme of homosexuality in conservative and 'holy, Catholic Ireland', where homosexuality was as yet illegal, and this in the context of a do-or-die attempt to save the company, may have been injudicious. Some audiences loved it; others stayed away.

By the end of 1988 the Arts Council baldly announced that the leadership model INB represented 'was not the most appropriate framework for dance development and that the £420,000 subsidy given to the company could be better spent elsewhere'. It was the end of the INB.

The company appealed to the Taoiseach of the day, Charles Haughey, a man who was known to be in sympathy with the arts, and he responded with an allocation of £120,000. It was roughly enough to pay off debts and redundancies, and dancers found out that their jobs were gone when they read it in the newspapers.

Aloys sent Joan a large greeting card with a picture of two magnificent, noble-eyed heavy shire horses on the front, galloping side by side in a field, against a clear sky.

'To my darling—
In memory of
Dreenagh
Easter 1990.'

After a decade and a half, their second child 'Dreenagh' was gone. It was his own special birthday, his eightieth, and it was time for him to pay a tribute to Joan. He knew that in spite of the love felt for her by the Cork Company, Joan remained bitterly disappointed. He typed out a letter to her, and folded it into the card:

'Anno Domini 80

'In all my eighty years, there has only been one dominant figure—the youthful warrioress-piper, the blithe and graceful dancer, the skilful and imaginative choreographer, the obstacle-surmounting administrator who single-handed (sic) created a new art-form for Ireland—above all a dear, wise, loveable, trusted friend.

'My darling, we have moved from a time of wonderful dreams, of their partial fulfilment, to a later time when there are still things to be done, but the real glories are the memories of all that has been—unforgettable, unspeakable, unquenchable.

'This Easter, my love, let there be a new summer ahead for you, and a new, quiet period of happiness.

'My gratitude, for all you have given me for a period of well over forty years. To bring back a figure from olden times, you are my alter ego, my epipsychidion.

'When the laburnum blooms again, I shall be making the annual offering to my goddess.

with all my love —
Colm.'

26

Honeymoon

Aloys Fleischmann remembered the large brown envelope from Miss Moriarty when he was sipping apple juice, waiting for a friend to arrive for lunch in Reardon's Mill pub, opposite the Courthouse in Cork. He could never bear to be idle. To fill in the brief time he waited, he opened his briefcase and slid the envelope into his lap. It contained a book and a postcard. Neither of them ever wrote inscriptions on flyleaves. They wrote on carefully-chosen cards, and slipped the cards into the books they chose, equally carefully, for each other.

He had received it on opening night of Ballet Week at the Opera House in Cork, as he stood in dressing room Number 8, distinguished and charming in full evening dress, preparing to conduct the Cork Symphony Orchestra. He knew that the brown envelope she quietly pressed into his hands, contained the latest annual gift to the conductor, from his colleague, the director of the Cork Ballet Company, Miss Joan Denise Moriarty. An exchange of gifts between them, presented with much cordial formality on opening night of Ballet Week at the Opera House, had been a tradition between them for more than forty years. He had known better than to open it at once.

Now he held up the postcard to his short-sighted eyes. It pictured a pair of lovers on a bed, deeply entwined in sexual intercourse. It was a print of a sensual work by Kerry artist, Pauline Bewick, entitled 'The Honeymoon Couple'. On the other side, in Joan's wandering, big scrawl, were the words, 'Need I say more?' and underneath it 'Nutcracker 1990'. The shiny new paperback on the eighty year-old professor's lap, was a copy of *The Love Poems* by W.B. Yeats. His wife was dead. The honeymoon was to begin.

The honeymoon period was to be celebrated with a special trip to Kerry the following summer. But even though he was now as free as she was, it was very soon after his wife's death, and they were both instantly recognisable in public. Since they did not want people talking, they agreed it would probably be better if they were to stay in separate hotels.

Joan had been laid low with a very bad 'flu the previous winter, and had been very ill with her chest. For years, good friends in the Cork Ballet Company had been looking after her. Detractors and subversives had no place near her, and those who embraced her mystique, perceived her to be too trusting, almost too kind and tolerant. She had always entered into the problems of her own company, and bought special little gifts in recognition of their anniversaries, and in the main, they loved her. For many years, she had kept every good luck message they ever sent her. She called them 'my family'. After she was deposed from the national company, members of the amateur company were specially concerned for her. Always able to inspire feelings of protectiveness, Miss Moriarty was now more closely cosseted by her inner circle. More than ever, people who might in any way upset her, were not allowed to get to her.

She had gone back to what she knew best. One thing that she had built her reputation on, which was absolutely authentic, was the asceticism. It was partly through this, rather than the glitter, that she had won the support of hardworking Irish people. It had always been her own way of perpetuating herself, and at no point did she let go of her pursuit of it.

The draughty halls, the bare, concrete floors and the 60W, unshaded lightbulbs were what Joan was all about. Though she did not realise it, it was there in the chill of privation that she felt most comfortable. Performing conditions which would appal most other dancers, were home to Joan—first and last base. In her last few years, she went out to places like Skibbereen once again, in headscarf and trousers, her back straight, preaching to a half-empty town hall, where sweet wrappers and Coke cans littered the floor. She was serene in places where there was no sound system, and young members of her corps danced to taped music on a noisy, unsprung stage that was too small, and by dancing standards, 'filthy'. She took her place where modern young dancers stoically complained backstage that conditions were terrible. She went back to it all, and when he could, Aloys accompanied her.

The pain in her foot was tormenting her, and yet she could still manage to look brilliant. She was slim and supple, her voice still mellow and gentle. Through all her debility and weakness, Joan was still able to impress her mentor. She had extensive cocktails of medication to alleviate the worst symptoms, and she took vitamins, but it was her ability to prevent her limbs from shaking with Parkinsonism when in public which astonished Aloys. Before summer came, however, her longstanding illnesses reached an acute episode, and she was in hospital again. There were tests, and she had an operation for one of the cataracts that had formed on her eyes, an effect of powerful asthma treatment.

One early November afternoon soon after his wife's death in 1990, alone in his lakeside house in the secluded Cork glen where white swans nested, the retired music professor hefted a locked metal strongbox from the dusty storeroom next to his study, and carried it downstairs. It was time to use his new privacy for taking stock.

In the big drawing room, a new fire of dry logs crackled. It was early to have a fire lit. At that time of day, he would normally be working upstairs in the study. He was expecting company later, but would be undisturbed for some hours yet. He'd forgotten where he'd hidden the key to the box. It could have been anywhere amongst the rambling, neglected acreage of shelves he'd crammed with hundreds and hundreds of books and music scores down the years. He'd hidden many things behind those books.

Laying the box down on the heavy oak dining table, he stood back on his heels for a moment, and ran a hand through thin hair, his thick, still-sensuous lower lip jutting. His memory was failing. He couldn't begin to look for the key now. An impatient man, it was impossible for him to wait. He'd made up his mind. He left the room at a stumbling run, into the dark hall, and through a cavernous, disused dining room towards the garden door, out into the little woodshed. There, in the place where he sometimes hid keys amongst the wood he'd cut and neatly stacked, he groped for the crowbar.

Bracing the box against his blue waistcoat in the drawing room, he roughly wrestled it against the metal bar with big hands, crudely wrenching the metal out of shape as he broke the lock open. Scores of letters tumbled out onto the old rug in front of the fire, love letters. Envelopes of folded letters fell out, all in the same extravagant, flowing hand; letters from forty years ago, from ten, twenty years ago, letters from last month, this month—a card from yesterday.

Crouched on the low firestool, he took one into his hands, and clumsily fumbled it out of the envelope. It was addressed to 'Colm'. With grave, grey eyes, he quickly scanned the page down to the flowing, playful signature. 'Maeve'. He tossed it into the flames. He picked up another. 'My darling', it began, and was unsigned. He flung it onto the fire. One by one he opened and read them in the firelight, some unsigned, some signed 'Joan' but all in the same big spidery scrawl. Bending close to the fire, the great dome of his ancient forehead glistening, he slowly destroyed them all, reprieving only a few cards and letters on which Joan had written some poems. For him it was time and he knew as he read them, that he would have to go to her hospital bedside, and ask her to do the same.

Lying in her bed at Shanakiel hospital, Joan immediately refused to burn the letters he had sent her over a period of forty-five years. When he gently insisted that she must, she replied that she could never bear to do it. But he pressed her as she lay looking with soft, diminished eyes out of her hospital window towards the winter sky, until eventually, for peace, she said yes, alright, as soon as she got home after this, she'd do it. He did not believe her. He knew that she had meant it when she had said she could never bear to destroy his letters.

He didn't understand quite why. He did not know how much his letters meant to her, any more than he could understand why she had kept every little message from every little pupil that had ever written to her. He could not possibly realise just how much he had validated her. He had no idea that destroying the letters for Joan, would be like destroying herself. Contained in those notes, and described in happy, transcendent terms, was the image, the model, the blueprint of herself that Joan had welcomed. Somewhere in there amongst the high praise, in the place where 'Maeve' the goddess, the muse dwelt, was the pure essence of Joan Denise Moriarty.

She had never grown up. Her dreams were the dreams of a virgin child-woman, and she was never to relinquish them. The real person who had suffered the cruelty of rejection, orphanage-life, cold, hunger, poverty, and above all loneliness, was someone that Joan Denise had closed her mind against. The bastard grand-daughter of a profligate Lord Justice of Appeal in Ireland, had kept her secrets well.

The most enduring feeling of her early life was the pain of loss. The only relative whom she had actually known, had committed suicide. Her own nervous breakdowns had proved to her terrified and inarticulate mind, that Joan Denise Moriarty was not stable enough, or strong enough, to survive.

Her gentle lover had been her father, her mentor, her protector, and her provider, as well as her romantic focus. It was through him that she had lived. He had brought poetry to her. He had conducted for her, the music of Tchaikovsky, Delibes, Mozart, Bax, and so many other composers. He had written his own music all for her. He had whispered his love to her, and he had transformed her life. He had fought for her, rescuing the ballet company from constant jeopardy, and he had made her a promise that he would look after her always. With his own enduring genius, he had created for her the person she wanted to be. And there in the letters, was evidence and proof that she was a wonderful person who was dearly and sweetly loved. She had no language that could tell the value of his letters, and wanted none.

His own panoply of tangible successes continued to swell. Macmillan publishers had agreed to take on his massive thematic index which would occupy several volumes. He had gone on composing, and conducting symphony concerts, and had automatically been accepted into the élite ranks of Aosdana, the organisation of government financial support for practising artists in Ireland.

Aloys still did not believe that Joan had received enough recognition. He began to refer to her as 'poor Miss Moriarty', and had resurrected the idea of getting her the Freedom of the City, as a compensation for all she had suffered, and for the loss of her company.

He had secured an appointment to see the Lord Mayor, The Rt Hon. Councillor Chrissie Aherne about the matter, and arranged to take with him one or two colleagues. He followed it up with a letter:

'Dear Lord Mayor,

'... it has since occurred to me that a list of the chief events of Miss Moriarty's career might be useful if you were good enough to consider her nomination. Of the various people you say have already been proposed, do you think any of them could produce a cv comparable to that which is enclosed?....

'One other thought has struck me—if you will forgive my suggesting it. Would you not consult the other Freeman of the City, Mr Jack Lynch, as to his views?...'

Aloys gave the Lord Mayor Jack Lynch's Dublin number, and enclosed ten copies of Joan's CV. But he had already taken the precaution of writing to Jack at home.

'... Despite her ill health and all her problems, Joan Denise managed to put on Coppelia recently, with full houses, expenditure covered, and a general verdict that it was the best production for the past ten years. We were really sorry that you and your dear wife were unable to be with us, just when it was such a success.

'Afterwards I conferred with Jim Corr and Pat Fenton....and we agreed that it would be very appropriate if a Lady Lord Mayor were to nominate Joan as the first Lady Freeman of the city, in view of her achievements. It would be some sort of compensation for all she has suffered, and the loss of her company. We arranged a meeting with the Lord Mayor.....she....most sympathetic...but already had seven nominations, and the pressures were enormous....

'...I also ventured to suggest that she should consult you, and hope you won't mind! If she does, I know you won't mention that I have been in touch with you.

'I enclose copies of all I have sent. Please on no account bother to acknowledge...'

He had taken copies of both letters over to Joan, but his hopes of presenting her with this gift were dashed; someone else was given the privilege of the Freedom of the City. He wanted the Firkin Crane building for her, but progress was irritatingly slow. When he was requested to consider co-operating in a full biography of Joan, with himself as the key figure in her life, he unhesitatingly agreed, making all his papers available. The biography of 'Miss Moriarty' was to be another gift from him for Joan, but he wanted it done quickly, so that she would see it. Bashing in the evenings on his primitive old typewriter, he attempted to contribute whole chapters himself—cursory, artificial things, crammed with unqualified and inappropriate praise and evaluation.

After another brief spell in hospital for Joan, the honeymoon began. They took off for six days of freedom in Kerry at the end of July 1991. Since she was rather frail and did not want to stay in a hotel on her own, they agreed that he would take another room in the same hotel. A mysterious lone male dolphin called Fungi swam off the Kerry coast, befriending swimmers and divers, and attracting tourists in summer. It was said, not just that Fungi would swim contentedly alongside his visitors, whose spirits he was able to lift, but that sick people had been known to go out to him expecting a 'cure'. Aloys resolved that the ailing Joan would go and spend an afternoon of her holiday visiting Fungi. If there was a cure to be had, he was going to put Joan in its way.

She was more than happy to comply. Delighted to be going back to her beloved Kerry, it had been her intention for some time to visit

Fungi. Rugged, wild Kerry was a place of the soul for Joan. Whatever pressures she met in her working life, the idea of going to Kerry was her dream of freedom from all pain. There, sitting watching the waterfalls with Aloys, and walking over unpopulated countryside, she could find a relief for the torments of the mind. Apart from reading, it was her only true relaxation, and she loved it. Since it was the only place, apart from her flat, where she had ever spent time privately with Aloys, it was also, down the years, associated with the magical bonding process of love. The waterfalls and the sea represented a fusing of their souls. Now Aloys was to guide her towards a mystical contact with the extraordinary creature of the sea.

However, it was not to be. As she stepped onto the gangway to get onto the boat that would take her out to see the dolphin, she slipped and fell. Whether it was the cataract on her eye, or whether she lost her balance for some other reason is irrelevant—Joan had fallen again, and this time she had hurt her back rather too badly to go on. Aloys became alarmed, exposed as they were, alone together in Kerry, on a holiday excursion, and so much in need of help.

She was in too much pain to enjoy the rest of the holiday. For both of them, the honeymoon had been a miserable disappointment, and they never returned to visit the dolphin. Aloys promised instead that they would return as soon as she was well. Back in Cork, Joan was admitted to hospital. Some of her ailments meant that she was not well enough to be operated on for other things. She was patched-up, sent home and began sifting through old letters.

That summer, Richard Collins agreed to come back from his home in America to do *Cinderella* for her. When he saw Joan he realised that she could no longer cope. He offered to take over the company for her. 'I don't want you to worry', he told her, the wondrous, drunken exploits of his early ballet days in Cork all flooding back to him. He had treated her cavalierly in his rich, arrogant and fun salad days. He had been known to lead dancers into taverns when they were meant to be *en route*, responding to her withering glances on arrival, with an incorrigible grin. Now he would make it up to her. 'I was irresponsible when I was a dancer,' he confessed gravely, as a mature choreographer. 'I am a different person now. I am going to do it. You'll be OK from now on. I'll see to everything.'

Before the show was due to open in November, Richard went back to America for a few weeks to attend to his affairs, and to prepare for a long stay in Cork. He was to come back in good time for all the last-minute preparations, but before the few brief summer weeks were over, Joan received sudden news from America that Richard Collins had been involved in a serious car crash, and had been killed.

Around October, Aloys began to notice a nagging pain in his back. He bashed on with life, as busy as ever, waiting for the pain to pass, but it kept bothering him. Even though he was eighty-two, the pain to him was just a 'wretched nuisance'—another fly to be swatted off. He'd never had a day's illness in his life. He was preoccupied with the orchestra. There were so many problems. He was getting tired of dragging the harp down so many flights of stairs for the harpist, but there was nobody else to do it. Now the first violin was threatening to resign unless someone of competence could be found to support him. The whole thing had been in jeopardy so many times, now it really was on the brink of being disbanded. Aloys had kept it going for so long, and had no desire to call it all off, after 58 years. He was already in the Guinness Book of Records because of it. He wanted to keep going for 60 years, and invite flautist James Galway to play for the special anniversary. He went on trying to ignore the pain; he still had the thematic index to finish.

Joan left her hospital bed in a wheelchair to attend the first night of *Cinderella*, for which Katherine Lewis had taken over as ballet mistress. Rachel Greenwood and Gilles Maidon danced the principal roles, and other guests were Roy Galvin and Donnachadh McCarthy. It was a cold night, and the only place where there was enough room for a wheelchair was in a box right up at the top of the house, past wide corridors full of wardrobe rails and skips.

At the end of the show, Aloys took someone up to meet Joan.

'Another great admirer of yours,' he murmured, as he always did, no matter whom he was presenting to her. Joan was in no state to meet people. She looked terrible. The tartan blanket that covered her bony frame was unable to conceal her wasted thinness; her cheeks and eyes were sunk deep into her once-lovely face. She looked up, stricken, into faces younger than her own, faces that were plump, animated; faces that were full of compassion; faces with eyes that shone with life.

'It's cold,' she said abruptly, turning her sickened head towards the boy who guided her wheelchair, as a chill wind blew across her soul. 'It is time to go.'

In Shanakiel, Aloys visited her every day. Company members brought videos of ballets to her room, but she refused to watch them. She did not want to see anything about ballet; she was only interested in old Hollywood movies. With all her longstanding disabilities, and in view of her age, the main medical worry was about Joan's chances of surviving an operation on her spine. She was in severe pain. If she decided to go ahead and have an operation, she was advised, it would be better to travel up to the Beaumont Hospital in Dublin for it. The decision, she was told, was hers. In Aloys' mind, there was no question about it; she was to go up, have the op, come back to Cork and recover. His optimism, as usual, was boundless, but Joan was very frightened.

Madeline O'Connor, 'Daddy' John's daughter came to visit, from Clydaville in Mallow, where many years before Joan had spent happy days playing tennis, and teasing her beloved 'Daddy'. The gentle woman was full of concern and love for Joan, whom she found in a state of despair. When she saw Madeline, Joan began to cry.

'You are alright', she sobbed, 'you have all your family round you: your sisters, your nieces and nephews. I have nobody; nobody at all.'

'But sure Joan,' said Madeline, taking Joan's hand, and embracing her, 'we are your family; we'll always be your family.'

It wasn't good enough for Joan. In her mind, the caring Madeline was not her family, and she had no confidence that Aloys was her family, or Billie, or Hilda, or any of the faithful Cork company. Everyone must face their final journey alone, but Joan's sense of isolation was overwhelming. At this stage of her life, surrounded by the utmost love, of all those dear ones who had been with her through so much, Joan perceived herself to be utterly alone.

She could not trust the optimism of Aloys. There was one crucial area in which he was useless to her—he did not believe in God. He had the usual liberal philosophical arguments that allowed for the probable existence of something that some people called 'God', but if pressed for his own view, he put forward the idea that death was final, and that there was no afterlife, no 'heaven'. Joan was a Catholic, someone who had always liked to attend Mass. She needed affirmation that she was not going to be extinguished forever, but she was insecure in faith. Aloys' unbelief unnerved her. She had always been afraid to die; he never had been.

In early January, Joan travelled to Dublin by ambulance. Aloys, as well known as he was, could not go with her in the ambulance, but promised to travel up after a day or so. The operation was to take place on the sixth, but was postponed until the thirteenth. Joan waited whilst Aloys kept in touch by phone. The following Monday he stood at his dining room table, surrounded by Christmas decorations still shining on the walls, and he filled a couple of briefcases with books for the journey. He began his visits to her, working on the thematic index as he travelled up by train. A preliminary investigation was undertaken, but the full operation would take place later again, they were told. Jack and Mairin went in to visit. Joan seemed fine.

At least, that was what she said. That was what she had always said. Drugged, facing an operation, waiting, reflecting, dreaming and dreading, what she was experiencing was the primary terror of abandonment, the experience she had spent a lifetime trying to forget.

Aloys duly arrived to comfort her just before the operation was due to take place. Joan had two questions she needed to ask him.

'Am I really going to die?,' she whispered.

'Of course you are not,' he retorted, softly. He believed it sincerely.

She turned her face up to him again. 'Will I ever see Kerry again?,' she pleaded.

'Of course you will,' he replied. He believed that, too. The pain in his back had begun to distract him. All the extra dashing about had caused him to lose weight. He looked haggard, and thin, but he shrugged it all off. He was fine, and she would be fine, too. He looked down at her for a brief moment. He had to dash for his train. He had to keep working. Half of his thoughts were on finishing his index, on which he would work for the whole of the return journey. He would keep in constant touch, as ever, he promised, and the moment she was out of the operating theatre, he would be back.

Aloys thought the operation had been a success. Billie Hunt, the old ballet hand, the woman who had served Joan's Sunday lunches every week, the matron who had looked after her in Shanakiel hospital, was the nearest thing Joan had to an official next-of-kin. It was Billie who made the final decision by phone, to rush Joan back into theatre in an attempt to save her life.

On 24th January, 1992, Joan Denise Moriarty died on an operating table at the Beaumont Hospital in Dublin, from a massive clot to the heart.

Epilogue

As unseen by the public as her real life had been, so she ordained it in death. In Ireland, the coffin is kept open prior to the removal, and a large attendance of friends and neighbours is encouraged to view the body, and to pay respects. Contrary to custom, Joan directed that her coffin was to be closed, and that nobody was to see her body.

She stage-managed her funeral. She requested that the Chieftains play the overture from *The Playboy* at the Mass in St Patrick's Church, but only two members were available—piper, Paddy Moloney and harpist, Derek Bell. The Vanbrugh String Quartet played other laments. Townspeople packed the church to pay their respects, and little girls from Joan's classes were brought by their ex-pupil mothers. Jack Lynch attended, also Fine Gael TD Peter Barry, and Kathleen Watkins represented the Arts Council.

Company board members and friends carried Joan's coffin, and a police escort led the cortège through the city of Cork. A lone piper from the Carrigaline Pipe Band, in full Highland dress, and playing a lament on the war pipes, led the funeral cortège into St Finbarr's cemetery, where Aloys delivered a graveside oration. Joan was buried in the plot reserved for her years before, by her chief mourner.

She left small bequests of money to her doctor, to her friends, to Aloys and to charity. The furniture was returned to the Fleischmann family. Her clothes, pictures and books, were distributed amongst her trustees, and her friends in the Cork Ballet Company. She left her schools to dance teacher, Breda Quinn. The four trustees—Aloys, Hilda, Pat Leonard and Pat Fleming—were requested to continue her amateur company and particularly its annual Opera House production.

Joan's gross estate was evaluated at £169,790, roughly two and a half times that of her protector, which was valued at £68,000.

In death, Joan relinquished her hold on the huge volume of love letters she had accumulated over forty-five years. Aloys recovered and burnt them all. He immediately commissioned a tombstone for Joan, intending to pay for it himself.

He went on fighting for her to the end. He picked over the obituaries with a critical eye, and found the one in *The Telegraph* offensive. It stated that she 'fatally restricted herself to her own choreography—which was limited—and to that of a few other local figures'. He wrote immediately, indignantly refuting the 'monstrous mis-statement' in the 'tissue of misinformation'. The unattributed obituary also offered the opinion that she 'proved incapable of rising to the challenges her enthusiasm created'. Aloys wrote that the obituary sounded as if it had been written by a 'disaffected member of her company', but privately, he wondered whether it had been written by someone like Peter Brinson.

Shortly after her death, the Firkin Crane was officially opened as a centre for the arts by Taoiseach Albert Reynolds. Aloys Fleischmann attended. Then, thin and ill, he went into hospital.

He lived for just six months. It was cancer of the spine that had given Aloys so much pain, and the first operation in the Bon Secours Hospital appeared successful. After another spell in a wing for the terminally ill, he was sent home. He worked ferociously through great pain and the disabling nausea that accompanies high doses of morphine, trying to finish his thematic index. On the day of his death, 21st July, 1992, he worked for several hours.

He was laid out in evening dress. The big funeral Mass in the cathedral, where his father and grandfather had played the organ, reflected his importance in the city and in the country. Aloys was buried adjacent to Joan, whilst her grave was still fresh, and before her tombstone was erected. Clustered around their graves, are those of composer Sir Arnold Bax, for whom Joan had first played the war pipes, and whom Aloys buried in the 1950s; music professor Sean Neeson, who had first engaged her, and his wife, ballet critic Geraldine; and pianist Charles Lynch, who had played for ITB in the 1960s, and whom Aloys had buried in the large plot he bought primarily for Joan.

Joan Denise Moriarty directed her trustees to destroy immediately after her death, all videos, notes and tapes pertaining to the Irish National Ballet, on the grounds that she did not want them to be reproduced.

Further recommendations of the Brinson Report on dance in Ireland were never implemented. The money that Joan's company had been previously granted by the Arts Council, was mainly redirected to other areas of the arts. Today, there is no national ballet company in Ireland.

In the year of her death, a tribute production by her own amateur Cork Ballet Company of *Giselle*, took place at the Opera House. In 1994, for the first time in forty-seven years, there was no Ballet Week in Cork.

Appendix

Sources are as quoted in the text. In addition, interviews with Joan took place at her studio on 3rd August 1988, and in Shanakiel Hospital on 5th September 1991. She also recounted her life story on audiotape on 4th May 1989.

Aloys Fleischmann provided numerous interviews and contributions between 1989 and 1992, including taped interviews in August 1989, September 1991 and in February 1992. Over 1990–91, he also independently wrote four chapters on his own version of Joan's life to assist the author, and these were consulted. Also consulted extensively was material written over many years by Aloys about Joan and the ballet; letters written by Joan, notes in margins of meetings, and also cards, letters and other correspondence between Joan and Aloys, dated as indicated in the text.

Several interviews have been drawn on over several chapters. Amongst these are interviews with Beatrice Hunt and Sean Cunningham on 28th March 1992, and another on 3rd April 1992, at which Tom Donnelly was also present and contributed. Information from interviews with Brenda Sexton and Madeline O'Connor, both on 17th February 1993 in Mallow was also used over several chapters. Interviews with Mairtin McCullough on 12th February 1992, and with Colm O'Briain and Arthur Lappin, both on 13th February 1992, were also consulted extensively.

Other sources are indicated as follows:

1 — Origins
Register of Births, Mallow.
Register of Births, Leeds.
Register of Births, Southport, near Liverpool.
Register of Births, St Catherine's House, UK.
Register of Births, Lombard Street, Dublin.
Register of Births, Scotland.
Interview with Peter, Lord Inchcape, 4th Earl, 20th March 1994 and correspondence.
Interview with Georgina, Lady Inchcape, wife of 4th Earl, 20th March 1994.

Irish Law Times (1915) details will of John Francis Moriarty.
Interviews and conversations with Aloys Fleishchmann 1989–1991.
Interviews with Joan Denise Moriarty 1988 and 1991.

2 — Orphan

Interview with Kieron Bolster, Mallow, 31st August 1992.
Interview with Myra and Catherine Greany, Mallow, 31st August 1992.
Drugs and drug prescriptions for JDM.

3 — Early Life Reinvented

Telephone conversation with Jane Pritchard, Rambert School 3/11/93.
Letters from Debbie Sparshott, Exams Manager, Royal Academy of Dancing 2/6/93 and 5/7/93; and phone conversation 3/11/93.
Letters from Catherine Browne, Head of UK Exams and Membership, Imperial Society of Teachers of Dance 12/11/93 and 17/1/94.

4 — Glenapp Castle

Interview with Georgina, Lady Inchcape, wife of 4th Earl, 20th March 1994.
Interviews with Joan Denise Moriarty 1988, 1990, 1991.

5 — Back in Ireland

Sid took low fees — Interview with Sheila Rafter, Mallow, 17/2/94.
Field class — Interview with Myra Greaney, Mallow, 31/8/92.
Interview with David Willis, Mallow 17/2/94.

6 — Friends

Taped interview with Ethel Beare, Manchester, 23/3/94.

7 — Soulmate

Aloys Fleischmann's CV 1959.
AF in Conversation with Tomas O'Canainn 1992.
Booklet Irish Composers No. 10 AF CMC Dublin.
Booklet AF Professor of Music UCC 1934–1980.
Self-Portrait Edward Sheehy at Glen House Cork.
Cork Echo 8/6/31.
Cork Echo 9/5/31.
Cork Echo 11/5/31.
Cork Echo 14/5/31.
The Cork Examiner 16/5/31.

8 — The Bad Years
Obituaries. Jack Moriarty, Gus Moriarty.

Interview Ethel Beare.

Interview Greany girls.

Interview JDM 1988.

Information from three former pupils of Joan's first class: Mary Conran, Margaret Barry and Patricia O'Gorman.

9 — Aloys' Life with Ann Madden
The information in this chapter on Aloys Fleischmann's marriage to Ann Madden, is drawn partly from his own version of it, related in during 1989–92, and also from other off-the-record sources.

Details of his provision for Joan's grave related by AF, October 1990.

10 — Collaboration
Interview of AF by Tomas O'Canainn *The Cork Examiner* 22/7/92.

Booklet AF UCC 1934–1980 UCC.

Programme Brochure for first performance June 1947.

The Cork Examiner review 2/6/47.

Information from three former pupils of JDM 28th January 1992.

13 — Irish Theatre Ballet
Interviews with INB dancers.

Interview with Pat Murray, 4/4/92.

Arts Council Annual Report 1965.

Draft letters from Aloys, 1959 and 1960.

Copy letters from Jennie Dowdall 1959/1960.

Thank you letters from: Australian Embassy, Dublin, 1958; from British Embassy, Dublin, 1960; from Austrian Embassy 1969; also from COS Command, Cork 1955.

Letter from Ninette de Valois 10/3/60.

Interview with Alan Foley 4/3/92.

14 — Dijon
Interview with Pat Murray, 4/4/92.

Interview with Pat Fleming, 27/2/92.

15 — Schools

Correspondence with Debbie Sparshott, Examinations Manager, RAD May and June 1993, and telephone conversation, 3/11/93.
Interviews with ex-pupils, Roz Crowley (14/2/92) and Alan Foley (4/3/92).
Author attendance CBC performance Skibbereen visit backstage, 21/5/90.
Interview with pupil Eileen Flynn, 13/5/94.

16 — Legend
Correspondence between Aloys and Joan.
Interview with Jack Lynch, 19/7/92.
The Cork Examiner 21/10/77.

18 — Irish Ballet Company
Arts Council Report 1976.
IBC financial statements 1974–76, FJ Grey and Co. Auditors and Accountants, 12, St Joseph's Lawn, Bishopstown, Cork.
Joan's IBC Board meeting from agendas, 1975.
Joan's lists.
Joan's folder "IBC Finance" 1975.
IBC Programmes 1975 and 1976.

19 — 76&77
Joan's salary — IBC finance.
Joan's wealth on death — will.
Agendas IBC board meetings 1975.
Minutes IBC board meeting 5th April 1977.
David Gordon's submission of idea for new work.
Interview with Pat Fleming. 27/2/92
Interview with Katherine Lewis 20/2/92.
Interview with Alan Foley 4/3/92.
Ninette and Tom Donnelly quotes: RTE radio programme on IBC, 1977.

20 — Playboy
Pat Murray's sets — *The Cork Examiner* (23/6/78).
Joan had never seen playboy — Seamus Kelly *The Irish Times* (4/7/78).
Honorary doctorate — Interview with Jack Lynch 19/7/92.
Clippings dated to November 1979, returned to Aloys from NUI January 1980.
IBC board meeting minutes.
Joan's video of *The Playboy of the Western World* performance by IBC.

21 — Cresting The Myth
Video tape of *The Late Late Show* 17/4/79.

Tom Donnelly — Morgan O'Sullivan radio interview February 1978.
Telegram from Jack and Mairin Lynch at the Irish Consulate in New York.
Evening Echo (28/12/80).
Playboy on RTE2 — 28 December 1979.
Festival details — *Irish Post* (6/10/79).
Rush for Chieftains and Planxty tickets. *Evening Press* (16/2/80).

22 — Crisis
Interview with dancer and equity representative Katherine Lewis, 20/2/92.
Interview with dancer Alan Foley, 4/3/92.
Arts Council Reports 1980–83.
Phoenix 14/10/83.
INB Board meeting minutes: 26/10/83, 25/2/82, 25/3/82,
19/1/83, 14/1/82, 16/4/82, 28/10/82, 27/5/82.
Dancers' contracts—Meeting with Equity Committee 26/5/82.
Dancers request financial statements. IBC Board Meeting 19/1/83.
Cut number of dancers, cut orchestra: notes on revised budget 82/83.
Muriel Large's contract; Tom Donnelly's contract.
Dancers' and stage manager's report autumn tour November 1981.
Salary List 82/83.
Contracts List 1982/83.
Ranelagh School—*Southside Express* 16/6/82.

23 — The Firkin Crane
IBC Trust Fund financial statements, 30/4/83 Cooper Magennis.
Firkin Crane — interview with Jack Lynch 19/7/92.
The Irish Times (25/6/80).
Determined to rebuild—*Evening Echo* (7/7/80).
Irish Independent (7/7/80).
The Sunday Press (20/7/80).
Minutes of meeting Emmet Place (15/7/80).
Minutes of meeting with Colm O'Briain at Merrion Square.
Correspondence between Joan and Pfizer Feb–May 1981.
Letter from Joan to Maurice O'Brien 25/9/81.
Bank loan for Wells Fee. Meeting 11/12/81.
Jamie's letter about costings to Joan 7/4/82.
Goddess of Dance. Joan's letter to Jamie 12/4/82.
Irish Independent 21/12/82. non disclosure of sum *The Cork Examiner* 21/12/82.
Trust Fund Meetings 1982.
Trust Fund account to (30/4/93) by Cooper Magennis, Cork.
Community Centre CE (21/12/82).

Joan champion of culture *Sunday Tribune* (11/3/84).
Nationwide appeal *The Irish Times* (2/3/84).
Eric Peard's report on trust fund (14/5/83).
Friends circular and application form.
Triskel — Aidan Dunne *The Sunday Press* 18/3/84.

24 — The Brinson Report

Arts Council policy on dance — reports 1982–88
Funds of Suitors — Seana Macreamoinn, *In Dublin* (9/8/84).
John McCarthy's tour report 1982.
Dancers' report on touring conditions 1982.
The Brinson Report — The Dancer and the Dance, Arts Council 1985.
Cost of Brinson Report — Arts Council Report 1985.

25 — Aftermath

Letters to Dame Ninette 21/6/85; 24/9/85.
Letter from Dame Ninette 12/7/85.
Rennes July 85. picture Joan in Rennes.
Interview with Katherine Lewis, 20/2/92.
Meeting INB and Arts Council Silversprings Hotel 7/9/85.
Jack Lynch presentation — *Evening Echo* (28/11/86).
Advance billing 40th birthday *The Cork Examiner* (13./10/87).
Markova (17/11/87); telegram.
Arts Council reports 1986–1988.
Doors from rotary club Mallow *Cork Echo* (19/12/85).

26 — Honeymoon

Death certificate of JDM.
Freedom of City copy letter from AF to Jack Lynch 9/1/89.
Copy letter from AF to Chrissie Aherne 6/12/89.
Author attendance at Skibbereen Town Hall performance of Cork Ballet Company 21/5/92.
Joan's vitamin preparations.

27 — Epilogue

Last Will and Testament of JDM.
Schedule of Assets of JDM.
Schedule of Assets of Aloys Fleischmann.
Author attendance at funeral of JDM 28/1/92.
Author attendance at removal and funeral of AF 22nd and 23rd July 1992.
The Telegraph obituary of Joan 8/2/92. Aloys draft letter of reply.

Bibliography

Inchcape, Hector Bolitho. John Murray.

The Munster Circuit, Maurice Healy.

Dancing in Ireland, Vol. 1 1983 Breandan Breathnach. Dal gCais.

A History of Mallow, Evelyn Bolster, Cork Historical Guides Committee 1971.

She Had To Do Something, A comedy in 3 Acts, Sean O'Faoilain, Cape 1938.

Aspects of the Liszt Tradition of Tilly Fleischmann. Adare Press, Cork.

The People's War 1939–45, Angus Calder, Cape 1969.

Myth Legend and Romance, Dr Daithiu O'Hogain.

Dictionary of Irish Mythology, Peter Berresford–Ellis, OUP.

The Táin, translated by Thomas Kinsella, OUP.

Object-choice (All You Need is Love), Claus Theweleit, Verso.

Index

A

Aherne, Chrissie 232
Aherne, Father 89
Anderson, Lavinia 88, 104
Andrews, Eamonn 179
Arrau, Claudio 90
Aspinall, Wayne 184

B

Bacon, Francis 222
Baker, Arthur 198, 201, 202
Barbirolli, Sir John 87
Barnes, Clive 174, 178
Barry, Margaret 61
Barry, Peter 238
Bax, Sir Arnold 48, 75, 125, 239
Beare, Ethel 44, 53, 54, 59, 96, 179
Beaver, Sir Hugh 102
Beck, Toni 164
Bell, Derek 238
Bewick, Pauline 254
Binchy, Maeve 180
Blum, Mabel 101
Bolster, Kieron 15
Boomtown Rats 179
Brenaa, Hans 153
Bridgeman, Fred 60
Brinson, Peter 188, 195, 207, 208, 213, 214, 220, 221, 225, 239
Brooke, Leonora 29
Buckley, Hilda 143, 162
Byrne, Gay 17–4
Byrne, Gerald 137

C

Callaghan, Domini 88
Chieftains 179, 238
Churchill, Lord 26
Ciuca, Radu 157
Coakley, John 129
Coakley, Maeve 88, 103, 112, 129, 157, 224
Colley, George 135, 142
Collins, George 44, 55, 59, 61, 88, 179
Collins, Maureen 44, 55, 59, 179
Collins, Richard 149, 152, 153, 157, 179, 186, 234
Conley, Sandra 137
Conran, Mary 61
Corr, Jim 233
Costello, John A. 82
Cotter, Julia 104
Crosbie, Donal 197
Crosbie, George 179
Crosbie, Patricia 153, 157
Cross, Eric 83
Cunningham, Sean 105, 106, 111
Curtis, Margaret 101
Czarny, Charles 153

D

Darrell, Peter 88, 90, 153
Davidson, Geoffrey 157
Davidson, Norris 89, 140
Davies, Richard 166
Davis, Colleen 225
Davis, Thomas 72
de Lutry, Michel 89, 153
de Valera, Eamonn 74, 78, 142
de Valois, Dame Ninette 102,

159, 166, 176, 179, 182, 187, 215, 220, 221
Dolin, Anton 153, 199
Dolphin, Mabel Agnes 3
Donnelly, Tom 161, 191, 196, 197, 201
Donovan, Anna 153
Dowdall, Jennie 100, 102, 130, 142, 174
Dowling, Noeleen 142, 157
Dromgoole, Nicholas 180
Drury, Martin 224
Dubreuil, Alain 137

E

Earl of Inchcape 2
Emperor Franz Josef 41
Espinoza School of Dance 17, 20

F

Farrell, Patrick 78, 80
Featherstone-Haugh, Susan 104
Fenton, Pat 233
Finegan, John 140, 169
Fitzgerald, Seamus 82
Fleischmann, Alan 67, 85, 179
Fleischmann, Aloys Georg 46, 65, 76, 87, 217
Fleischmann, Ann 83
Fleischmann, Tilly 65, 87, 114, 217
Fleischmann, Vanessa 179
Fleming, Pat 88, 238
Fonteyn, Dame Margot 176
Friel, Brian 179
Fungi 233

G

Galbraith, Mark 183, 184
Galvin, Roy 235
Galway, James 235
Gandara, Babil 153, 221

Gavin, Monica 162
Gibson, Eric 157
Gillespie, Elgy 136, 139
Goddess of Dance 21, 201
Goldberg, Gerald 59, 87
Graham, Desmond 191, 201, 205
Greaney, Mrs 12
Greaney, Myra 57
Green, John 201, 202
Greenwood, Rachel 235
Grey, Joe 189
Grizzell, Terence 157

H

Hanf, Mary 137
Harty, Hamilton 89
Harvey, Sir Charles 102
Haughey, Charles 227
Healy, Gus 165
Heaney, Seamus 179
Hillary, Sir Edmund 89
Horne, Leslie 82, 88, 113
Hunt, Beatrice 67, 88, 108, 110, 115, 147, 174, 236, 237
Hutson, Cherry 89
Hutson, Marshall 78

I

Ingoldsby, Mona 88

J

Jacob, WR 201
Jones, Alun 104
Judson, Stanley 90, 103, 104

K

Kellermann, Berthold 46
Kelly, Seamus 104, 140–2, 157, 163, 166, 170, 171
Kelly, T.C. 104
Kennedy, Dr Eamonn 179
Kilbracken, Lord 26

Kir, Canon 112
Knight, Beverly 186

L

Lambert, Gordon 201
Lappin, Arthur 190, 205, 210
Larchet, Professor 80
Large, Muriel 146, 152, 186, 191, 197, 210, 224
Lemass, Sean 84, 100, 101
Leonard, Pat 88, 139, 142, 224, 238
Lewis, Janet 181
Lewis, Katherine 219, 235
Little, P.J. 78, 80
Lucas, A.T. 59
Lynch, Charles 23, 68, 78, 239
Lynch, Jack 100, 129, 138, 141, 162, 168, 174, 200–4, 225, 238
Lynch, Mairin 129, 174, 201, 225

M

Mackay, Elsie 28, 31
Mackay, James Lyle 25, 27, 31
Mackay, Kenneth 1–4, 24, 26
Mackay, Patricia 5, 24, 26, 27, 29, 38
MacLiammoir, Michael 80
Maconchy, Elizabeth 82
Madden, Nancy Ann 52, 64–9, 87
Maidon, Gilles 235
Markova, Alicia 88, 102, 225
Maynard, Victor 104
McCarry, Deirdre 140
McCarthy, Denis 58
McCarthy, Donnachadh 186, 235
McCarthy, John 213
McCullough, Mairtin 205, 224
McKenna, TP 179
McLaughlin, Kay 104

McSwiney, Anne 48
McSwiney, Mary 48
Melville, Kenneth 90
Miller, Sheila 104
Moeran, E.J. 78, 104
Moffat, Tony 43
Moloney, Paddy 167, 238
Moore, Madeline 104
Moriarty, Denis 15, 32, 57
Moriarty, Gus 15, 32, 57, 58
Moriarty, Jack 14, 32, 43, 58
Moriarty, James 11
Moriarty, Joan 2, 3, 24, 26, 29, 38, 40
Moriarty, John Francis 2, 3, 11, 39
Moriarty, Marguerite 2–4, 10, 40
Moriarty, Marion 11–4, 16–8, 24, 31, 35, 38, 39, 53, 54, 56, 57
Moriarty, Michael Augustus 10, 11, 12, 57
Muldoon, Royston 153
Mulholland, Patricia 89
Munnelly, Adrian 224
Murphy, Nellie 57, 58
Murray, Pat 88, 108, 112, 142, 143, 151, 154, 157, 168, 224, 226

N

Nealon, Ted 194, 212
Neeson, Geraldine 162
Neeson, Sean 45, 49, 72, 239
Nicassio, Susan 137
Nowlan, David 141, 142, 213
Nureyev, Rudolf 199, 215

O

O Mullane, Meta 162
O'Briain, Colm 160, 169, 189,

191, 198, 226
O'Brien, Edna 179
O'Brien, Maurice 197
O'Brien, Patricia 104
O'Connor, Bobbie 34
O'Connor, John 40, 43
O'Connor, Lana 34
O'Connor, Madeline 54, 56, 57, 236
O'Connor, Mummy 56
O'Connor, Wendy 43, 58
O'Dea, Tom 191
O'Donoghue, Robert 157
O'Donovan, James 44, 88, 101, 102, 120, 130, 142, 146, 191, 192, 196, 201, 221, 224
O'Faolain, Sean 80, 84, 214
O'Gallchobhair, Eamonn 82, 84
O'Gorman, Patricia 61
O'Mahoney, Eoin 39
O'Reilly, Dr Tony 201, 203
O'Reilly, Patricia 82
O'Riada, Sean 84, 130, 131, 147, 167
O'Sullivan, Louis 187
O'Sullivan, Mrs 59
Ormston, Andy 195

P

Patricia Ryan Company 111
Pavarotti, Luciano 199
Pavlova, Anna 90
Peard, Eric 202, 205
Pearson, Noel 169, 178
Percival, John 169
Planxty 179
Pope Pius X 46
Potts, Sean 178
Professor St John Lacey 49
Proudley, Gilde 104

Purcell, Henry 82

Q

Quinn, Breda 238

R

Raikes, Kathleen 101
Rajah of Sarawak 29
Rambert School 22
Rambert, Dame Marie 22, 23, 37, 75, 88, 102, 104, 150, 182
Rawlinson, Lord 26
Reiter-Soffer, Domy 110, 147, 148, 149, 151, 153, 154, 158, 164, 176, 179, 186, 189, 221, 226
Reynolds, Albert 239
Ridley, Leith 186
Roosevelt, Mrs Kermit 'Belle' 101
Rosse, Earl of 203
Royal Academy of Dance 23

S

Salkeld, Cecil 84
Sanquest, Frank 78, 108
Sanquest, Paul 104
Senn, Leo 104
Sexton, Brenda 34, 43, 57
Sheehy, Edward 50, 51, 67
Sheila Elliot Clarke School 17, 20
Smale, Juanita 104
Smith, Brendan 179
Smith, Kathleen 152, 153, 186, 213
Smurfit, Michael 203
Solymosi, Zoltan 225
Spring, Mrs 204
Starr, Helen 137, 144
Stavenhagen, Bernhard 46
Sutton, Sir Abraham 103

Svetlova, Marina 90, 104
Swertz, Hans Conrad 46

T

Thin Lizzy 179
Torode, Sandra 104

W

Wade, Roger 185
Watkins, Kathleen 238

Weldon, Maureen 104
Woodward, Ian 180
Wyndham, Dennis 28

Y

Yeats, Jack B. 98
Yeats, WB 243